INTEGRATING AGILE DEVELOPMENT IN THE REAL WORLD

INTEGRATING AGILE DEVELOPMENT IN THE REAL WORLD

PETER SCHUH

CHARLES RIVER MEDIA, INC.
Hingham, Massachusetts

Acquisitions Editor: James Walsh
Cover Design: The Printed Image

Jeffries/Anderson/Hendrickson, EXTREME PROGRAMMING INSTALLED, p. 20, p. 80, © 2001 Pearson Education, Inc. Reprinted by permission of Pearson Education, Inc. Publishing as Pearson Addison Wesley.

CHARLES RIVER MEDIA, INC.
10 Downer Avenue
Hingham, Massachusetts 02043
781-740-0400
781-740-8816 (FAX)
info@charlesriver.com
www.charlesriver.com

This book is printed on acid-free paper.

Peter Schuh. *Integrating Agile Development in the Real World.*
ISBN: 1-58450-364-5

Library of Congress Cataloging-in-Publication Data
Schuh, Peter.
    Integrating agile development in the real world / Peter Schuh.— 1st ed.
        p. cm.
    Includes index.
    ISBN 1-58450-364-5 (pbk. : alk. paper)
    1. Computer software—Development—Management. I. Title.
    QA76.76.D47S315 2005
    005.1'068—dc22
                                2004022221

Printed in the United States of America
04 7 6 5 4 3 2 First Edition

CHARLES RIVER MEDIA titles are available for site license or bulk purchase by institutions, user groups, corporations, etc. For additional information, please contact the Special Sales Department at 781-740-0400.

To Katja

Contents

Acknowledgments

Many people contributed to the completion of this book. Significant thanks go to Mike Cohn, Mike Griffiths, and Kent McDonald for reviewing large portions or all of the text. Thanks also to Eric Meyer and Eamon Kearns for serving as both co-conspirators and guinea pigs for a year and a half, in addition to multiple follow-up phone calls and conversations about agile programming practices. Thanks to Herzum Software for accommodating me with a flexible work schedule. Thanks as well to my family for giving me the time, space, and support required to complete this tremendous project, which often seemed to defy all attempts at management.

Introduction

Consistently successful software development is the result of skilled professionals engaged in a collaborative process of continuous planning and disciplined execution. The methodologies of agile development do not have the corner on this market, but they have rightly identified many of the practices, processes, and values that make it possible. An agile approach to software development may be summed up in the following principles:

- The delivery of useable and user-valued software is the single most important goal of a software development project.
- Project teams perform best when they are working toward near-term, realizable, and recognizably valuable goals.
- Customers are happiest when they feel they have control over what is being developed and see regular, tangible results.
- Short and regular feedback loops are necessary to both gauge and direct the progress of a software project.
- Process streamlining and automation (of both management and programming activity) free people to do more valuable and interesting work.

One proposal of this book is that a final principle might be added to this mix:

- A project team should adapt its environment to fit its needs and the needs of the system under development. However, where this is not possible and when the demands are not unreasonable, the team must adapt itself and its processes to fit its environment.

To this end, this book tackles head-on the challenge of getting hands-on with agile development. There is not a lot of theory in this book. There are plenty of other well-written books on the underpinnings of and philosophy behind agile development and the agile methodologies. This book does not care what agile methodology a project team has selected or if a project team has not selected an agile methodology at all. This book is focused on the practice of getting a project done and how any and all agile practices and processes can help a team do that.

WHO SHOULD READ THIS BOOK

This book is meant to appeal to anyone who is implementing agile development (regardless of methodology) in anything less than an ideal environment. Specific individuals whom this book hopes to target are:

- A programmer or manager who knows a thing or two about agile development and wants to start experimenting with it but cannot or does not want to start with the full implementation of a named methodology.
- An experienced agile practitioner who has found himself in a project environment that is beyond the bounds of the methodology in which he is versed. Such an environment may be waterfall driven, heavy process, fixed cost, or otherwise significantly non-agile.
- Experienced managers or team leads who are taking their first—or a renewed—look at agile development and agile practices.
- A handful of programmers on a team following traditional development processes who need guidance on how to begin effectively adopting agile practices without rocking the project boat.
- A manager with little experience in agile development who has just found himself managing an agile team.

Basically, this book is intended for anyone working in the field of software development who is using agile or interested in using agile and requires a resource to help address and tackle the real-world problems that will almost undoubtedly arise.

HOW TO READ THIS BOOK

This book is meant to serve both the cover-to-cover reader and the practitioner in the field who has time only to locate and read about specific topics on demand. The book is organized into topical chapters that build upon one another and chapter sections that are meant to make it easy for the practitioner to target and review an area of interest.

- There are, of course, some recommended paths that may be taken through this book.
- Readers who are relatively new to agile development should start with the first chapter and read all the way through.
- Programmers with some knowledge of agile might choose to start with Chapter 5 or 6, especially if they are in the middle of an ongoing project.
- Project managers with some knowledge of agile might review Chapters 5 and 6 and then proceed to Chapter 10.
- Anyone contemplating an agile approach on a new project may want to start with Chapters 2 through 4.

One final note. Customer buy-in and participation are integral to the implementation of a fully agile approach to software development. The many aspects of the relationship between the project team and the customer are discussed in Chapter 15, including identifying the right customer, engaging the customer, and working with less than ideal customers. You should skip ahead to this chapter if you believe that a lack of customer involvement is one of the bigger impediments to success on your project.

STARTING MONDAY

This section heading is inspired by a study that came out late in 2003. The study suggests that neither hackers, viruses, worms, nor Microsoft Windows® is the leading cause of Web server crashes. Instead, it turns out, the leading cause is all of us. Specifically, the single greatest cause of Web site crashes is IT professionals inflicting their "weekend inspirations" on Web servers come Monday morning [Middleton03].

This anecdote should reveal the irony in the heading. On the one hand, the "Starting Monday" sections in the book are meant to give the reader bits of advice and direction. On the other hand, one must be mindful of adversely affecting the team with half-baked ideas that seemed good at the time. Therefore, one might consider the following steps before implementing any knowledge gleaned from this or any other book on agile development:

- State a clear goal for the project and how the information gleaned from the book will make that goal attainable
- Discuss the idea with trusted members of the project team
- Consider all the consequences
- Act

Yes, this is common sense, but sometimes it is all too easy to get caught up in the moment.

1 Agile Development Primer

In This Chapter

- What Is Agile Development?
- The Agile Methodologies
- Agile Values
- Agile Practices
- Agile Principles

Readers of this book have gleaned their knowledge of agile development by various means. Some may have used an agile methodology for a couple years and are now venturing beyond that methodology's self-described limitations. Others may be relatively new to agile development, with a few months or a few practices under their belts, but have already faced real-world issues that the named methodologies have not addressed. Others may be project managers or team leads who have seen some of what agile practices can deliver but are not yet convinced that agile development can adapt itself to their heavy-process, fixed-cost, complex-system, or otherwise change-adverse environments. While this book is not intended as an introduction to agile development, it is intended not to alienate but rather to welcome the reader who has some hands-on experience with agile development but has chosen this as his first book to read on the topic. This chapter provides a quick synopsis of agile development. It will provide the less-informed reader with the background he needs to start reading this book.

WHAT IS AGILE DEVELOPMENT?

Agile development is a method of building software by empowering and trusting people, acknowledging change as a norm, and promoting constant feedback.

Agile development is a countermovement to 30 years of increasingly heavy-handed process meant to refashion computer programming into software engineering, rendering it as manageable and predictable as any other engineering discipline. It is a direct refutation of the notions that people are fungible resources and that software modules can be stamped out like so many widgets off a factory line.

The practices of agile development are not new. Agilists readily admit that for decades there have been teams that have written reusable tests, delivered frequent and small releases, and even programmed in pairs. Rather, agile development is novel because the people behind the movement have catalogued and proofed these agile practices, fused them with core values about people and project environments, and stated in real and valuable ways how to go about building software better.

THE AGILE METHODOLOGIES

Agile development is an umbrella term used to describe a specific group of methodologies that arose out of a growing discontent with the way software development has been approached for the past 30 years. It is important to note that agile development itself is not a methodology. Instead, agile development is a set of fundamental principles about how software should be developed. The best known of a growing number of software development methodologies that subscribe to the principles underpinning agile development include:

- Adaptive Software Development (ASD)
- The Crystal Methodologies
- Dynamic Systems Development Method (DSDM)
- Extreme Programming (XP)
- Feature-Driven Development (FDD)
- Lean Software Development
- Scrum

Although they have similar values and practices, each of these methodologies approaches software development differently. Some are more management and communication focused (such as Scrum and ASD), while others zero in on programmers and development practices (such as XP). Similarly, some methodologies specify clearly what processes a team should follow (such as FDD), and others advocate tailored processes for every project (Crystal).

AGILE VALUES

The values behind agile development are best summarized by the *Manifesto for Agile Software Development* [Manifesto01]:

> We are uncovering better ways of developing software by doing it and helping others do it. Through this work we have come to value:
>
> > *Individuals and interactions* over processes and tools
> >
> > *Working software* over comprehensive documentation
> >
> > *Customer collaboration* over contract negotiation
> >
> > *Responding to change* over following a plan
>
> That is, while there is value in the items on the right, we value the items on the left more.[1]

This is much more than a pretty piece of prose. Each of the four points embedded within the declaration first identifies a fundamental value in agile development and then anchors it to a necessary (though less valuable) aspect of software development. The Agile Manifesto (admittedly highfalutin language) brings us back to the basics of software development.

Individuals and Interactions

People work together to write software. Agile development puts a high value on those professionals who comprise a project team because the success of that team relies upon the skills, effort, and actions of each of its members. For their project to succeed, a team of individuals must select and implement a set of processes and tools that fits its environment, its technology, and its goal. A team with a prefabricated set of tools and process forced upon it is as likely to succeed as it is to fail.

Working Software

Software is meant to do something, and what the software does should be useful. Agile development recognizes that no stack of requirements, analysis, architecture, or design documentation—no matter how high—has value if it does not accompany an operational system. Working software should be the first measure by which a project is evaluated. Documentation can foster the continued delivery of working software, but excessive documentation too early in the development process can at the very least be a waste of time (if it is neglected after it is written) and at the very worst can kill a project (when updating documentation becomes more important than writing code).

Customer Collaboration

Agile development believes IT professionals work in teams to write software for customers. This may sound utterly obvious, but only until one works on a few non-agile projects. The unfortunate truth is that process, tools, and documentation (implemented from both within and outside of the development team) can and too often does separate the project from its purpose. Too often things go bad because the project team is too busy working to the letter of the contract, or things have gone bad so the project team starts working to the letter of the contract (this being the same difference). Agile teams follow practices that keep them focused on the needs of their customers. Agile development advocates only those contractual relationships that encourage the project team to work with and for its customer.

Responding to Change

Change happens. Either a project team fashions itself to work with change or it delivers lower-value software. Agile development stresses practices that enable teams to adjust to changing requirements and system environments. Short feedback loops are an essential component of many of these practices. They help to provide all individuals on the team (whether members of development, management, or the business) with the information they need to make timely decisions. High quality and flexible code is an essential goal among many agile practices. Timely response to change is possible only when the system being developed is amenable to change. Finally, when requirements and environments change, plans must be made so that they can follow.

In short, agile development strives for an empowered development team that responds to change and collaborates with its customer to deliver software with real business value. Processes, tools, plans, documentation, and contracts must be tailored and applied as necessary to achieve this goal.

AGILE PRACTICES

These are the tools of the agile trade. They are the things agile teams do on a daily basis to stay disciplined, foster communication, remain flexible, and deliver software. Agile practices include many well-known techniques such as automated testing, continuous integration, daily Scrum, collocated team, and pair programming. These practices are shared across the agile methodologies. Not all of them (such as pair programming) are endorsed by every methodology, nor will two project teams following the same methodology necessarily implement the same set of agile practices. Each agile methodology recommends and each team selects a set of practices that best fits the environment and needs of a given project.

Many agile practices address the activities of programmers, while others speak to management processes. Agile practices operate in conjunction with and in support of agile values. They are shared across the agile methodologies. Some methodologies, such as XP, are very specific in the practices they prescribe; others, such as Crystal, leave it almost entirely up to the project team to decide.

Most agile practices did not start with agile development. Project teams have been following them for decades. Agile development, however, has done us the great service of exploring these practices in depth, documenting them extensively, marking routes and hazards, and—where necessary—blazing trails.

Agile practices are only as good as the programmers and managers who select, apply, modify, and follow them. They can be applied at the wrong times, and they can be applied incorrectly. As with any other development process, the misuse of an agile practice can slow down a team, and its use as a bludgeon can beat down a team. Of course, all of this rarely happens when teams adhere to agile values.

Finally, the agile practices discussed in this book are all prefaced with "Agile Practice" so as to be readily identifiable and easy to locate.

AGILE PRINCIPLES

The authors of the *Manifesto for Agile Software Development* also penned a short document known as the "Principles Behind the Agile Manifesto." To the agile methodologies and those who practice them, this document is something more than recommended guidelines and something a bit less than creed [Manifesto01].

We follow these principles:

- Our highest priority is to satisfy the customer through early and continuous delivery of valuable software.
- Welcome changing requirements, even late in development. Agile processes harness change for the customer's competitive advantage.
- Deliver working software frequently, from a couple of weeks to a couple of months, with a preference to the shorter timescale.
- Business people and developers must work together daily throughout the project.
- Build projects around motivated individuals.

■ Give them the environment and support they need, and trust them to get the job done.

■ The most efficient and effective method of conveying information to and within a development team is face-to-face conversation.

■ Working software is the primary measure of progress.

■ Agile processes promote sustainable development.

■ The sponsors, developers, and users should be able to maintain a constant pace indefinitely.

■ Continuous attention to technical excellence and good design enhances agility.

■ Simplicity—the art of maximizing the amount of work not done—is essential.

■ The best architectures, requirements, and designs emerge from self-organizing teams.

■ At regular intervals, the team reflects on how to become more effective, then tunes and adjusts its behavior accordingly.

All agile methodologies are meant to adhere to these principles. They are good thoughts to keep in mind and worth revisiting on occasion.

Nonetheless, throughout this book, we will address projects, situations, and environments where one or more of these principles must be compromised. Fortunately, we are talking about shipping quality software—not life or death.

2 Agile Characteristics

In This Chapter

- The Characteristics of an Agile Project
- The Development Team
- Agile Practices, Non-Agile Values
- What Projects Can Benefit from Agile Development?
- Starting Monday: Assessing Your Project Environment

Going agile really is a two-way street. You may think you are ready for agile, but is agile ready for you? Agile does not just hang out with anyone. She has her standards, and sometimes they can be a bit tough to meet.

If your team is planning to tango with agile, or even step through a practice or two, it is a good idea to know what she expects from a project team. This chapter will detail and elaborate on the characteristics of agile project environments, discussing both what agile is and is not.

THE CHARACTERISTICS OF AN AGILE PROJECT

Agile methodologists have good reason to be choosy about the environments in which they execute their projects. This is no different than a general identifying the ground on which his army is most suited to fight. Recognizing that high, sunny ground is a force multiplier (while difficult and hemmed-in ground are force divisors), Agilists have invested significant time identifying the project characteristics that best foster positive and successful development environments. Similarly, Agilists believe it is worth investing significant effort to influence or even reshape environments so that project teams are best poised for success. The type of environment that the agile methodologies strive for can be seen in Figure 2.1.

Project Environment		Project Characteristic	
Category	Variable	Agile	Non-Agile
The Development Team	**Communication Style**	Regular Collaboration	Only When Necessary
	Location	Collocated	Distributed
	Size	Up to 50 People	More than 50 People
	Continuous Learning	Embraced	Discouraged
Project Management	**Management Culture**	Responsive	Command and Control
	Team Participation	Mandatory	Unwelcome
	Planning	Continuous	Up Front
	Feedback Mechanisms	Several	Not Available
The Customer	**Involvement**	Throughout the Project	During Analysis Phase
	Availability	Easily Accessible	Hard to Reach
Processes and Tools	**Team Input**	Team Has the Last Word	Team is Told What to Use
	Amount	Just Enough	More Than Enough
	Adaptability	May be Changed	May not be Changed
The Contract	**Requirements and Dates**	Flexible	Fixed
	Cost	Time and Materials	Fixed

FIGURE 2.1   Project characteristics—agile versus non-agile.

In Figure 2.1, project variables are grouped into categories, and an agile and a non-agile characteristic is listed for each variable. Non-agile characteristics are provided both to help frame the agile characteristic and to indicate some of the non-agile characteristics that often need to be overcome in agile environments. It is worth noting that nearly every agile team has some non-agile project characteristic that it must overcome.

THE DEVELOPMENT TEAM

The agile methodologies require teams of individuals who openly communicate and collaborate and who are committed to continuous learning. They also are geared toward teams of up to 50 individuals who work either alongside or within close proximity to one another (although specific methodologies such as Scrum, FDD, and DSDM can scale to larger project team sizes).

A successful agile project is one staffed with programmers who like to work with others, not programmers who like to work alone behind a closed door. Agile focuses on communication both within the team and between the team and its customer. Communication within the team is a no-brainer—a team cannot work effectively if its individual members do not raise issues, provide feedback to one another, and strive to resolve different points of view. When it comes to communicating with the customer, programmers need to be the sort of people who are willing to start conversations, raise questions, and discuss options—instead of guessing—when they encounter the empty spaces between requirements.

Collaboration is essential to share knowledge of the code base and to identify and implement optimal solutions. It is achievable by promoting a culture in which a programmer is given the time and encouragement to grab the guy next to him and strike up an impromptu design discussion or call over another team member to pair program with through an unfamiliar or technically tricky patch of code.

Furthermore, the agile methodologies want individuals who are open to and take enjoyment in learning new things, individuals who are naturally inquisitive and willing to adapt to changing situations. Such individuals will make the most of agile methodologies and practices by implementing, tailoring, and switching them to meet shifting requirements, technologies, and project environments.

Finally, team size and collocation are important because of many of the other characteristics of agile development. Smaller groups that work within the same physical space require fewer lines of communications, can operate on less-formal processes, can come to agreement more easily, and can adapt to change more rapidly. A larger or distributed team may take a significant hit on productivity because more time is spent on communication and coordination activities than would be required—proportionally—to steer a smaller, collocated team. As noted earlier, team size does vary by methodology, and larger teams are not unheard of. FDD took its maiden voyage on a 50-person project and can handle larger teams. Scrum also has a history of running larger teams. Similarly, projects with distributed teams have executed successfully following a variety of agile methodologies. However, all these cases demand a greater degree of skill, diligence, and expertise in implementing agile development.

Project Management

Agile teams require a management structure that is responsive to the needs of the team, over which the team has some influence, and that provides mechanisms for regular feedback to evaluate progress and processes.

Agile development all but requires an environment in which project management is receptive to the needs of the team and their desire to employ an agile methodology. Most management-related agile practices (such as short iterations, small releases, and the maintenance of a sustainable pace) cannot be implemented without the consent and cooperation of project management. At the extreme, even many development practices (such as testing and refactoring) cannot be followed if a project's management does not value those practices and is too much of a miser to allow programmers to allocate their own time.

Agile methodologies vary over how much control a team needs to have in its own management, although all agree that the team should have at least a hand in making decisions. XP, for example, calls for teams where each programmer communicates directly with the customer as needed, and the team is overseen by a coach who is also a programmer. In this textbook implementation of XP, there may be no need for a project manager, and the team can be entirely self managed. Crystal, on the other hand, allows for teams that vary in structure from self-management to heavy process, depending on the size and criticality of the project. In general, Agilists agree that it becomes very difficult for a team to remain agile if management refuses to listen and respond to the needs of the team.

Finally, agile development requires feedback mechanisms so that the team can regularly evaluate whether it and its practices are on target. Agile teams need to collect and evaluate both verbal and metrics-related feedback in order to measure overall progress, to determine whether specific practices are working, to identify when something stops working, and to respond to change in either requirements or environment. A good example of a management-related structure that facilitates useful feedback is the practice of short iterations, which provides a regular interval for gauging progress and collecting metrics. While typical project plans demonstrate whether the team is ahead of or behind schedule, consecutive iterations can depict whether a team is growing more productive (and catching up to schedule) or slowing down (and losing its ahead-of-schedule cushion). Meanwhile, metrics collected over consecutive iterations, such as the number of unit tests written or the number of defects uncovered, can be used to measure whether newly implemented or tweaked processes are adding value to the team.

Agile management concepts are addressed specifically in Chapter 10, "Agile Management." Activities related to managing agile projects are discussed throughout this text but are concentrated in the second half of the book.

The Customer

Agile development requires a customer who is involved throughout the lifecycle of the project and is easily accessible to team members. The customer does not need to be a single person, but the customer must be one or more individuals who are familiar with the project, are empowered to make functionality related decisions, can speak with a single voice, and, ideally, have a vested interest in the outcome of the project.

Agile methodologies want customer involvement throughout the entire project for both practical and agile reasons. First, speaking practically, it is simply common sense that any project will deliver a better product when it has a knowledgeable and interested individual on call to provide input and direction. Second, continuous customer involvement is required by the just-in-time nature of many agile management practices. More specifically, small releases and short iterations—which spread planning and requirement decisions across the lifetime of the project—require the regular engagement and participation of the customer.

Different methodologies request different levels of customer availability, ranging from daily access to an individual who sits with and works alongside the team. Regardless of methodology, the goal is the same. An easily accessible and communicative customer means requirements can be refined when the majority of questions arise: during low-level design and coding.

Typically, a customer cannot merely be assigned to an agile team and be expected to provide the team with what it needs. Agile teams need to take the time necessary to acquaint a customer with an agile approach and ensure he is comfortable with defining, explaining, and planning new bits of functionality on a regular basis. These topics are discussed in depth in Chapter 15, "The Customer."

Processes and Tools

Development processes and tools should be agreed to by the team and should be of the "just-enough" variety. That is, the team should employ those processes and tools that provide sufficient checks and structure to keep it disciplined and on target, but nothing more. For example, a team might choose to use a source control tool because of the obvious perils that arise from not having an identified gold standard for the state of the code at any give time. Or, a team might commit itself to checking code several times a day because each programmer wants to avoid the time that would otherwise and inevitably be lost if code were left on individual workstations to grow in disparate directions over several days.

Any process or tool that is not accepted by the team or that goes beyond providing just enough structure for the team is unnecessary baggage. Whenever possible, agile methodologies seek to pitch this baggage back onto the platform before the train leaves the station. Satchels of documentation are often the first thing programmers ditch. Project plans that spell out packet-by-packet how the work will be performed but have no basis in reality quickly follow. Sometimes the team clears out the train and starts rolling down the track. Too often, however, the customer (or the testing team or the database administrator) is right there on the platform tossing, smuggling, or otherwise trying to get some of that baggage back onto the train.

In my experience, most of the teams that make the effort have managed to strike some form of compromise with the relevant parties, where some of the heaviest tools, processes, and trunks get booted from the train, and some of the baggage the customer really wants stays on. The customer may have good reason to ask for some of these things. In a multisystem environment, other projects may require artifacts that the team itself does not find useful. In large companies, the customer may not have the authority to permit the team to shirk a given process or not use a specific tool.

Of course, there is a point at which so much process and so many tool requirements get thrust on an otherwise agile team that it begins to feel downright unagile. Been there. Done that. At some point, if the train cars fill up with enough baggage that the programmers and manager cannot remove, an agile team may need to follow tracks that do not align with any named methodology.

Implementing and remaining agile in heavy process environments will be discussed in Chapter 20, "Real-World Environments."

The Contract

Possibly because agile development is so focused on accepting and being prepared for change, sometimes it seems to have a little problem with commitment. Specifically, this is a commitment to cost, requirements, and timeline. The agile methodologies are shy on these topics for two reasons. First is change itself. Agile projects thrive in environments where change is the norm. In fact, one of agile's best selling points is that it allows and even encourages customers to change their minds about requirements late in the project. Since requirement changes are typically thought to have an effect on both price and timelines, one can begin to appreciate Agilists' reluctance to enter into such rigid contracts.

Second, contracts with hard numbers and dates can encourage both vendor and client to focus on the wrong thing—namely, the contract. Agilists note that these parties can readily lose track of the spirit of the contract by focusing on its letter. In the face of a changing business climate for the client, the vendor may grow focused on delivering the functionality spelled out in the contract. In spite of flexibility and a willingness to adjust to change on the part of the vendor, the client may refuse to budge from the contract price. Either scenario, Agilists would argue, sticks one of the parties with the short end of the stick and will discolor future engagements.

The use of contracts in agile development, including those based on fixed-cost engagements, is discussed more in Chapter 20.

AGILE PRACTICES, NON-AGILE VALUES

A development team does not become agile merely by adopting a set of practices and policies. Agile development is really a mindset [Cockburn02]. To be truly agile, a project and the individuals who oversee and regularly interact with it must subscribe to the values and principals laid out in Chapter 1, "Agile Development Primer," and re-examined here. That is, to be truly agile, a project culture must trust its people, foster communication and collaboration, value the ability to respond to change, and never forget that the goal of the project is to deliver software that is useful to the customer.

On real-world projects, it is sometimes impossible to get an entire team to shift over to an agile value set, much less the customer, stakeholders, or directors who oversee the project. For example, consider a single project of eight people, embedded in the IT department of a *Fortune* 500 company that is pursuing CMM Level 3 certification and already has in place a waterfall process with a strict regiment of end-of-phase tollgates to ensure that analysis is completed before design, design before build, and so on. This project could not successfully turn a sufficient number of related parties (information managers, architects, users, stakeholders) to an agile mindset. By trying, it would prove an old Japanese proverb: The nail that sticks up gets hammered down.

Ultimately, a project is not agile if its culture does not support agile values. Such a project, however, may still benefit from adopting agile practices.

WHAT PROJECTS CAN BENEFIT FROM AGILE DEVELOPMENT?

Almost any project can benefit from agile development to some degree. Failure to meet one or more of the characteristics discussed in this chapter is not a deal breaker for teams that want to go agile. Failure to meet certain characteristics can rule out the use of one or more named methodologies. Failure to satisfy any characteristic in a single category (from those listed in Figure 2.1) will probably rule out the strict adherence to a named methodology, but a named methodology may certainly (and probably should) be employed as a guide for a project that chooses to pursue agile development. None of these outcomes is necessarily bad. A team can still adhere to agile values under these circumstances.

A failure to meet a majority of the agile characteristics described in this chapter can pose real challenges for a project that wishes to go agile. Any team in this situation has two options available to it. First, the project may endeavor to change its environment. Depending on the specifics of a project, this may involve making an appeal to the project stakeholders, initiating a discussion with a higher level of management, or attempting to alter the project's relationship with its customer. While none of these actions sounds particularly appealing, adjusting the project's environment to a more agile mindset and foundation will be in the long-term interests of the project.

Second, the project may chose to implement agile practices on a gradual and opportunistic basis. If a project team cannot change its environment, then that project really cannot call itself agile. But what is in a name? There is nothing to stop the team from slowly, determinedly, and cautiously adopting agile practices. Automating the build, implementing a unit test framework, organizing requirements into features, and executing task cycles are all activities that any team may be able to adopt, and there are others. Perhaps the team is not adopting agile practices but instead best practices that happen to have been thoroughly investigated and embraced by the agile methodologies. Still, there is no qualitative difference.

Most any project can benefit from adopting even a single agile practice, but here is the caveat: That single practice must be correctly chosen, embraced by the team, given the appropriate time to take hold, and adhered to. There is no guarantee, but if the first practice does not take hold, there should be nothing to stop a project team from trying again. Still, a team that slowly and successfully adopts one practice after another may see those once rigid environmental constraints crumbling away until it finds itself in a place that it can truly call agile.

The correct application of agile practices and adherence to agile values can bring tremendous results in a wide variety of environments. My experience has included successful projects in a selection of markedly non-agile environments. Operating in such environments can, however, make implementing agile practice more difficult, reduce the productivity of a team, threaten morale, and significantly slope up the agile learning curve. Whenever possible, it is best to make the project environment more agile, but of course there are perils to that, as well. We will pick up the discussion of altering your project environment in Chapter 5, "Going Agile."

STARTING MONDAY: ASSESSING YOUR PROJECT ENVIRONMENT

After reading this chapter, you may want to determine just how agile your project environment is. This activity may help in selecting which agile path your project will embark upon, and the information you collect can feed directly into the topics discussed and questions raised in Chapter 5 and Chapter 6, "Agile Practices." Figure 2.2 provides a checklist that you may use to complete this assessment.

The Agile Environment Checklist

Your Development Team

☐ Do members of your team communicate and collaborate easily and often?

☐ Is your team located all in one space?

☐ Is your team less than 50 people?

☐ Are the members of your team interested in learning new things and changing the way they work as a result of the things they learn?

Your Project Management

☐ Does project management listen and respond to the needs of the team?

☐ Does your team have a hand in the way it is managed?

☐ Are there feedback mechanisms in place that allow your team to evaluate its progress and processes?

Your Customer

☐ Does your customer want to be involved throughout the lifetime of the project?

☐ Is your customer willing to make himself available for requirements and functionality-related questions as they arise?

Your Processes and Tools

☐ Does your team have a significant say in what processes and tools it uses?

☐ Is your team allowed to drop processes and tools it does not consider valuable?

☐ Can your team alter the process and tools it uses to better fit its needs?

Your Contract

☐ Are your project's requirements and milestone dates fixed?

☐ Is the cost of your project fixed?

FIGURE 2.2   Assessing your project environment.

This is not an exhaustive list of criteria, nor does it take into account the specific aspects of particular methodologies. DSDM, for example, has a more detailed list of questions known as a Suitability/Risk List [Stapleton03]. This list should, however, provide a team lead or project manager with a sufficient amount of input to guide the selection of an agile methodology (when reading Chapter 3, "The Agile Methodologies") and determine whether (and how) the project will strike a balance between an agile approach and a more traditional approach to software development.

One cautionary note: Do not make a big to-do out of this exercise. Rather, it is something you might complete on your own or share with one or two trusted members of the team. In short, keep a low profile. For reasons discussed later in the book, it is often best not to draw undue attention to your project when going agile.

3   The Agile Methodologies

In This Chapter

- Common Themes
- Methodology Descriptions
- Extreme Programming (XP)
- Scrum
- Feature-Driven Development (FDD)
- The Crystal Methodologies
- Adaptive Software Development (ASD)
- Dynamic Systems Development Method (DSDM)
- Lean Software Development
- Starting Monday: Investigate Further

The agile methodologies are as similar as they are different. The goal of this chapter is to provide the reader with a feel for each methodology so as to determine whether one or more of them is a good fit for a project or organization.

COMMON THEMES

So as to avoid repetition, themes common to all the agile methodologies have been left out of the descriptions. So that they are not overlooked completely, those common themes are listed here.

- Agile teams focus on completing features as opposed to simply checking off tasks.

- Agile teams attempt to work with change instead of preventing it.
- Documentation is secondary to working functionality.
- Timeboxing is not used to make people work harder but to ensure that tough decisions are not deferred and that the most important bits of work are prioritized accordingly.
- Planning and estimation are team activities and should not be performed by a lone project manager.
- Feedback collected near the end of the project arrives too late to be of any use to the project. Feedback should be elicited regularly so that the team can make adjustments during the project. Short iterations provide an excellent mechanism for feedback loops.
- Projects must be able to adjust their direction as the result of internal feedback and external events.
- Agile development is not about reusing techniques that work in every situation. It is about creating a project environment and culture that allow skilled professionals to adapt to changing requirements and situations.
- While process is a necessary component of software development, an over-specified process slows down a project.
- No amount of process can replace good people.

These points are not meant to reiterate the agile values or principles listed in Chapter 1, "Agile Development Primer," though in some cases one or more may be restated in plainer English.

METHODOLOGY DESCRIPTIONS

Each methodology is described in depth in the pages that follow. As much as possible, the descriptions of the methodologies are both thorough and consistent. For the sake of consistency, each methodology description should include the following information when available:

- The methodology's approach to management and programming activity
- How the methodology fosters a culture of communication and collaboration
- The methodology's conception of an iterative project flow
- The methodology's tolerance for diverse project environments

The most visible indication of this approach is in the process diagrams for each methodology. Each diagram has been built from the same toolkit of circles, boxes, and arrows, and the more commonly recognized process diagrams for some methodologies such as Scrum, FDD, and DSDM have not been included. This is intended to make the process diagrams more readily comparable across methodologies.

Finally, the exception to this unified description approach is Lean Software Development, which is not a methodology in the same sense as the other six.

EXTREME PROGRAMMING (XP)

The best-known and most widely used agile methodology is *extreme programming* (XP). It is also the only agile methodology that focuses primarily on the programming side of software development.

The impact of XP has been significant and far reaching. Many of the practices that XP has embraced and fostered are regularly adopted by agile and even non-agile teams. Several of those practices will be discussed in the book as agile practices. Furthermore, the XP community continues to develop, explore, and refine software development practices that can benefit a wide variety of teams.

Programmer-Centric, Test-Infected

One often gets the impression that every person on an XP team is a programmer. This is not far from the truth. Even the management roles on an XP team (the coach and the tracker) are meant to be held by individuals who also complete programming tasks. While XP teams typically can and do incorporate dedicated managers, analysts, and testers into their ranks, there is no position on an XP team that cannot be filled by a programmer (and that includes the job of the customer) [Jeffries00]. This is, in fact, a strength of XP. By making programmers responsible for their own analysis and management, XP cuts out many of the levels of (and barriers to) communication associated with traditional development processes. There are no walls that project plans, requirement documents, or hand grenades can be thrown over. Since they will be stuck with the plans they draft, XP teams tend to be more responsible with the system they build and realistic with the goals they set.

Additionally, XP is unique among the agile methodologies because of its laser-like focus on testing [Fowler03]. Although the other agile methodologies recognize testing as an important component of software development, XP is the only methodology to prescribe how testing should be fit into the development process. XP could not be implemented without testing. Furthermore, many XP-inspired agile practices (such as continuous integration, simple design, and refactoring) are of little use and potentially dangerous to teams that have not embraced testing.

Four Values, Twelve Practices

XP is founded on four values: communication, simplicity, feedback, and courage. These values are meant to guide the decisions and actions of an XP team. Set firmly atop those four values are the 12 practices of XP. The 12 practices are the muscle of the methodology. They stipulate how the team goes about its daily programming and planning activities. When strictly followed by a group of skilled and motivated programmers, they lead to a high-discipline, low-defect, results-oriented and effective project team.

XP's 12 practices have shifted slightly over time (and may continue to do so). Such change is merely indicative of a healthy, evolving, and relevant methodology. At present, the 12 practices (in no particular order) are as follows [Wiki04]:

Test-driven development: The practice of writing unit tests prior to writing code, which serves to aid the design and development process. Discussed as an agile practice in Chapter 8, "Testing."

Planning game: A set of rules and moves that may be used to simplify the release planning process. Discussed as an agile practice in Chapter 13, "Small Releases."

Whole team: The programming team, management, the customer, and all other pertinent parties work within the same open workspace to get the project done [Martin02]. This practice is the evolution of two former XP practices: onsite customer and collocated team. Onsite customer is discussed as an agile practice in Chapter 15, "The Customer," and collocated team is discussed as an agile practice in Chapter 17, "Communication and Collaboration."

Pair programming: Two programmers working at one workstation can actually produce better quality code without costing extra time over the life of the project. Discussed as an agile practice in Chapter 7, "Design and Programming."

Continuous integration: If each programmer checks in working code several times a day, the system should never be far from a production state. Discussed as an agile practice in Chapter 7.

Design improvement: The team needs to keep the code clean by regularly taking the opportunity to clean and simplify complicated or confusing sections. This practice was once referred to as refactoring, which is discussed as an agile practice in Chapter 7.

Small releases: Chapter 13 and Chapter 14, "Executing Iterative Development," discuss this common agile approach in depth.

Simple design: Programmers must design and code a system that works today, not one that may be needed in the future, because budgets, business conditions, and all manner of things can cause the future to change. Discussed as an agile practice in Chapter 7.

Metaphor: The project team should write and keep a simple statement that says what the system does and how it does it. This metaphor ensures that the entire team shares a common vision of the system. Discussed in Chapter 12, "Project Initiation."

Collective code ownership: The whole team owns the code for the entire system. Therefore, each programmer may work in whatever part of the code he needs to in order to complete a new feature or otherwise improve the system. Discussed in Chapter 7.

Coding standard: A common coding standard used by the entire team ensures that the code is easily understood and accessible by any programmer.

Sustainable pace: Teams that work too hard burn out, and projects with burned-out teams fail. Sustainable pace focuses on keeping team members working when they are in good shape and letting them stop when they are tired. This practice was once called the 40-hour workweek and is discussed in Chapter 10, "Agile Management."

Highly Iterative

An XP project runs under a steady percussion of one- to four-week iterations (illustrated in Figure 3.1). Just about all project activity may be stuffed into XP iterations,

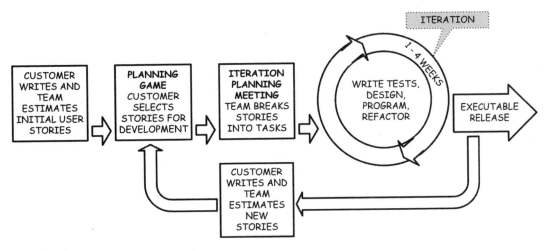

FIGURE 3.1 The highly iterative XP project flow.

including the creation of user stories (the artifacts that XP uses to identify and communicate project requirements). Arguably, the only three things an XP project requires to initiate its first iteration are an iteration's worth of user stories, a decision on the technology that will be used to complete those stories, and funding. These make XP a very handy tool for rapid prototyping and systems intended for rapidly changing business environments.

At the end of each iteration, the team delivers a fully programmed, fully tested, production-worthy version of the system (irrespective of whether that version goes into production or on the shelf). Therefore, in XP every one- to four-week iteration may be treated as a release. In practice, because the delivery of a new system every few weeks can be disruptive for many businesses, XP teams often will group a specific number of iterations into a release and deliver new software into production at an acceptably less frequent and consistent pace.

Small Teams, Engaged Customer

In its pure form, XP works best with smallish, collocated teams of up to a dozen programmers. There are other significant project characteristics that XP requires to be truly effective. These include:

- A knowledgeable member of the business who is assigned to and sits with the team.
- No plan that stipulates the delivery of specific functionality on a specific date.
- A minimal level of documentation.
- An open workspace (discussed in Chapter 17).

XP teams can and do manage to adjust when one or two of these project characteristics are out of whack, but a pure implementation of XP can bend only so far. Ultimately, a project team operating within an environment that does not conform to the majority of these characteristics will implement something less than pure XP.

See Also

- Browse over to Don Wells's "Extreme Programming: A Gentle Introduction" at *http://www.extremeprogramming.org*.
- Ron Jeffries also hosts a good site at *http://www.xprogramming.com*.
- The entire XP series, starting with Kent Beck's *Extreme Programming Explained: Embrace Change* [Beck99].
- ObjectMentor (at *www.objectmentor.com*) provides good-quality and well-respected XP training courses.

SCRUM

Scrum is a management-focused agile methodology that is relatively straightforward and can be enacted in a wide variety of project environments. The methodology provides the guidance necessary to direct a project in an environment of high changeability and where different parties within the customer may have conflicting or competing interests. Scrum is rather light on the programming side of things. While it does stipulate that the team deliver tested and working functionality, it does not prescribe how the team should go about achieving this goal.

The values upon which the Scrum methodology rests are commitment, focus, openness, respect, and courage.

Empirical Process Control

Scrum is founded on the concept of empirical process control. This concept is a contrast to defined process control, where the production process for a product is defined and refined to meet an acceptable convergence of cost and quality. The complexity and unpredictability of a software development project (in terms of requirements, goals, technologies, and the general business climate) often render the use of a defined process impractical. This is where Scrum enters the game. Through the use of empirical process control, users of the methodology control quality and cost by [Schwaber04]:

■ Making the aspects of the development process that most affect the project's outcome visible to the customer.
■ Allowing the customer to inspect the product regularly and ensure little variance from stated objectives.
■ If an inspection shows a variation beyond acceptable limits, enabling the customer to quickly adapt the development process or product.

In Scrum, empirical process control is used to steer both day-to-day and iteration-to-iteration activity.

Self-Managed Team, Scrum Master, Product Owner, and Everyone Else

Scrum makes a clear distinction between the team whose responsibility it is to deliver the project (programmers, testers, analysts, and technical writers) and everyone else (stakeholders, business users, and upper management). While the latter party selects the system's features and gets a regular view into the team's activity, the programmers perform the day-to-day management necessary to build the system. Even more than XP, Scrum puts the project team's success or failure in its own hands. While the customer has a clear and daily view into the activity of the team and is expected to exert control on the project at the outset of each 30-day sprint (an iteration in Scrum), the customer is not allowed to interfere with the team's activity at any time during the sprint. While in a sprint, the team is given the time, clearance, and trust necessary to make the right decisions and complete its work. The customer then has the opportunity to address any issues that may have arisen during the sprint prior to or at the onset of the next sprint.

The project team is led by a *Scrum master* (this may be the team lead or project manager). This individual bridges the gap between the project team and the customer and ensures that both groups are adhering to the rules and values of Scrum [Schwaber04].

Scrum recognizes that there may be lots of individuals related to a project (stakeholders and customers) with competing interests, worries, and needs, but Scrum designates a single individual, the product owner, to tell the team what it will develop at the beginning of each sprint. It is the job of the product owner (who may be a product or project manager in real life) to communicate and negotiate with the project's variety of stakeholders and interested parties and prioritize the product backlog, which contains an evolving list of functional and technical features for the system under development. In Scrum, the product owner must be a single individual (and not a group or committee).

Timeboxed and Sprint Driven

Timeboxing is an important feature of the 30-day sprint. This forces tough decisions about functionality and design. The more things different customers request at once, the longer it will take for the project to produce anything of value; meanwhile, there is always a more elegant design solution if the programmers would keep looking. The timeboxed sprint keeps the team from entering into such low-productivity quagmires by forcing the customers to agree on the features the team will produce in the next 30 days and by giving the team a hard deadline to deliver as much of those features as possible.

Scrum uses the daily Scrum meeting, which facilitates daily communication from the programmers on the project to the otherwise unengaged stakeholders. This meeting (discussed as an agile practice in Chapter 17) ensures that the team communicates frequently, that no one ever wanders far off course, and that customers are made aware of roadblocks in a timely manner. Figure 3.2 illustrates this process.

Each sprint ends with a product increment that demonstrably furthers the progress of the project, whether it is a release into production, a substantial and usable step forward in functionality, or the proofing of a particularly risky component. It is important to note that this sprint goal is not fixed in stone. It may be moved by agreement of the team and its product owner if the team appears to be ahead of or behind schedule.

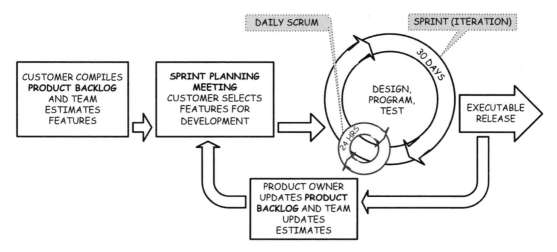

FIGURE 3.2   The sprint-driven Scrum project flow.

Little Assembly Required and Scalable

Of all the agile methodologies, Scrum is probably the one that can be established—without customization—in the widest variety of environments. This stems from its lightweight management processes and lack of specific programmer policies. This lightweight nature means that Scrum can wrapper existing programming practices, usually without significant changes to the way the team does its daily work. Scrum does, nonetheless, make some real demands on the customer. Mainly, Scrum requires that the customer not meddle with the team while in sprint and accept that the team may alter sprint goals as required by the difficulty or ease of its tasks.

Scrum out-of-the-box is formulated for smaller teams. However, it comes packaged with a scaling strategy, based on a Scrum of Scrums, that is claimed to have been applied to an 800-person project [Cohn04]. This approach will be discussed in Chapter 20, "Real-World Environments."

See Also

- Up-to-date information on Scrum and Scrum master certification can be found at *http://www.controlchaos.com*.
- *Agile Software Development with Scrum* by Ken Schwaber and Mike Beedle [Schwaber01].
- *Agile Project Management with Scrum* by Ken Schwaber [Schwaber04].

FEATURE-DRIVEN DEVELOPMENT (FDD)

Feature-Driven Development (FDD) tackles both management and programming activity, and it does it with scale, having clocked in a 250-person, 18-month project [Highsmith02]. In order to scale to this extreme, FDD calls for system-wide modeling activity at the outset of the project. This, combined with a penchant for providing an initial (but flexible) plan up front, has caused some to criticize FDD as not being very agile [Boehm04]. This is an unfair criticism. An FDD project is highly iterative, performs low-level analysis and design activities in the same iteration that it completes functionality, engages its customer through the entire lifecycle of the project, and is tuned to recognize and respond to change.

Nonetheless, FDD does celebrate its divergent opinions from some other mainstream agile methodologies. In particular, it values design-first activity, provides its customer with an upfront plan, and mandates that programmers own specific parts of the code [DeLuca04]. Of course, there are more than a few customers who might find such sentiments appealing.

Eight Best Practices

A successful implementation of FDD is founded upon eight best practices. As with XP's 12 practices, teams may gain some benefit from adopting one or more FDD best practices, but the practices are built to reinforce one another, and their full benefit can be obtained only when all eight are being followed. The eight best practices of FDD are [Palmer02]:

Domain object modeling: The domain model is an overall roadmap of the system to be built. It consists of a handful of high-level diagrams that depict the relationship between classes and sequence diagrams that demonstrate behavior. This approach is discussed more in Chapter 12.

Develop by feature: This is a premise common to all the agile methodologies (and a cornerstone of agile development). Features are discussed in Chapter 11, "Features and User Stories," and iterative development is discussed in Chapter 14.

Class ownership: The code class is an encapsulation mechanism that is common among object-oriented programming languages. Class ownership is the enactment of code ownership, where each class within a system is assigned to a specific programmer. It is the opposite of XP's collective ownership.

Feature teams: This practice is founded on the strict application of class ownership. The method is employed by class owners to complete features that span multiple classes. Since features commonly involve more than one class, feature teams are the common approach to design and development in FDD. Feature teams are discussed as an agile practice in Chapter 7.

Inspections: Inspections that focus on the identification of defects and do not intimidate or humiliate the programmer can significantly increase the quality of a system. Secondary benefits to inspections include improved transfer of knowledge and greater conformance to coding and design standards.

Regular build schedule: Teams need to build the complete system at regular intervals to identify integration errors early and so that an up-to-date and functional version of the system is always at hand (for activities such as client demos). The build may be performed hourly, daily, or even weekly, depending on the size of the project and the amount of time it takes to perform a complete system compile and integration. This practice is similar to the automated build agile practice, discussed in Chapter 7.

Configuration management: Code needs to be stored and versioned at a level that meets the demands of the team. Products with multiple installed and supported releases, for example, will need a much more complex versioning tool than a system that is deployed on only one server. Analysis, design, and testing artifacts also need to be versioned throughout the lifetime of the project. An audit trail of this sort is often necessary to meet legal or other business requirements.

Reporting/visibility of results: Regular and easy-to-understand updates of status are necessary to guide a project. Additionally, they keep the customer and stakeholders aware of the project's status, so that they can plan and act accordingly. FDD's approach to collecting and reporting status is discussed in Chapter 16, "Reviewing and Reporting Progress."

There are six key roles on an FDD project: project manager, chief architect, development manager, chief programmers, class owners, and domain experts (users, stakeholders, analysts, and so on).

Model Initiated, Feature Driven, Reporting Minded

As illustrated in Figure 3.3, an FDD project wends its way through the following five processes:

- Develop an overall model
- Build a features list
- Plan by feature
- Design by feature (DBF)
- Build by feature (BBF)

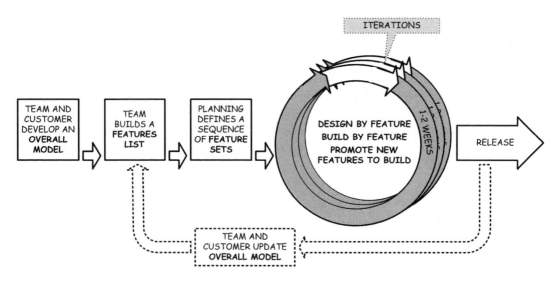

FIGURE 3.3   The design-first FDD project flow.

Each process is built on an entry-task-verification-exit (ETVX) pattern. That is, project teams have specific activities that should be completed prior to entering and exiting each process.

The observant reader may note two visual effects that make the process diagram for FDD different from the diagram for the other agile methodologies discussed thus far. First, the iteration circle is drawn three times. This is meant to signify that there are multiple feature teams on an FDD project working simultaneously and not all operating on the same iterative rhythm. Instead, each feature team starts and completes an iteration based on the planning of its chief programmer.

Second, note the arrows and box in dots at the bottom of the diagram. An optional (but not widely advertised) option in FDD is to iterate through the entire five processes (as opposed to the last two) on a less frequent basis. This approach may allow a project team to employ FDD within the more common small-releases, short-iterations approach taken by the other agile methodologies.

FDD keeps a thumb on the pulse of the project at all times. It tracks and reports progress by rolling up metrics based on the status of each individual feature through a low-overhead reporting approach that provides both feature-level progress tracking and executive-level project overviews (see Chapter 16). FDD highly values the ability to know the state of the project at any given time. When new or changing requirements cause a significant change in the overall schedule of the project, the project manager on an FDD project will go to upper management, exhibit and explain the deviations, and request a change in scope or schedule.

Frontload Some Architecture and Planning

This is where an FDD project takes shape. The first three FDD processes are performed only once in their entirety. However, projects return to these activities if the amount or timing of work changes significantly.

In the first process, the team works with the customer to produce an overall model of the system. The model is meant only to be completed to the "shapes" that will make up the system and is intended to force individual ideas and assumptions out into the open at the beginning of the project. The approach resolves misunderstandings early and ensures that the entire team has a more complete conception of the system. FDD also believes that some upfront work for the domain model will lead to better initial designs and reduce the need for future refactoring [Palmer03].

In the second process, the project's management uses the overall model to produce a features list. The system is broken down into features (bits of functionality that are each useful to the customer) and grouped into feature sets. On larger projects, feature sets are grouped into a hierarchy of feature sets. The feature sets are prioritized, and a minimally complete system is identified (this being the minimum features required for the system to be valuable to the customer) [Coad99].

In the third process, the project schedule is fleshed out in the form of a sequence of feature sets. Each feature set is planned for completion in a specific month (FDD does not give exact dates). Chief programmers meet to divvy up ownership of the different feature sets. At this point, all programmers on the project team are assigned to specific classes identified in the overall model.

Design and Build by Feature

The completion of each feature set takes place over one or more iterations of DDF and DBF activities (with each iteration lasting no more than one to two weeks). Each chief programmer works through his list of feature sets, creating a new feature team for each feature set, which is constituted by gathering together the owners of the classes related to the features in the feature set. The feature set is then completed with the guidance of a chief programmer (feature teams are discussed as an agile practice in Chapter 7). Feature sets are refined with the assistance of a domain expert, designed as part of a group activity, built and unit tested, reviewed by the feature team, and then integrated into the system.

It is worth noting that, although FDD does call for specific high- and mid-level programming activities, such as reinforcing an object-oriented design, mandating unit testing, and requiring design sessions and code reviews, it still does not step down to the low-level prescriptions (such as TDD and pair programming) associated with XP. Decisions regarding such low-level programming activity are left to the discretion of individual project teams.

Scalable, Prefabricated Approach

FDD lends itself to an approach that is more structured and design forward than other agile methodologies, while still enabling a streamlined management process founded on agile foundations such as short iterations, customer involvement, and testing. Teams operating in an environment where upfront design is required or highly valued might find FDD to be the right approach to blend agile developments with their existing development process. Larger projects that must follow an established and proven process or projects required to provide upfront (but still malleable) schedules may also find some real value in FDD.

See Also

- Peter Coad keeps a digital copy of the original FDD write-up (see Chapter 6 of *Java Modeling in Color with UML*) on his Web site at *http://www.pcoad.com/download/bookpdfs/jmcuch06.pdf* [Coad99].
- Stephen Palmer and John Felsing's *A Practical Guide to Feature-Driven Development* [Palmer02].
- The FDD discussion forum site at *www.featuredrivendevelopment.com.*
- Jeff DeLuca's FDD Web site at *www.nebulon.com/fdd.*
- David Anderson's *www.agilemanagement.net* has several good articles and blog entries about FDD.

THE CRYSTAL METHODOLOGIES

Crystal is based on the idea that different projects need different sorts of methodologies. The Crystal family is a set of methodologies that all share the same principles and building blocks, with each individual methodology geared toward a different project situation. Crystal should not be confused with a toolkit approach, such as the one employed by the Rational Unified Process (RUP), which provides a development kit of processes, practices, and documents that is meant to be tailored for each project. Instead, the Crystal approach is to collect and catalogue sample methodologies. A project selects a base methodology from that catalogue and tailors it to its particular environment and circumstances [Cockburn01a].

The Crystal methodologies are people focused, communication-centric, and highly tolerant—described by one agile practitioner as "the least dogmatic process conceivable" [Marick04]. Nonetheless, there are two restrictions on all the Crystal methodologies: they do not currently address life-critical systems, and they are based on collocated teams [Cockburn01a]. The three properties that are central to every Crystal methodology are frequent delivery, close communication, and reflective improvement [Cockburn04].

Project Size and Criticality

Crystal catalogs its methodologies by project size and criticality, as illustrated in Figure 3.4. In the catalog, project size is denoted by color (clear, yellow, orange, red, and so on) and criticality by letter (C for comfort, D for discretionary money, E for essential money). Project size is measured by the number of people on the team. Crystal recognizes that as the team gets larger, a heavier methodology is required. Criticality measures the severity of damage that may result from a defect or other error occurring in the delivered system. Criticality is therefore translated into the amount of rigor required from the methodology. A defect in the document management system for a small company may be a pain in the neck, but the worst result that may come of it is lost time and tempers (a C-level methodology will do here). Meanwhile, a defect in a financial trading system could result in the loss of significant sums of money, someone's job, and even the entire company (an E-level methodology is required here). Currently, the Crystal methodologies are indexed by color, so each methodology discussed here (Crystal Clear and Crystal Orange) is based on a given project size and can be tuned to fit more than one level of criticality. Finally, the astute observer will notice that a catalogue of Crystal methodologies extends beyond the area described here and depicted in Figure 3.4 [Cockburn01a].

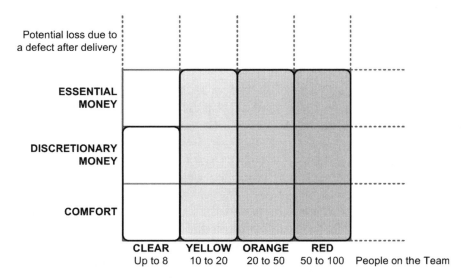

FIGURE 3.4   A corner in the family of Crystal methodologies [Cockburn04].

Working with Human Nature

All Crystal methodologies are based on the observation that the more disciplined a methodology is the harder it becomes to get everyone on the team to follow it. Therefore, each Crystal methodology strives to define the least disciplined process that could still succeed, maximizing the likelihood that everyone on the team will follow it. Through this approach, the Crystal methodologies explicitly trade efficiency (cost savings and time) for an increased chance of success (since more people will follow the less efficient process) [Cockburn01a].

Crystal has seven properties in total. The first three are mentioned earlier in this section (frequent delivery, close communication, and reflective improvement). The last four are personal safety (the ability to speak without fear of reprisal), focus (knowing what to do and having the time to do it), easy access to expert users, and a technical environment with automated testing, configuration management, and frequent integration. While the first three properties are mandatory to every Crystal project, the remaining four push the team further into the safety zone, the position in which the project is most likely to succeed [Cockburn04]. Each Crystal methodology is derived from the same pool of priorities, properties, principles, and sample techniques [Cockburn04]

Finally, Crystal Clear and Crystal Orange, like FDD, call for class ownership instead of collective ownership [Cockburn04]. Medium and large project teams using Crystal may want to take a look at the feature teams practice in Chapter 7 if coordinating work across classes has become an issue.

Crystal Clear

Crystal Clear is meant for a project of up to eight people on one team and working in the same area. Crystal Clear ratchets up the Crystal principle of close communication to osmotic communication, which is, in essence, a requirement that teams work together in an open workspace (see the agile practice in Chapter 17) .

Crystal Clear, like other Crystal methodologies, is focused on eliciting feedback, reflection, and tuning. Teams have a well-defined chartering period during which they define and validate the project, prior to the initiation of delivery cycles (as illustrated in Figure 3.5). During this period, the team is brought together, an Exploratory 360 is performed, the methodology is fine-tuned to the project environment, and an initial project plan is created. Crystal Clear projects must complete at least two delivery cycles and release functionality at least twice during the project, allowing it to gain real feedback from the customer in the middle of the project while there is still time to adjust. During each delivery cycle, the customer is entitled to view the progress of the system at least twice. Finally, reflection workshops are used to tune the current and future projects [Cockburn01a].

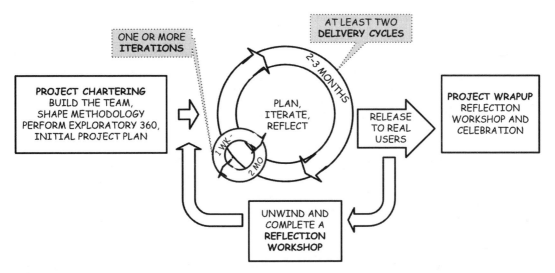

FIGURE 3.5 The Crystal Clear project flow, built around the delivery cycle [Cockburn04].

There are three essential roles on a Crystal Clear project: the executive sponsor, the lead designer, and the ambassador user [Cockburn04].

Crystal Clear may serve as either a fallback or stepping stone for teams that cannot currently operate under the high-discipline atmosphere of XP. It allows programmers greater flexibility in the way they perform project work. Crystal Clear teams have much greater freedom in identifying which agile practices and techniques they will employ, as long as they are in line with the overall methodology [Cockburn01a].

Crystal Orange

Cockburn originally introduced the Crystal Orange methodology in 1997, prior to all of the current hubbub over agile development [Cockburn97]. More recently, Cockburn has said he would use the methodology again, but only as a base methodology that would need to be tuned to a new project, since technologies, work products, and needs for interaction have shifted over the last several years [Cockburn01a]. The methodology is discussed here as a base methodology that one might investigate further and to illustrate how two methodologies like Crystal Clear and Crystal Orange may draw from the same building blocks to fit two significantly different project environments.

Crystal Orange was designed for projects where both cost and time to market are important, that involve from 20 to 50 people, and will run one to two years. It can be used for projects where discretionary money is at risk and may be extended to suit projects associated with essential money by adding additional verification-testing activities. Because of the larger project size, Crystal Orange provides 14 roles that individual team members may take (eight more than Crystal Clear), focuses on creation and makeup of subteams, and places additional emphasis on documentation (including the addition of requirements and user-interface documentation) [Cockburn01a].

Crystal Orange follows a similar project flow to Crystal Clear (as illustrated in Figure 3.5), but the length of a delivery cycle may be extended up to four months. The longer delivery cycle is meant to balance between complete releases that are production worthy and extensible and flexible requirements [Cockburn01a]. Crystal Orange also calls for three "deep" iterations in each delivery cycle, where the user has time to examine and give feedback on either a mocked-up or functioning system. Each delivery cycle may contain an additional number of "shallow" iterations [Cockburn97].

Finally, the methodology has an offshoot, Crystal Orange Web, that—as opposed to addressing a single project—takes on a steady stream of initiatives [Cockburn01a].

Just Enough Process and Very Flexible

The every-project-is-unique mindset that is built into the Crystal methodologies should make them amenable to a wide variety of individuals and environments. The methodologies are immediately useable but highly configurable by the fact that they come with specific policies and processes but readily allow the substitution of other, equivalent policies and processes [Cockburn01a]. Small, collocated teams that find XP too strict and Scrum too quiet on programming processes may identify Crystal Clear as just the right thing. Now that there is an entire book devoted to Crystal Clear (listed in "See Also" later in this section), project teams may be able to easily locate all the information they need on it.

Finally, the Crystal approach may have very real appeal for an organization that is attempting to execute many diverse projects. While it may entail a significant investment, the Crystal methodologies may help to rationalize a portfolio of projects by providing a set of base methodologies that provide just enough process across the organization.

See Also

- The Crystal Main Foyer at *http://alistair.cockburn.us/crystal/*. At last view it looked a bit dated, but it also contained some new and useful information [Cockburn04].
- Alistair Cockburn's new book, *Crystal Clear* [Cockburn04a], spells out this approach to agile development in a simple, insightful, and intelligent manner.

■ Another Cockburn book, *Agile Software Development,* discusses the Crystal approach and some of the notions behind it [Cockburn01a].

■ Finally, Crystal Orange is discussed in Chapter 4 of Cockburn's *Surviving Object-Oriented Projects* [Cockburn97].

ADAPTIVE SOFTWARE DEVELOPMENT (ASD)

ASD is focused at the project management level and its relationship with the organization it serves. The methodology has some trappings of traditional project management, including formal project initiation and review procedures. Unlike XP and Scrum, ASD folds the planning of future iterations into an initial stage of the project. Like other agile methodologies, ASD argues that command and control is a liability in high change environments because it slows the sharing of information and impedes quick decisions. ASD envisions the project manager as someone who enables a collaborative environment, helps to identify project goals, removes obstacles, and then steps back to let results happen [Highsmith00].

An ASD project is mission focused, feature based, iterative, timeboxed, risk driven, and change tolerant.

The Adaptive Lifecycle

As illustrated in Figure 3.6, ASD follows a project flow that is broken into three phases: speculate, collaborate, and learn. While an ASD project cycles through all three phases every four to eight weeks (registering an iteration length that is longer than most other agile methodologies), portions of the speculate and learn phases also serve to bookend the project. The focus on project initiation reveals ASD's organization-minded nature. During this activity, as well as at other periods throughout the ASD lifecycle, vital information is exchanged between the project and the organization within which it exists. This availability and sharing of information, bundled with the iterative nature of ASD, are meant to foster an environment in which the project leaders collaborate with the organization as iterations are completed to adapt the direction of the project toward the most desirable outcome.

Speculate

ASD replaces project planning with speculation. This phase is meant to help the project and its organization appreciate the uncertainty behind the system they are about to build. Speculation does not mean that planning should not be done; it just means that the planning should be understood as tenuous. This portion of an ASD lifecycle is unlike other agile methodologies that we have discussed so far in that it includes specific documentation recommendations. These documents are relatively

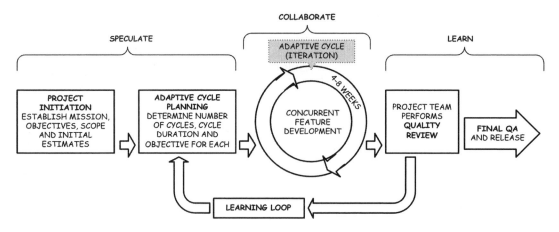

FIGURE 3.6   ASD's adaptive project flow.

simple and straightforward and are meant to serve as a guide and be refined throughout the life of the project. (The documents are a project charter, data sheet, and specification outline, and they will be discussed in Chapter 18, "Documentation.")

There are five steps in the speculation phase of ASD. The first step involves gathering information, including project mission, objectives, initial size, scope, estimates, and key project risks. Second, the entire project length is determined. Third, the number and length of iterations are decided. Fourth, the objective for each iteration is identified. Finally, features are assigned to each iteration [Highsmith00].

Collaborate

This is where programming activity occurs. Each cycle must deliver something useful to the customer, but there is no requirement that the iteration deliverables be production worthy. Like Scrum, ASD does not state how programmers should go about performing technical activities.

Instead of focusing on design, build, and testing activities, ASD calls for the project manager to focus on instilling a collaborative culture across the project team. Emphasizing collaborations is seen as an effective counter to excessive individualism, is a necessary catalyst of self-organizing teams, enables high-performance teams, and encourages individuals to focus their energies on merging diverse opinions and perspectives [Highsmith00]. There is no sure procedure for fostering collaboration within a project. For smaller projects, it could entail the institution of agile practices such as collective ownership and pair programming; on larger projects, much more effort and creativity may be required [Highsmith00a]. Ultimately, most any process, practice, or parlor trick that gets individuals on the team to communicate and collaborate more effectively is fair game.

Learn

ASD highlights the importance of people-based feedback more than the average agile methodology. Each iteration finishes with a quality review. During the review, the project team solicits and considers all input from the customer (priority number one), the mindset of the programmers, the quality of the delivered features, and the overall status of the project. It is assumed that the result of the quality review may have an effect on the content of future iterations (even though they were planned in advance).

ASD recommends, and explores in some detail, three techniques for the learning process: focus group reviews with the customer, technical reviews of the software, and a project-wide postmortem.

Foster Collaboration Among Individuals and with the Organization

ASD lends itself to culture-based and organization-minded implementations. For example, in its speculation phase, ASD addresses organizational activity that is not discussed by other agile methodologies. These activities may provide a leaner, more agile method of constructing, evaluating, and green-lighting project-level business cases. ASD may also work well in organizations that choose to retain some of the activities of traditional project management, including formalized project definition and review processes.

It should be noted that ASD has been criticized for not providing enough specific direction to everyday teams that wish to follow it as a methodology [Boehm04]. Nonetheless, through its focus upon and insight into techniques intended to foster project-wide collaboration, ASD might also make a good complement to a more structured agile methodology. XP has been proposed as an agile methodology that ASD might complement well [Fowler03].

See Also

- Jim Highsmith, an ASD founder, has written a book on the methodology: *Adaptive Software Development* [Highsmith00].
- You can also browse Highsmith's Web site at *www.adaptivesd.com*.
- A digital description of the methodology can be obtained at *http://www. jimhighsmith.com/articles/Dinosaurs.pdf* [Highsmith00a].

DYNAMIC SYSTEMS DEVELOPMENT METHOD (DSDM™)[1]

DSDM advocates agile techniques similar to many of those endorsed by the methodologies previously discussed. The approach calls for a collaborate relationship between a project team and its customer, the use of timeboxing to control scope and focus on business value, and a focus on testing to ensure the quality, reliability, and maintainability of developed systems.

DSDM purports to support all parts of system development from the conception of a project idea to the retirement of the system spawned by that idea. This includes determining whether the project is a fit for DSDM and maintaining the system after the project team has been disbanded. DSDM takes the same approach to process and work products as Crystal, providing what DSDM methodologists believe to be a bare minimum of process and work products that projects can tailor to their specific technical and business environments.

The Nine Principles of DSDM

DSDM focuses on building systems in a short time, in small increments, with participation of the entire team and users, and with an explicit mindset that tradeoffs need to be made between more valuable and less valuable features. It uses the following nine principles to meet these goals:

- Active user involvement is imperative.
- The team must be empowered to make decisions.
- The focus is on frequent delivery of products.
- Fitness for business purpose is the essential criterion for acceptance of deliverables.
- Iterative and incremental development is necessary to converge on an accurate business solution.
- All changes during development are reversible.
- Requirements are baselined at a high level.
- Testing is integrated throughout the lifecycle.
- Collaboration and cooperation between all stakeholders is essential.

Similar themes reverberate between these nine principals and the values and principles of the Agile Manifesto. In fact, the DSDM principles were the starting point for the principles laid out in the Agile Manifesto. DSDM views a failure to adhere to one or more of its nine principles—without the implementation of an accepted mitigation strategy—as the introduction of a significant risk into a project [Stapelton03].

DSDM teams are typically composed of two to six people; several teams can serve together within a single project. Important roles on a DSDM team are the developer (incorporating the traditional roles of programmer, designer, and analysts), tester, technical coordinator, ambassador user, and the visionary (usually the person who initiated the project and has a vision for it). DSDM purports to address the needs of all the relevant participants in a project and spells out a total of 12 roles that individuals may take on a project.

A Seven-Phase Approach

A DSDM project wends its way through seven phases. Five of these occur during the execution of the project, and two others cover the rest of the software development phase. Three of these phases (the functional model, design and build, and implementation iterations) address the main activities within a project and are included in the process flow in Figure 3.7.

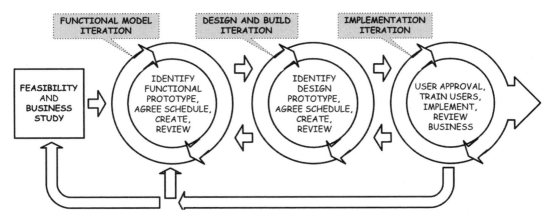

FIGURE 3.7 DSDM's flexible project flow.

How a project works through these three cycles is up to the individual project. Within DSDM, a single project team may transition forward and backward between these three phases (and even back to completing new feasibility and business studies) as it pursues an iterative approach. A team may even iterate its way through each phase sequentially, although this would result in a traditional waterfall approach to the project.

DSDM schedules work within timeboxes of two to six weeks. Each of these timeboxes may contain multiple cycles of each of the iteration phases seen in Figure 3.7. DSDM uses this timeboxing approach both to ensure that tough decisions regarding functionality and technical requirements are made and to enable regular and rapid feedback.

Tried, Tested, and Enterprise Ready

DSDM has one significant downside: In order to use it, an organization must pay to become a member of the DSDM Consortium (where it also has the opportunity to influence the evolution of the methodology). This may deter small projects from dabbling in the methodology. DSDM, however, might be very interesting to medium or large organizations with enterprise systems that want to adopt a supported process with a defined set of work products and documents. Additionally, the DSDM Consortium believes its approach is well suited to work within an outsourcing environment as well as alongside a variety of other project approaches, including ISO 9000-3, CMM, RUP, and XP [Stapelton03]. With it reliance on short iterations, testing, modeling, prototyping, and forays into a variety of process environments, DSDM may deliver the right amount of agile to such an organization.

See Also

- The DSDM Consortium's Web site at *http://www.dsdm.org.*
- Jennifer Stapleton's *DSDM: Business Focused Development* [Stapleton03].

LEAN SOFTWARE DEVELOPMENT

Lean Software Development defines the maturity of an organization by how quickly and reliably it can serve its customers. Process, documentation, and even best practices all take a back seat to the overriding goal of operational excellence [Poppendieck03a].

Lean Software Development is not a methodology in the same sense as those described earlier in this chapter. It does not propose a specific set of practices to follow nor does it subscribe to any specific process flow. Rather, Lean Software Development is a toolkit of principles, ideas that guide but that are not concrete instruction of what to do, that may be used by managers and team leads to identify, shape, and implement practices for the project team and organization [Poppendieck03].

Lean Thinking

Lean Software Development is based on the theory and principles behind lean production, which was pioneered by the once-upstart Toyota automobile company. The Toyota Production System did not take on a brute force mass production approach that was common in the day, including running machines to produce as much as possible regardless of need and always having plenty of stock waiting to be sent through the line. Instead, Toyota focused on eliminating waste in both the process and parts being used in the manufacturing system and dramatically reducing the turnaround time once an order had been placed. The approach, for example, sees inventory and raw materials that sit unused as waste, taking up space that has to be paid for. Similarly, decisions that are made earlier than necessary make a commitment to a specific direction and are expensive to undo, adding unnecessary waste.

The lean production approach swept through the American automobile industry in the 1990s. Of course, it did not stop there [Poppendieck01].

Seven Principles[2]

Lean development takes lean manufacturing principles and applies them to software development. Lean development is founded on the following seven principles [Poppendieck03].

Eliminate Waste

Waste is any activity, artifact, or output that does not add value to the system. This includes documents that are not required, components that are built but then not used, any features programmed that are not immediately needed, and even the handing off of activities from one group to another. Basically, whatever slows down the project team from giving the customer what he needs is considered waste.

Amplify Learning

This principle distinguishes the development process from the production process. While the production process is focused on reducing variation, the development process is focused on defining the right product or system. Project teams need to put processes in place and shape their environments so as to amplify learning.

Decide as Late as Possible

This principle tackles environments of high and rapid change head on. Delaying decisions allows a project team to wait until the future is closer and easier to predict. Keeping options open in terms of design requirements and code enables a project team to move quickly on new and even unexpected pieces of information.

Deliver as Fast as Possible

Delivering working software quickly and as needed instead of all at once and after substantial investment and effort helps reinforce the three priciples just discussed. By focusing on delivering what is needed now, we are able to hold off on decisions about what may be needed later. Learning is amplified because early deliveries enable the customer and the team to better understand and give feedback on the portions of the system that have yet to be developed. Finally, reducing the time between a request for functionality and the delivery of that functionality also reduces waste.

Empower the Team

Decisions cannot be put off until as late as possible if they all need to be made by managers and other high-level people. When programmers are provided with appropriate guidance and engaged in activities related to design and process, they make better decisions on their own than anyone else could make for them.

Build In Integrity

Integrity means that the product or system is put together well, operates smoothly, will continue to be useful over time, can be extended, is easy to use, and is not difficult to maintain. Integrity comes from good leadership, domain knowledge, communication, and discipline, not simply good practice and process.

See the Whole

Complex systems require expertise that is both broad and deep. A common pitfall in product development is the tendency to overemphasize one's expertise in a given area to the detriment of the entire system. A lopsided approach can be taken at the individual, project, and even organizational level because in each case the entity will want to maximize performance in its own area of specialization. The integrity of a system is based on how well its parts work together, not simply the quality of each individual part.

See Also

- Mary and Tom Poppendieck's Web site at *www.poppendieck.com* contains information and articles on lean software development.
- The Poppendiecks' book, *Lean Software Development* [Poppendieck03].

STARTING MONDAY: INVESTIGATE FURTHER

If you are inclined toward one of these methodologies, spend some time getting to know more about it. Sit for half an hour in the coffee shop of your local bookstore. Do some investigation online. Talk to someone who has done it. Do not take any one person's word for it.

If a project team chooses to follow a strict interpretation of one of these methodologies, this book can still be of assistance. Inevitably, the team will encounter resistance when trying to roll out some practice of process. Also, no matter how much a project environment can be shaped, adjustments will need to be made to fit in the methodology.

4 Selecting an Approach That Fits

In This Chapter

■ Choosing Between an Agile and a Traditional Approach
■ Selecting the Right Agile Approach

D eciding whether to take a project team agile and then plotting the course of that team's adoption of agile development can take significant thought and deliberation. Although it is the project team that is in the best position to contemplate and make such a decision, a number of factors that stretch well beyond the opinions of the team may bear upon the outcome.

CHOOSING BETWEEN AN AGILE AND A TRADITIONAL APPROACH

While any project may benefit from adopting one or more agile practices, it is not a given that every project would be better off by transitioning to an agile methodology.

Each of the variables depicted as sliders in Figure 4.1 may help to determine how suitable a given project is for an agile, traditional, or blended approach. These variables include two dimensions used to catalogue the Crystal methodologies (size and criticality), an additional dimensions introduced by Boehm and Turner (personnel), and the project team's environment, as discussed in Chapter 2, "Agile Characteristics."

When all the sliders for a project rest at either a high or low setting, then that project may be considered rooted in either an agile or traditional approach. These regions may also be referred to as the home grounds for each of the two approaches [Boehm04].

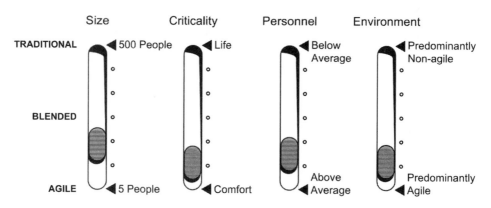

FIGURE 4.1   The variables for determining a project approach.

If all of a project's sliders are set low, that project is a model candidate for agile development. If all of a project's sliders are set high, then a traditional approach is best, although the team may cautiously adopt a handful of agile practices. If one slider is high and the others are low, the project may be able to proceed with agile development, although this would need to be determined on a case-by-case basis.

What follows is an explanation of each slider and the affect its position may have on a project's ability to adopt an agile methodology.

Size

While there are agile methodologies that address larger projects, team size cannot be entirely discounted when contemplating whether a project can follow an agile approach. Large teams rely on more lines of communication and more formal processes. This typically means more upfront planning and documentation, which take a bite out of both the team's productivity and its ability to react quickly to feedback and respond to change.

Size by itself should not be considered a deal breaker until it reaches at least 100 people, which is still within the normal tolerance of the Scrum, FDD, and DSDM methodologies. Size does not have to be a deal breaker above 100 people, but such an endeavor is best undertaken with the assistance of several individuals who are highly experienced in the domain, the technology, and the agile methodology to be used.

Criticality

As defined by Cockburn, criticality represents the potential for loss due to a defect in the delivered system, ranked from loss of comfort to loss of life, as discussed in Chapter 3, "The Agile Methodologies." Agile teams routinely tackle projects where errors may result in the loss of comfort, discretionary money, and essential money. No agile methodology has yet made a lot of noise about its suitability for projects where a single defect may result in the loss of human life. That is not to say the agile methodologies are unsuitable for such levels of criticality—nor that agile projects have not been successfully completed in environments of high criticality—simply that at this time there has not been enough work done in this realm to reach any definite conclusions. Therefore, high criticality is a potential (though not definite) deal breaker for pursuing an agile approach.

As criticality goes up, projects typically employ more upfront planning. In addition, these projects will require greater amounts of process and work products—and the more tested, tried, and proven they are the better. FDD, with its emphasis on upfront modeling and planning, and DSDM, with a defined and thorough set of processes and work products, may be best suited (or at least make the organization behind the project feel more secure) for higher-criticality projects. Again, however, loss of life is not a topic addressed frequently by even these methodologies.

Personnel

Several factors go into determining whether the people on a project are ready and capable to pursue an agile approach. This slider applies to programmers, managers, and customers—basically, anyone who can claim to be on an agile project team. While competent people are required for both agile and traditional approaches, more competent people are required for an agile approach [Boehm04].

Assuming a basic level of competence for every individual, these are the qualities most needed in project personnel:

1. Ability to communicate and collaborate
2. Technical skill
3. Experience with agile development

These qualities are ranked by order of importance and the level of difficulty entailed in attaining this quality when it is absent in an individual.

Every agile methodology requires a project full of people who can communicate effectively and collaborate on at least a basic level. Technical skills are important but not as essential to agile development because a group of amicable (that is, communicative and collaborative) people can help train one another. Experience with agile development is useful but easier to learn than technical skills [Lyndvall02].

Therefore, a lack of agile experience on a team can be overlooked rather easily. Solid agile experience but a lack of technical knowledge can often be overcome. For example, a programmer with lots of experience in C++ and agile development should have a minimal amount of difficulty starting on a project that uses Java and follows XP. However, even truly communicative and collaborative people may begin to encounter real hurdles when they need to learn too much at once, such as the new technology and agile development.

Environment

How a project's environment affects its ability to go agile is discussed in detail in Chapter 20. The categories of project environment characteristics include the development team, project management, the customer, the process and tools, and the contract. If a project's environment is not conducive to agile development in one of these categories, an agile approach may still be achievable. Each of the agile methodologies can flex to a certain extent to handle environments that include the following:

- A large and distributed team
- A waterfall plan
- An unavailable or aloof customer
- Heavy process and tools
- Fixed cost and scope

It is important to remember, however, that working in such an environment may both slow the adoption of an agile methodology and limit its overall effectiveness. Additionally, this advice applies to project environments that experience only one of these constraints, possibly two if they are mild, and under no condition three or more.

If a majority of these categories is deemed non-agile, the project team at best may pursue a blended approach, one in which the project selects an agile methodology and adapts as much of it as its project environment will allow. If the project environment is predominantly non-agile, then the team may be able only to gradually select and adopt those agile practices that will still fit within the non-agile constraints of its environment.

SELECTING THE RIGHT AGILE APPROACH

Once a project team has identified one or more methodologies that it is interested in and assessed its compatibility with an agile approach to software development, the team may still find itself considering just how deep a plunge it wants to take into any one methodology in particular or agile development in general. Four possibilities are discussed in this section. They serve to demonstrate the many options available to such teams, and no one option is necessarily correct. Finally, many projects never get nearly as close to the pure implementation as they would like, but they benefit nonetheless.

By the Book

When possible, it is best to adopt an agile methodology by the book. Scrum and DSDM, for example, both highly recommend starting by the book and tailoring it only after a project has become proficient with the approach. XP has occasional and raging debates on this issue, with no certain conclusion but lots of opinions. The important thing about the by-the-book approach is to ensure that the project sliders discussed in the previous section all indicate that the project is suitable for a pure agile application. Implementing XP on a fixed-cost project, Scrum with a dictatorial or abusive customer, or FDD in a CMM environment—without first making adjustments to the approach—is all but certain to result in a train wreck.

Modified or Partial Implementation

A project may modify the methodology as it implements it for several reasons, varying from the desire to substitute a single process with something that better suits the project's environment to a partial adoption in order to blend an agile approach with an environment that has high regard for traditional values, such as a plan-driven or architecture-first approach.

Process substitution is simply the replacement of one agile process or practice with another. Crystal Clear, for example, specifically endorses this practice. So, for example, a project may follow all of Crystal Clear but use a Scrum-like approach to planning iterations [Cockburn04]. Cross-pollination of processes and practices, after all, has been occurring within the agile methodologies for some time.

More significant is the partial implementation of a methodology. This approach is frowned upon by many strict methodologists, who argue that the project environment must be altered to reflect the values and principles of the methodology before its processes and practices are applied. While correcting the project environment first is a valid recommendation, many project teams simply have no chance of making good on it. The IT organization, long-established and enterprise-wide processes, or an entrenched business may pose a significant rampart that a lone project will not be able to overcome. In those cases, the project that hopes to become agile and has only one or two significant constraints in the way can implement as much of the methodology as its environment will allow. Then, possibly, once the methodology has borne fruit, the project may actually be able to use its progress to argue effectively for the removal of the constraints that prevent full adoption.

Finally, project teams that have only the time, ability, or interest in dabbling in agile development may select a single methodology and begin to incorporate the aspects of it that they find most interesting. Such a project team may also be interested in applying a mix and match approach, as discussed near the end of this section.

Embedded XP

XP stands out among the agile methodologies for being so explicit in how programmers should perform their day-to-day activities. Many projects and even organizations may look to the XP programming practices as how they would like development to be done while (justified or not) preferring a more defined and document-friendly project planning approach. Several agile methodologies that put more focus on planning or work artifacts than XP regularly flirt with its programming practices. Scrum and DSDM, for example, have some established processes for embedding XP programming practices within their planning frameworks [Stapelton03] [Mar04].

One approach to blending Scrum and XP, for example, is to implement Scrum in its entirety while folding the programming-level XP practices. The XP practices to be included are simple design, TDD, refactoring, pair programming, collective ownership, continuous integration, and a coding standard. In this approach, Scrum processes handle the iteration planning, execution, and tracking, and XP practices control and maintain the quality of the system [Mar04].

It should be noted that there are some conflicts specifically between FDD and XP associated with code ownership; FDD has it, and XP espouses collective ownership. This difference of opinion, in addition to FDD's upfront modeling activities, creates incompatibilities between FDD and XP at a programming level. XP programming practices that may add little value to an FDD project include simple design, refactoring, and even continuous integration.

Finally, an embedded XP approach even extends beyond the world of agile methodologies. The Rational Unified Process (RUP), for example, has an XP add-in.

Mix and Match

There is an option to transition to agile development without following any agile methodology. Instead, a project team may simply identify those processes and practices that it believes may benefit it most. Such a team may even identify practices as it goes, taking the time to select and adopt one or two practices, reassess its situation and needs, and then move on to select the next practices that will help it the most.

The mix and match approach, what some Agilists may more properly refer to as a team tailoring its own methodology, is a very legitimate solution for some projects [Highsmith02] [Cockburn01]. Moreover, a team that finds itself with too many sliders positioned toward a traditional software development approach may find that this is the only way to transition to a more agile approach. However, unless it has a team of crack programmers with solid agile experience, a project is likely to move more slowly when adapting agile processes and practices in this ad hoc manner.

The mix and match approach happens no matter what. Whether the team actually brings the process coach in on the secret and whether they are viewed as hacks or enhancements, individuals and teams are constantly tweaking, modifying, and augmenting whatever processes they are given to use [Oldfield03]. Also, as has been noted previously in this book, whatever helps to make software better, faster, and more useful to the customer should be considered fair game.

5 Going Agile

A team can approach the process of going agile from a variety of directions and with a variety of intentions. Some intentions can be very specific: "We want to start doing automated testing and test-driven development." Others can be more vague and far reaching: "We are already doing a good job at testing, but we want to get agile into our project management." Others, still, can sound specific but lead to many new questions: "We've been given permission to adopt extreme programming, but we must do it while continuing to complete the project." Occasionally, a team gets the chance to do it by the book: "Management has said we can pause the project at the end of this release and adopt Scrum." But even this scenario can pose challenges related to the project environment, the team learning process, and individuals, both on the team and business.

IS THE TEAM READY?

Sometimes going agile is a rocky experience. Knowing the project environment and where the team is headed (in addition to going slow) can steady the ship.

Hopefully, any project that is about to start adopting agile development has taken its bearings and knows the very basics of how it will start off in a more agile direction. Nonetheless, the following list may serve as a good double-check:

- Is there a customer?
- What methodology will be followed?
- How closely will the project stick to the guidelines of that methodology?
- Will the project go agile gradually or all at once?
- How well is the project environment suited for the planned changes?
- How much will the project environment need to adapt to meet agile?
- How difficult will it be for the necessary changes to be made?

These are all questions that should have been considered by now. There certainly will not be answers for everything, but if a project team has not at least thought through one or more of these questions, now is the time to do so. Answers to these questions will help a project's advocates for agile—whether they are programmers, the project manager, a higher level of management, or any combination—determine the steps that need to be taken before going agile, select the specific practices that should be adopted first, identify potential pitfalls, and choose the speed at which everything should proceed.

Preliminary answers to these questions will do. After all, a plan to go agile should be just as flexible as the practices that will be implemented and the project that will implement them.

ANNOUNCING THE TEAM'S INTENTION TO GO AGILE

It really is not in any project's interest to bill itself as Team Agile. In fact, projects going agile may benefit the most from trying to bring as little additional attention to themselves as is possible. The team will need time to work through even a single practice, to measure its benefit, to tweak its implementation, and ultimately to embrace or reject it. No team wants to have its hands tied to a well-publicized experiment or feel as though it is developing software while under a microscope.

Full Transition

A lot of people are going to know, because the project team will need to have sold the concept to the project's customer, the business, and upper management. But a team can also draw additional (and unnecessary) attention to itself by foretelling all the valuable things it is going to do with agile and claiming that it will become the role model for the rest of the organization. Such proclamations can actually raise the bar so high that the team will be unable to reach it. They can also build up resentment from other project teams.

Gradual Adoption

A plan based on gradual adoption should result in less immediate attention being focused on the team. First, because the project team will create fewer waves at start-up. Second, because a successful start-up will provide achievements that may be used to justify future changes to the project environment that may be required to implement additional practices and processes. Typically, it is easier to get someone to agree to use something when it is proven to work or at least is closely related to something else that has proven to work.

With this approach, it is even possible that a team will not need to ever make a big deal to anyone about going agile. If the project team has bought into going agile and decided to adopt it one or two practices at a time, the team may choose to put off announcing its new agile tendencies until it needs buy-in from individuals outside the project (such as the customer and higher-level managers) to implement practices such as user stories and frequent releases. The downside to this approach, of course, is that it is slower going than an immediate transition, but this by itself is not a bad thing.

The same approach may apply for a few programmers on a team who want to begin experimenting with agile but for whatever reason are not able to get the project's manager to seriously consider a full-fledged agile approach. The team may simply identify and adopt an agile programming practice that will not influence its overall velocity. Then, the successful implementation of that one practice may be used to justify a greater time investment for the next one. For example, a team lead might bring up the topic with the PM: "Remember that automated build we started using last month? Well, that went really well, so we'd like to try another agile practice to work alongside it—testing."

As much as possible, let the results of the team's foray into agile speak for itself. If the team's performance is improved, the customer, the boss, and the customer's boss are all likely to notice. Answering that agile practices were the key to the project's success will serve the team much better than heralding the results that agile practices are going to bring to the project once they've been explained to everyone, and once the team has implemented them, worked through all the issues, and then explained why it all took longer than they thought.

ENCOUNTERING, ADDRESSING, AND OVERCOMING RESISTANCE

A transition to agile development (or even the adoption of a handful of practices) can be met with resistance and even be seen as threatening to a wide variety of individuals and groups. In many cases, people have simply established a specific method of doing things and do not want to change. Overcoming the resistance of individuals and groups can be a key challenge to some project teams that choose to go agile. This may especially be the case in heavy process environments.

There are a lot of types of resistance project teams may encounter when going agile. Ultimately, each must be addressed on a case-by-case basis. Some of the most common are discussed in this section.

People Who Like Meetings and Documents

In many environments, the unfortunate reality is that people are all but encouraged to measure their progress by things that may not actually be productive but are easy to measure, such as the number of meetings they attend or the number of pages written in design documentation. Because such behavior may be the result of years of conditioning, no one can reasonably expect these habits to change overnight. As the team transitions to agile development, these individuals will find reasons to attend and hold more meetings and generate and cling to more documents than would otherwise be necessary. Confronting these individuals directly may not produce desirable results.

The most important thing for programmers on a team with such individuals to do is simply to avoid taking part in any unnecessary meetings or documents initiated by those individuals. The most important thing for the team lead and project manager to do is to be ready to step in if and only if the additional meetings and documents are reducing the productivity of other members of the team.

Agile practices are geared toward specific and useful goals such as fully integrated code and completed features at the end of each iteration. Hopefully, over time, these goals may wean individuals away from their meetings and their documents and onto better measures for defining their personal productivity.

Fears of Micromanagement

Constantly asking for estimates, regularly setting short term goals, holding daily meetings (no matter how short), and frequently checking on progress can stir fears of micromanagement within many sane individuals. When such practices are used in the wrong manner, people are justified in having these fears, but some individuals will not wait long enough to find out whether their fears are justifiable. From day one, these individuals may treat some agile practices and processes with suspicion.

To overcome these fears, project managers and team leads need to emphasize the reasons agile projects use these practices, but they should do so through actions, not words. Managers need to show interest in the obstacles standing in the way of team members and demonstrate that they can and will act quickly to remove them. Furthermore, managers must be respectful of the changeability and uncertainty of estimates [Cohn03]. One sure way to confirm fears of micromanagement is to react negatively when a task turns out to take longer than planned.

Business and Upper Management Do Not Want to Give Up Control

Even when everyone knows that detailed schedules cannot actually be adhered to and estimates are just estimates, it can be very difficult for managers and customers to let go of the project schedules, Gant charts, functionality-specific milestones, and commitment dates they are accustomed to. No matter that few projects in the organization actually meet those targets, managers and customers fear how much worse it would be if the targets did not exist at all.

If simply knowing what is actually going on is the problem, it may help to explain the process used by agile projects to track progress very specifically through the collection of a few reliable metrics, as discussed in Chapter 16, "Reviewing and Reporting Progress." If control is the problem—that is, management or the business is concerned they will not have a strong enough hand in the direction of the project—then explaining the process of planning iterations and releases and the amount of control provided may be in order (discussed in Chapters 10 through 14). Finally, if there's just no way around it, and the schedule has to be there and documents have to be written, the project team should still be able to manage a compromise between some agile and traditional processes (see Chapter 20, "Real-World Environments").

Ultimately, it will take time to change the opinion of managers and customers who have dug into their positions over years of working with projects that miss deadlines, deliver low quality, throw up change control walls, and the like. This is where adopting agile practices and processes gradually may matter most. A team will need early victories and may have to show significant progress before asking others to make significant changes.

Analysts and Testers

Testers and analysts can feel as though they have been given no place within the new vision of an agile project. This certainly will not be the case on all projects, but in some cases the traditional role of the tester may be adopted by programmers, and the traditional role of the analyst will seem to have been divvied up between the customer and the programmer.

In some cases, the roles of these individuals may not change dramatically. Analysts may still work with the customer to define new functionality, act as domain experts, and assist programmers with domain modeling. The organization (or the system) may require enough testing activities that cannot be covered by the programmers alone. In fact, testers may even find their roles enhanced because the project team will be interested in discussing testing at the beginning of the project rather than seeing it as an unavoidable obstacle at the end.

In other cases, however, extra attention will need to be given to these individuals to help them find their place in the new team. Testers may need to learn to work with the programmers throughout the project instead of just near its end. Analysts may need to transition away from heavy documentation and acting as a filter between the customer and the programmers and embrace a role that facilitates a timely and high-quality mode of interaction directly between the customer and the programmers.

When Agile Is a Four-Letter Word

Agile development—or at least discussion of it, opinions about it, and claims to have done it—is becoming ever more common. Unfortunately, there are places where agile has become a dirty word. It may be for completely groundless reasons (somebody told somebody about a team somebody else had worked on), but it is an issue nonetheless. If these opinions appear unalterable and are held by individuals who have influence over the direction of the project, then they really need to be taken into account when determining how the team will adopt agile.

One can imagine the perils awaiting a team that chooses to perform a speedy transition to agile in a hostile environment. In such a situation, even if the team manages a successful transition, once the word agile comes out, the project may not be judged on the merits of its work. In an environment that is unfriendly to agile, gradual and cautious adoption is recommended.

The team may find itself with new options if it can determine the actual concern that is held about agile. Is it something that the team can draw a chalk line around (such as the agile tendency against documentation or toward TDD) and simply agree not to go there? Conversely, the team may need to agree to something extra, such as a separate multi-week phase to perform integration and system testing. Either way, the powers that be may be more amenable if they believe their concerns are being acknowledged and accommodated. Even if the team has to throw out "that whole agile planning thing" to gain approval to implement development-level practices, then it is better off. After six months of successful, continuous integration and test-driven development, perhaps the answer about agile planning will be different.

If it appears that agile itself is simply a tainted term, then the team might make some headway by detaching the practices from agile. In this case, each practice that needs approval in order to be implemented would be presented based on the benefit it would provide to the project and not its association to agile. That does not sound so bad, does it? Someone may also be able to scrape up some literature on the practice that predates agile. This may help if the real concern about agile is that it is new, untested, or unproven.

Chapter 17, "Communication and Collaboration," and Chapter 19, "People," discuss topics that may be helpful in addressing issues that arise from resistance in the face of a transition to agile development.

STARTING WITH THE BARE MINIMUM

It is easier to build up from a bare minimum methodology than it is to pare down from a one-size-fits-all approach [Stapleton03] [Cockburn04] [Boehm04]. Starting with too much in the way of process and work products is a problem because too often the superfluous stuff never is gotten rid of. Additionally, with too much process, it becomes difficult to identify what really works and what just gets in the way. When a whole load of process is dumped on a project all at once, a team typically begins to follow bits of the process, but typically the individuals do not follow the same bits. When the team tries to do too much at once, the result may be that it is unable to give a fair shot to anything. Some practices, such as automated unit testing and continuous integration, are of greatest benefit to the team only when they are followed by all or nearly all members of the team. Teams have adopted these and other agile practices and then dismissed them because not every member of the team invested time in their implementation. As a result, the experiment was deemed a failure, and agile was blamed.

Starting with as little process as necessary is a theme that is repeated throughout this book. It is discussed with regard to the creation of documents, the use of tools, and (as already begun) the adoption of agile practices and processes themselves.

ALTERING THE PROJECT ENVIRONMENT

As noted in Chapter 2, "Agile Characteristics," the best thing to do prior to implementing agile development is to make the project environment as conducive to agile as possible. In an ideal setting, this means training customers and programmers to collaborate with one another, convincing stakeholders and upper management that continuous planning really can produce better results than an upfront plan, ensuring that the project team has the ability to set its estimates and identify the processes it needs to operate most effectively, and focusing everyone on the development and delivery of useful and useable software.

In many environments, such changes simply cannot be made. Whether it is because agile is being advocated by only the programmers on the project or because the organization with which the project exists is simply too large and set in its ways to adjust, the result is the same. The environment cannot be dramatically altered, and the project team will simply have to adjust. Nonetheless, there are still little things that a project team in such a situation may be able to do to shave off some of the roughest edges of a stubborn project environment.

Adjust with Many Microtouches

Requesting that environments or even people change in significant ways can be like poking at a hornet nest without a stick. Often, instead of shifting to a more desired behavior, the organization or individual can actually become defensive and even more difficult to work with. Alistair Cockburn proposes a technique called *microtouch intervention* for making significant changes in project environments without stirring up a nest full of angry hornets [Cockburn01].

Cockburn proposes a series of small changes intended to have a large impact. Each microtouch consists of a small change in the project team (such as a seating assignment) or a small request of an individual (some sort of simple favor). The effect of these many small but coordinated changes can be significant. Obstacles may be overcome. Goals may become more aligned. Individuals may feel less friction between one another and find more areas of mutual benefit.

Eliminate Waste

Any activity or artifact completed by a project team that does not provide a benefit to the customer is a waste. Depending upon the situation of any given project, examples of such waste may include documentation that does not have an immediate and valuable purpose, requirements analysis that does not result in developed functionality, and even features that are not absolutely required for the upcoming release.

In *Lean Software Development,* the Poppendiecks present seven categories of waste in a software development project [Poppendieck03]:

Partially done work: This is an investment that has yet to provide any return. Work (such as the fine-grained analysis of a feature) that is left undone can quickly grow obsolete so that it needs to be completely redone. Even when partially done work is completed, it often takes a significant amount of additional time to update and integrate because the system has evolved since the partially done portion was completed.

Extra processes: Documentation, meetings, and official sign-offs all take time to complete. Reducing and removing unnecessary processes is a mantra of agile development and a theme of this book.

Extra features: Adding a feature because it may be needed typically seems like a good idea. We do such things because we are trying to think forward and act instead of having to look back and react. Features that go unused, however, have a real cost associated with them, not only in terms of initial development time but also in terms of integration, tracking, debugging, deployment, and support activities. An extra feature, unfortunately, may be just as likely to necessitate an emergency release as it is to be of benefit.

Task switching: No matter how thin and sharp the blade, matter is always lost when an object is sliced in two. Similarly, whenever someone has to stop and put down one thing in order to pick up another, time is lost in the transition. Teams and individuals complete work most efficiently and quickly by completing one thing before moving on to the next.

Waiting: People cost money and time. Unnecessary waiting, for whatever reason, results in waste.

Motion: Just as waiting is waste, unnecessary movements are also waste. Programmers needing to seek out analysts or the customer to ask a question is waste. Document sign-offs and hand-offs are also motion and, when unnecessary, are similarly wasteful.

Defects: Fixing a defect takes time that could have been spent on something more productive. Defects typically take more effort to fix the longer they go unnoticed. Therefore, adjusting processes to find defects faster can eliminate waste.

Reducing waste lightens the load that the project team needs to carry at any given time, increasing its overall productivity and responsiveness. Demonstrating that a given activity, process, or document may be wasteful in time or money can be a successful strategy to initiate change.

ITERATION ZERO

Agile teams strive to deliver functionality that can be appreciated by the customer at the end of the first iteration. Sometimes, however, it makes sense for the team to focus on building its foundation before delivering functionality. This may be the case especially when a team is new to agile development. Regardless of what practices it initially adopts, a team new to agile development may consider employing an iteration zero strategy. (ASD refers to this technique as Cycle 0 [Highsmith00a].)

An iteration zero does not deliver any functionality to the customer. Instead, the project team focuses on the simple processes that will be required for the adoption and use of most agile practices. From a programming point of view, the features delivered in an iteration zero may include:

- Source control system installed and operational
- Initial build scripts written and checked into source control
- Initial build promotion and deployment scripts written and checked into source control
- Automated test framework selected and implemented with an empty test suite
- Construction of a rudimentary continuous integration process

One good method of performing these activities is to wrap them around a Hello World program. Hello World can then be the first piece of functionality to pass a test in the unit test framework. It can be the first thing to be automatically compiled, run through the continuous integration process, checked into the source control, promoted to the testing environment, and automatically deployed.

From a management point of view, iteration zero outputs may include:

- Initial list of features identified and prioritized
- Project planning mechanism (spreadsheet, simple database, index cards, or other planning tool) identified and agreed upon
- Identification of and agreement upon a team customer, essential stakeholders, and business users and the nature of the iterative planning process, such as the time of planning meetings and the length of iterations

The activities performed in an iteration zero are analogous to learning the letters and numbers of a foreign language. Before learning to read a foreign language, we need to know how to pronounce the letters in that language. Similarly, before writing tests, we need to have a unit test framework, and before prioritizing and planning features, we need to have a simple system to track and organize those features. Finally, assigning this foundation-level activity to a single short iteration timeboxes the work, which guards against gold-plating, analysis paralysis, and a host of other project villains.

DISCONTINUE A PROCESS ONCE IT HAS SERVED ITS PURPOSE

The processes employed by project teams can be split into two categories. Some processes need to be followed all the time, such as deploying the new release of an enterprise application into the production environment. Other processes serve to train and cement new habits, such as sticking a mark on a calendar to signify that the last daily run of the team's new automated test suite finished successfully. While the first type of process may be altered or amended, it is something the team will always need to do. For example, the risk of letting someone shove the new release of an application into an enterprise environment without first backing up the old system, then bringing down other dependent systems, then deploying the new system, and then running a system diagnostic is just too great.

The latter kind of process, however, should be removed. Transitioning to agile development may entail a number of these little processes—such as asking at the daily stand up whether anyone did not check in their code yesterday (see Chapter 17), tracking a temporary metric (see Chapter 16), or citing specific rules that must be followed during release planning (see Chapter 13, "Small Releases"). They will likely be necessary to help team members break old habits and learn new ones. However, each process must be discarded once it has served its purpose. If not, people may continue to strive to meet the goal of the process even though it is no longer particularly valuable to the team. If a multitude of little processes begins to accumulate, they can bog down the team. Finally, in an extreme scenario, too many mostly harmless but useless processes left in place can even threaten morale.

FALSE AGILE PRACTITIONERS AND PROJECTS

False agile practitioners are not necessarily disingenuous or ill-intentioned individuals. They may honestly believe they are doing agile development, for example, because this is what others they have worked with have told them. Further, as stated repeatedly throughout this book, there is nothing wrong with melding agile practices onto a traditional software development process (or vice versa, for that matter).

What is dangerous about false agile is the discordance and potential failure that will ultimately result when a project founded on a standard development process declares itself agile, does not change any of its non-agile underpinnings, and yet begins to take on agile habits without a genuine understanding of the practices and principles on which they are based. Such a project is headed down a bad path for a variety of reasons.

First, false agile projects may only do themselves more harm by trying to do some of the things agile projects do, such as not freezing requirements and releasing often, without following many of agile development's disciplined practices, such as automated testing, continuous testing, and simple design. Second, there is a significant potential for real misunderstandings between different parties on the project. Stakeholders and users who have been sold on iterations and user stories may not recognize that many agile practices require their regular participation and that estimates are not timeline commitments. An old-fashioned manager who controls the information conduit between programmers and users but does not really comprehend user stories could wreak absolute havoc on timelines and deliverables by miscommunicating estimates, requirements, and priorities. Ultimately, false agile practitioners and projects threaten real harm to both themselves and the movement as a whole.

Traditional development processes masquerading as agile can sometimes be obvious. At other times, however, some real investigation may be necessary. Pete McBreen, in an insightful article titled "Pretending to Be Agile," has provided a list of the top 10 signs that a project is just pretending to be agile [McBreen02]. The items below paraphrase his list:

10. The project plan slates the first release 18 months into the project.
9. Deliverables are handed off from analysts to architects and architects to developers.
8. Architects are proud of not writing any code.
7. The project hierarchy puts programmers and testers at the end of a long food chain.
6. The team keeps asking the business to sign off on requirements.
5. Programmers complain when change requests sneak through change control.

4. Two months into the project and the team cannot show any working code.
3. The team is encouraged to document instead of communicate.
2. Testing and quality assurance act as the end of the process and not part of the development team.
1. Tasks are assigned to individuals who complete them alone.

The astute observer may note that several of these items relate to project culture. This is why one must use care and caution when melding agile practices and a standard development process. Most agile processes are predicated on the four core agile values: individuals and interactions, working software, customer collaboration, and responding to change. When some or all of those values are not there, one must evaluate the agile practice and the non-agile project to make sure they are still an appropriate fit. This means employing the advice discussed earlier in this chapter and elsewhere in this book.

STARTING MONDAY: MEASURING THE TEAM'S PROGRESS

Some project teams may want to measure their progress at adopting agile. A team that is interested in doing this might use the following scale to rate its progress toward achieving agile nirvana:

1. The project has decided to start implementing agile development.
2. The project has successfully implemented its first agile practice and has posted a copy of the Agile Manifesto in inch-high letters on a common wall near the team's location.
3. The project has adopted a second practice while collecting metrics and holding review meetings to measure its level of agility.
4. The project is regularly adopting additional agile practices and actively monitoring its level of agility.
5. The project has not checked its level of agility for months and is altogether focused on adopting or adapting any practice that will result in better communication, higher quality code, and a system that most accurately meets the needs of the business.

The point? Project teams should not fret over how agile they have or have not become. Rather, if a team needs to measure progress, it should focus on whether it and the business are communicating better; whether the code is cleaner, easier to maintain and less prone to defects; and whether, ultimately, the business is receiving more of what it has been asking for. Ultimately, a team should not really care whether it is more agile if all the rest of this activity is taking place.

6 Agile Practices

Agile practices are the things that agile teams do every day to write quality code, deliver useful features, plan and track progress, and react to change.

WHERE TO START?

If a team is not starting a brand new project with agile development—or unless that team has been given permission to pull its live project to a full stop, distribute books, hold lots of discussions, and start again at half-speed—the team will have to figure out how it is going to start phasing in agile practices. This is an activity that will require some thought and attention. Simply touting agile practices and then expecting the team to find its way toward agile nirvana, for example, will likely result only in a confusion of half-adopted practices.

Every team needs a plan for adopting agile practices. Teams with plenty of time to spare should seriously consider simply selecting an agile methodology and adopting all its processes at once by the book—no joke. Assuming that team does not have significant quantities of spare time on its hands, the plan can be very simple. First, identify one or more practices to adopt. Second, implement the practice or practices, evaluate the implementation, and make adjustments as necessary. Third, either accept or reject the continued use of each practice. Finally, return to the first step. This process is illustrated in Figure 6.1.

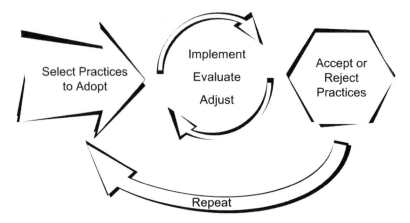

FIGURE 6.1   The ideal model for rolling out agile practices.

When going agile, the details behind any two plans will likely be different, although potential similarities are discussed later in this chapter and elsewhere in this book. The way a team implements agile practices depends on the methodology it is following, the speed at which it is adopting agile, and the project level that is being targeted (development, management, or both). A lot will depend on the individuals on and associated with the team. A lot may depend on the company culture and the technology that is being used.

Ultimately, each team going though this process must come up with its own right answer. When following a named agile methodology, a project team may sometimes come across a specific process (and practice or work product) about which the team is unsure. The team as a whole and even key individuals may be uncertain whether to follow the recommendation of the methodology or refrain from implementing the specific process. Boehm and Turner suggest a simple but intriguing query that may be asked in such a situation: Is it riskier to adopt or not adopt the process in question? The answer to this query may not decide the fate of the process in question, but it may help to frame the debate [Boehm04].

Speaking for most any process, if the project team is responding positively and the results are easy to perceive, keep it up. If a new process causes strife and its benefit cannot be easily discerned, then the project team should stop doing it, evaluate what has been done, and choose a different direction, which may mean trying the same process again or dropping that process and trying a different one.

SELECTING THE NEXT PRACTICE

The following sections discuss three methods that may be used to select the next practices the team will adopt.

Current Worst Problem

This approach asks where the team is hurting most. Next, is the team hurting most at the development or management level? Is the problem related to testing, integration, planning, or communication with the customer? The rationale behind this approach is that you are continuously zeroing in on that area where the team should be most willing to throw its whole weight behind a more agile solution.

The approach is based on the following process (which is a modification of one proposed by Don Wells) [Beck99]:

- Identify your project's worst problem.
- Pair it with the agile practice that best addresses it.
- Get buy-in from the relevant parties.
- When that is no longer your worst problem, repeat.

Biggest Bang for the Buck

What agile practice, implemented today, could deliver the best combination of fastest and greatest return on investment? This practice may be the team's current worst problem, but it does not have to be. The biggest bang for the buck should be something that takes limited time to implement, has the greatest likelihood for success, and will have a visibly positive effect on the project. It may be an automated build or short iterations.

There are two major benefits to selecting a practice in this manner. First, the swift and successful implementation of one or two agile practices can be a boost to morale and rally the team around the effort to go agile. Second, if necessary, the results of that swift and successful implementation may be used to persuade the powers that be to permit the project additional latitude in adopting agile.

Easiest Thing First, Hardest Second

This approach, which is a strategy of Crystal Clear, combines the previous two approaches. Initially, it steers the project team toward an "early victory" to boost morale and build team confidence. Then the team takes its newfound morale and confidence and turns toward tackling its worst problem. The strategy cautions that the team should ask if its hardest problem is still too hard (is success too uncertain or will it come at too high a cost). If so, the team should zero in on the hardest problem it has where success is very likely [Cockburn04].

REJECTING A PRACTICE

Not every practice is suitable for every project team. While one would hope that a team typically understands itself and agile development well enough to know in advance which practices are good matches, this is not always the case. No team should be afraid of abandoning an agile practice now and then if that practice has been deemed an unsuitable fit by the team. A team loses momentum when it begins flailing at a practice that it is unable to implement. It will regain much of that momentum simply by dropping the failing practice. It may then gain additional momentum by selecting another, better-suited practice to implement.

If a team finds it necessary to abandon a practice, then it should take the time to evaluate why that practice was rejected. Some important questions to consider are these:

- Was there another agile practice that the team should have implemented before trying to implement this practice?
- Did everyone associated with the practice (members of the team, the PM, and the customer) really understand the practice before the team attempted to implement it, and do they really understand it now?
- Is the project trying to go agile too quickly?
- Is the project going agile too slowly?
- Did the practice fail simply because there was no second or third practice to help reinforce it?
- Was there something about the project's environment or technology that caused the implementation of the practice to fail?
- Should the team attempt another implementation of this practice in the future?
- Are there other practices similar to this one that the team may encounter trouble implementing?

Answers to these questions may lead a team to all manner of conclusions and actions. These might be rather simple and basic, such as a better understanding into selecting future practices to adopt, or they might have wider ranging effects, such as a decision to alter its physical location or relationship with the business. Ultimately, what is essential is the determination to do something with the information gleamed from the postmortem.

ADOPT PRACTICES BEFORE TOOLS

Agile practices are meant to be adopted and adapted by teams in order to help them produce better, more valuable functionality faster. Tools also can help us do things better and faster, but tools are not as malleable as practices. Tools implicitly retain the assumptions and biases of their makers; this can cloud, skew, or impede the learning process for teams that are trying to adopt both a new agile practice and a tool related to that practice. People may learn the tool instead of the practice and therefore go through the motions of the practice without comprehending its real value or actually benefiting from that practice. Worse yet, tools can take a significant amount of time to put in place and learn. You do not want to be on a team that has the misfortune of trying an agile practice through the implementation of a tool only to go sour on the practice because team members could never master the tool.

XPers often argue that paper, pencil, and marker board are the tools a team should always start with [Beck99]. This is valuable advice. Once the team learns a practice and grows to value it, then of course it can and should consider tools to make that practice even more useful. See Figure 6.2.

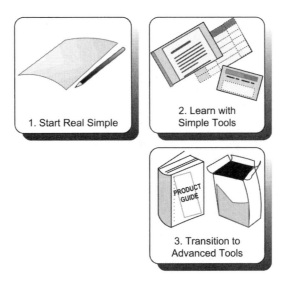

1. Start Real Simple

2. Learn with Simple Tools

3. Transition to Advanced Tools

FIGURE 6.2 Adopt agile practices before complex tools.

There are notable exceptions to this rule. Some agile practices such as automated builds and automated testing benefit from or rely on little tools (such as Ant and JUnit). Additionally, a spreadsheet application is a fine place to start cataloguing and tracking planned features and user stories. Finally, as we have discussed earlier, teams cannot always control everything that goes on with their project environment. Sometimes a team is required to use a given tool for project activities, such as a third-party testing or planning tool. In such cases, the team may need to take both extra time and extra care to learn the practice and implement it through the requisite tool.

LEARN PROGRAMMING PRACTICES IN PAIRS

Even if a project team has no pair programming experience, it could benefit from trying to learn and teach many of the agile programming practices such as automated testing, simple design, refactoring, test-driven development, mock objects, and ObjectMother through pair programming. The practice is described in Chapter 7, "Design and Programming," but at its most basic, pair programming is simply two programmers sitting down at one workstation to complete a programming task.

There are two reasons for working in pairs when adopting agile programming practices. First, two programmers working together will typically learn faster and with fewer mistakes than one programmer learning on his own. Second, once the first pair on a team has learned the practice, then that pair can break up; each programmer can then pair up with and teach the practice to another member of the team. This can happen while each pair is programming real code and contributing to the completion of the project. To be clear, using pair programming in this fashion does not mean that the entire team needs to be pair programming the entire day or even half the time. If pair programming sessions were targeted to occur only at those times when two heads will most certainly be able to learn faster than one, it should be easy to imagine how a pair-learning approach can cause new agile practices to ripple quickly through the project team—possibly without even causing a significant disruption in the completion of work.

AGILE PRACTICES IN THIS BOOK

The agile practices discussed in this book are listed on the back cover. The practices themselves are distributed throughout the book and discussed in the chapters to which they most directly apply. The majority of these practices are called out specifically as agile practices, which is really just a label to indicate that the practice will be discussed in a specific manner, as explained in this section. The list contains two practices central to agile development—small releases and short iterations—that serve as the foundation for Chapters 13, "Small Releases," and 14, "Executing Iterative Development," respectively. Finally, the list contains several other agile practices and techniques that, while discussed with less focus in this book, can be an important aspect of some implementations of agile development.

Agile Practices Explained

Each practice that is called out as an agile practice is broken into up to six sections, allowing for easy location of important information.

Purpose and Benefits

A short explanation of the rationale behind the use of the practice and what value it will bring to a project team. This section, plus the short blurb that precedes it, should provide someone who knows little or nothing about the practice with the information he needs to determine whether the practice could suit his needs and whether he should continue on and read more about it.

Prerequisites

Things a team should or must have in place prior to implementing the practice. Typically this section will include other agile practices. Sometimes it will include other project environment characteristics. This section should help project teams determine whether they are ready to begin a practice. If it is omitted, then there are no prerequisites for the practice.

Detail

This section provides all the specifics required to learn and adopt a practice. Typically it is included only when an agile practice is less well known or when that practice is not well documented elsewhere.

Implementation

An in-depth discussion about how to implement the practice in everyday project environments. The section includes practical information on how to introduce the practice on both new and existing projects and how to make the most of it.

When a detail section is not included for the practice, this section will also provide a basic overview of the inner workings of the practice.

Opportunities and Obstacles

This is a mix of notes on the practice. Most typically, the section addresses extraordinary hurdles the team may happen upon and highlights potential opportunities that may come from adjusting or extending the team's use of the practice.

See Also

This section includes a list of other online and print resources that may prove useful when implementing the practice. Except on rare occasions, this section avoids revisiting See Also links already listed in Chapter 3, "Agile Methodologies," or materials listed in Chapter 21, "Seeking Additional Assistance."

Whenever possible, freely available and online (but trustworthy and credible) resources have been included in this section, so the reader does not get the feeling that every time he wants to explore a topic further, he needs to run out and buy another book.

Why These Practices Were Chosen

Obviously, there are more agile practices than those specifically called out and discussed in this book. This book addresses the practices that it does for one or more of the following reasons:

- It is a core practice of multiple agile methodologies
- Benefits can be reaped from its application and acceptance in a wide variety of project environments
- It relates to other material discussed in this book

Just like the children of Lake Wobegon, all agile practices are above average, regardless of whether they are mentioned by name in this book.

Finally, the astute observer may notice that most of the agile programming practices discussed in this book (specifically those discussed in Chapter 7 and Chapter 8, "Testing") originated out of XP. Of all the agile methodologies, XP is the only one to prescribe in detail how programmers should go about their design, development, and testing activities. The other methodologies only go so far as to specify the duration and nature of iterations, permit the simultaneous execution of analysis and design and development activity, or define the non-software artifacts that the programmers should produce and deliver. This lack of deeper programming-level direction on the part of the other methodologies may be evidenced by their tendency to tag-team their more management-level approach with XP programming practices. This is evidenced most often with Scrum and DSDM.

7 Design and Programming

For programmers on an agile project, this is where the tires meet the road. The topics and practices discussed in this chapter and Chapter 8, "Testing," are the tools of the trade.

IMPLEMENTING AGILE PROGRAMMING PRACTICES

The practices discussed in this chapter may be adopted by a team of programmers with the consent and assistance of a team lead. These practices do not require a change in the team's relationship with the business or a hands-off project manager. A project manager who works closely with the team (a good thing) or micromanages (not a good thing) will need to adjust with some of the practices. Pair programming and collective ownership, for example, may change the way work is assigned and scheduled. Simple design and refactoring, meanwhile, may change the way work is structured. If these changes will affect how the project manager interacts with the team, then he should definitely be included in the preliminary discussions and decisions regarding any new agile practice.

Most of these practices will take time to learn, adjust, and fine-tune. Depending upon the practice, the team may need to have significant control over its own time management activities. If time is rigorously metered by the business or an otherwise hands-off project manager, then the team may need to make the case for a given practice before proceeding.

Finally, the practices in the chapter are roughly ordered from simplest to most advanced. This is a rough ordering because no true ranking does or should exist.

PRACTICES FOR THE LONE AGILE PROGRAMMER

A programmer working alone or the lone agile-minded programmer on a project team can still implement as many as four of the practices discussed in this chapter. These include automated build, automated deployment, simple design, and refactoring. Another two practices from Chapter 8 may also be implemented: automated testing and test-driven development (TDD).

The team as a whole may not see a lot of benefit from the lone agile programmer's endeavors. However, after successfully adopting even a single practice, the programmer may notice a productivity gain and could even find new enjoyment in his work. The rules on time allocation apply to a lone Agilist the same way they would for a team of programmers. Specifically, a micromanaging PM or team lead may keep the programmer from finding sufficient time to initiate some of these practices. Finally, remember to not sing the praises of agile too loudly. Otherwise, the first time you make an entirely understandable mistake they may blame agile.

MISPERCEPTIONS ABOUT AGILE DESIGN

A lot has been said about agile programming in the last few years. Here are a couple of misperceptions or misrepresentations that may be encountered and suggestions for addressing them.

Design Less

One charge regularly levied against agile programming practices is that development is done without design. This is entirely unfair and unfounded. While one might admit that agile has unfortunately been used as an excuse for not doing design, agile itself advocates nothing of the sort. In fact, several agile programming practices are focused on producing better designs; these include refactoring, test-driven design, pair programming, and the admittedly poorly named simple design.

Agile is culpable for two things: drastically reducing the time between design and coding and stipulating that whoever performs the low-level design also writes the code. Admittedly, this may make heavy upfront documentation difficult, and it might also restrict a non-programming architect from inserting himself too deeply into the mix, but these are separate beefs and should be debated on their own merit.

Undisciplined

Another charge that agile programmers get flogged with on a regular basis is that they are undisciplined. This is mind boggling. Any set of programmers that follows half a dozen of the practices listed in this chapter and Chapter 8 is farther along the road to discipline than most any team that has not. Recent studies are beginning to back this assertion. A study by the British Computer Society found that the majority of project difficulties arise from a failure to follow and implement best practices [BCS04]. They did not specifically say that these included agile best practices, but everyone is allowed to take some small liberty with research.

AGILE PRACTICE: BUILD AUTOMATION[1]

This practice should provide the biggest and quickest bang for your project buck. The traditional process a project team should run away from screaming is that of an anointed team buildmaster performing a half-hour-long manual ritual on a daily or even weekly basis. The goal is to reduce the build process to a simple push-of-a-button action and to let every programmer on the team use it.

Purpose and Benefits

An automated build reduces the time programmers spend on unnecessary tasks and removes a bottleneck (namely, the team's reliance on one or a small number of individuals to perform a build) from the development process, thereby enabling the team to respond faster to change. The benefits of an automated build manifest themselves in a number of ways. First an automated build frees programmers from performing mundane and repetitive work, leaving that time to be spent on more important and interesting activities. Thirty minutes a day adds up, both in real time and motivation.

Second, an automated build that can be performed by any programmer can increase the team's response time. The same programmer who makes a small, critical fix can then make the application ready for redeployment. No one needs to be pulled from other activities or lunch.

Third, an automated build that is useable by the entire team will reduce the time the team spends chasing down compilation and convergence issues, because a programmer no longer needs to wait hours or perform a set of arduous tasks to confirm that the code he has just written compiles. Moments after he has written his code, he can know that the code (at least from the standpoint of compiling) plays well with the other children in the codebase. What is the motivation of an individual programmer to use this new tool? That's simple. Most any competent programmer will intuitively understand that a few minutes of building is well spent when it decreases the likelihood that he will be stuck at work late with the build-master or called at home by a fellow programmer to sort out his code. Furthermore, ultra-quick builds that take 30 seconds or less are a joy because you can literally run the build every few lines of code. This is a benefit when working with or in little-known classes and regions.

Finally, a streamlined and shared build process provides the foundation for many other agile programming practices.

Implementation

First, let's address a couple of terms used earlier:

> **The build:** This should entail all the code related to the application, regardless of what component or interface a programmer is working on. Compiling all the code helps to verify the correctness of assumptions, recent checkouts, and unknown dependencies.
>
> **Push-of-a-button:** This means that a build process should be easily portable to a programmer's workstation, very simple to learn, and not time consuming.

As discussed later in this section, these terms refer to ideal conditions. They should be considered the optimal solution, but perhaps not worth the effort in all situations.

Builds can be automated with batch and shell scripts or by employing a build tool such as Ant (for Java). If a project team has time, it could investigate and perhaps implement a build tool. The advantages gained from a build tool include the application of an approach that has already been tested by others, a predetermined syntax and structure that should ensure a form of scripting standards, and the increased potential to reuse build frameworks on new projects.

The scripts used to automate the code should be checked into source control alongside the code. This will allow programmers to update the scripts as necessary.

Making changes to the build scripts at the same time related changes are made to the code will ensure that other programmers receive the updates when they are required.

If the Project Has Not Written Any Code

The team should select a build tool and set up the build scripts straightaway. One or more programmers should write a Hello World program to use to test the build scripts. This will provide the kernel around which the rest of the codebase can be built.

If the Project Has Code

Now the project team has to make a cost-benefit analysis. How hairy is the current build process? How many programmers know how to complete it? How much time does the team have to spare, keeping in mind that the return on investment from an automated build can come rather quickly? The members of the team have at least two questions to answer: How close to the optimal solution do they need to get, and do they have time to select a build tool? These are real-world questions that involve the trade-off of time spent in the short run for time saved farther down the road.

Opportunities and Obstacles

Automating the build can be a huge boon to the team. Here are a couple of pointers and a potential issue to keep in mind.

Keep Compile Time Short

Compile time matters. Long compile times (as little as 10 minutes) can become a significant impediment to programmers building on a regular basis—especially when a programmer cannot simply leave the build to compile in the background while focusing his attention on something else. Not only is time lost as programmers wait for builds to complete, but if builds take too long, programmers will go a long time without performing them, removing much of the value a shared and automated build is meant to provide.

There are several strategies that may be employed to speed up build times. These include incremental compilation, faster compilers (such as jikes in place of javac), memory upgrades for workstations, and cleaner code.

Mind the Twenty-Eighty Rule

Making the entire build push-of-a-button and sharing it across the whole team is an optimal solution. Large, complex codebases and third-party tools in which automation may not have been an emphasis can make full automation a time-consuming process. Reporting tools, for example, can be woefully inadequate when it comes to ease-of-automation. The organizational culture within which the project operates can also put a damper on sharing the build across the entire team. The good thing about an automated build is that it is not an all-or-nothing proposition. The team benefits if three programmers can perform it instead of one, if compile time is shortened, or if the process is made less error prone.

The Buildmaster May Take Offense at Being Replaced by an Automated Process

This is an unfortunate reality. Some people value and guard their busy work and their territory. There is a difficult conversation here that will need to be had. In a situation where the buildmaster is territorial, this impending conversation is all the more essential. Several years ago, on one of my projects with a pre-agile team, we had a testy and temperamental buildmaster who felt it appropriate to communicate his displeasure with team members through performing (or not performing) his duties. When he was in a bad mood, hours of productivity were lost. Eventually management correctly labeled him as "burnt out" and rolled him off the project. Fortunately, he was replaced with an automated process.

See Also

■   The Apache Ant Project's site can be found at *ant.apache.org*.

AGILE PRACTICE: AUTOMATED DEPLOYMENT

Let's call this a virtual practice. Automated deployment really is an extension of build automation, but it has received its own practice title in this chapter so that it does not get lost in these 300-plus pages and relegated to a line in the index. The goal of this practice is to streamline and make predictable the process of promoting builds from development through testing environments and into production. We really want to get away from the haphazardness that too often arises the first time a project, after months of cutting code, has to coax its way into user acceptance testing and then fumble its way into production.

Purpose and Benefits

Automating build deployment provides testers and customers with the latest and greatest code faster, minimizes the time the team will spend on this activity, and drastically reduces the mix-ups that too often result from both manual build deployment and promotion.

In my experience, UAT deployments for teams using a manual build promotion process are particularly prone to both frustrating errors and hours of lost time.

First, there is the possibility that no one has ever done it before. In that case, whoever is promoting the build is inventing the process from scratch and probably not taking notes. Second, even if the build has been promoted previously, there is no telling what surprise a less-than-disciplined programmer might have coded into the release. On one project, we had a programmer who implemented an e-mail-notification component via the sendmail program on a development server. This kludge, of course, would not have worked even in UAT. Fortunately, it was caught by another programmer who was working in the same area a week later. Thank heaven for collective ownership. Third, how often are UAT deployments performed at 2 a.m. the day after the code was due? Is this when you want your team proofing the build promotion process?

Finally, frequent (if not automated) build promotion is implied in and essential to the agile practices of short iterations and small releases because these management-related practices are dependent upon delivering new and useful (working) functionality every few weeks.

Implementation

Many of the tools intended for compiling code can also be used for automating build promotion and deployment activities.

If the Project Has Not Written Any Code

Before they write any functional code, a team should write a Hello World test and automate the process of promoting it as close as they can to production. You can set some regular schedule (usually once a day) for promoting the current build to a neutral machine in the development environment. Make the target machine resemble the production environment as much as possible. Then run your automated tests on the target machine to see if anything breaks.

This process is extremely useful when programmers are writing code in one operating system for deployment in another (such as Java being written on a Windows machine and deployed in a UNIX environment). This has helped many projects (including those in non-agile environments) identify and address compilation and functional issues well before the crunch time of the UAT deploy.

If the Project Has Code

Once again you face a time-today versus more-time-in-the-future tradeoff. If you can spare the time, you should at least have someone perform a test deploy and thoroughly document the process. It is even better to document it in executable scripts.

Opportunities and Obstacles

Once you have automated the production and deployment process, consider letting non-programmers take advantage of it. In my experience, everyone benefits when the programmers make the build promotion and deployment processes available to the rest of the team. For example, on one medium-size (20 people) team, the programmers had gradually shifted their work hours from starting at 8:30 a.m. to starting at 10 a.m. This schedule shift became an increasing irritation to the early-bird testers and analysts, and eventually the senior analysts approached the team lead to demand that at least one programmer be at the office every day at 8:30 to provide support for the rest of the team. Someone applied a dose of reality therapy and inquired as to what the analysts and testers really needed at that time of day. It turned out that the single biggest issue was that the other members of the team were losing time in the morning because no programmer was available to promote new builds for testing. The team already had an automated deployment process and offered to share it with the non-programmers on the team. The programmers also agreed to have someone on call, but not necessarily at the office, at 8:30 a.m. The testers and analysts first began promoting builds into the testing environments in the mornings, and when they realized they could do the process faster on their own, happily began promoting builds at all times of the day.

AGILE PRACTICE: CONTINUOUS INTEGRATION[2]

The benefit of continuous integration is less obvious than an automated build or test framework, but its potential to save programmers time and reduce defect rates is huge. The traditional process that we are trying to bump off (with prejudice) is the practice of allowing separate branches of code to reside on programmer workstations and the daily, weekly, or (you can't be serious) monthly convergence of that code into a single workable build. In its place we want to institute a process in which small bits of functionality are integrated as they are completed into an up-to-date and clean codebase.

Purpose and Benefits

Continuous integration, practiced regularly and team-wide, is like slapping a homing beacon on the code convergence gremlin. Click the build and test button and you will spot the little twerp almost every time. The obvious benefit is that many (some say, most) defects are discovered hours after they are introduced into the codebase, not weeks later and after days of digging.

Prerequisites

Continuous integration can be implemented without an automated build or automated tests. However, such an implementation will provide limited value because of the time it may take to perform the manual integration process and because simply verifying a clean compile falls far from the goal of ensuring that new code will not adversely affect old.

If you have not done so, seriously consider adopting the build automation and automated testing practices before moving on to continuous integration.

Implementation

Continuous integration has two manifestations, as illustrated in Figure 7.1. The first is a serialized process where programmers queue up one at a time to integrate their completed code into the current codebase [Beck99]. This queuing can be enforced through the use of a team-owned workstation or through the use of a build token (any stuffed or otherwise non-fragile object will do). In either case, the programmer sitting at the team workstation or with the build token in his cube is the only programmer allowed to check in. This ensures that only one programmer checks in at a time, and the next programmer gets to merge [Beck99]. This first approach does not require an automated build, but again, it is not too helpful without some form of testing to verify that new code has not adversely affected the old.

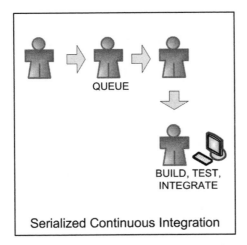
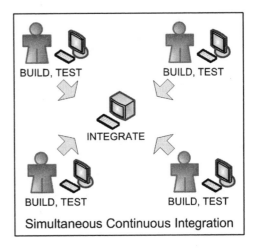

FIGURE 7.1 Approaches to continuous integration.

The second approach to continuous integration, which does rely on fully automated build and testing frameworks, is based on a build machine that frequently checks out all the code and automatically compiles and tests the current codebase. Frequent is a relative term here, but it should be at least once a day, and the best system is one that monitors the source control and executes after detecting a check-in. In this scenario, the programmer is expected to perform a build and test on his own workstation before checking in any code. The build machine serves as a failsafe in case a programmer forgets to check in a bit of code or forgets to perform a clean build before checking in. This approach works especially well for large teams or teams with programmers not physically located in the same space.

There are tools available (both open source and closed) for implementing the second flavor of continuous integration. Some work well, especially for large teams. But starting with them is not recommended, for reasons explained in Chapter 6, "Agile Practices." Instead, when adopting continuous integration, you should consider implementing a nightly build to supplement and act as a safety net for the continuous integration activities of the team. The nightly build process could entail a simple procedure that checks out the code on a nightly basis, shuttles it off to the build machine, compiles the code and runs the tests, and then notifies the team by e-mail in the morning if anything went wrong. This means any obviously bad code introduced into source control will be ferreted out within 24 hours, early enough that it is still easy for a programmer to go back, find it, and fix it. Once you have outgrown this simple method, then by all means select a tool and put a more advanced system in place.

Continuous integration relies on programmers checking in their code as they complete small bits of functionality (typically every few hours). This can be the tough part about continuous integration because it can take some real explanation and—unfortunately and too often—a significant amount of justification to get programmers to do it. For some reason, the benefit of everyone checking in small increments of working code—so as to ensure hours or even days are not lost to code collision and conversion—is simply not obvious. In my experience, only competent programmers get it, and no amount of cajoling or finger wagging will get less-than-competent programmers to follow the rules.

One tactic that may be employed to encourage continuous integration when a team is first adopting the practice is to ask during the daily stand up meeting (this practice is discussed in Chapter 17, "Communication and Collaboration") whether anyone did not perform a check-in the previous day. Any programmer who did not check in then has to explain why. Sometimes it is because he did not write any code. Sometimes the programmer does not have a particularly good reason, but as long as this only happens once in a while it is not a problem. Occasionally it is because a junior programmer has gotten in over his head on a particular task and, now that the team knows it, a more experienced programmer can offer to pair with him for a few hours.

Opportunities and Obstacles

Implementing continuous integration can benefit from a watchful eye for improvement and must be based on real teamwork.

Getting into the Habit of Checking In Code Every Few Hours

As mentioned above, this can be a difficult habit for programmers to get into. First, it will be all but impossible if it takes more than a few minutes for a programmer to do a build (an incremental compile is fine) and run the unit tests associated with the patch of code he is working within.

On an individual level, programmers may make a conscious attempt to never wander far from a clean build. In practice, this means writing a few lines of code, running the build to confirm that the tests still pass, then writing a few more lines of code and testing again. This approach is rather simple, but it can feel rather unusual for the sort of people who fix a toaster by taking it completely apart and then putting it back together again (you know who you are). Ultimately, however, sticking close to that clean build helps to keep a programmer from wandering off onto hours of ultimately fruitless work, means that a programmer is much less likely to walk away from his work and be completely lost when he returns to it, and ensures that there is never a piece missing from the rebuilt toaster.

At the team level, programming tasks may be cut finely enough that they do not take more than half a day to complete. This approach provides programmers with no excuse—assuming that they are completing their tasks one at a time—to not check in code at least twice a day. Once the team has transitioned to more frequent check-in and recognized the value, programming tasks can again be broken into more coarse-grained chunks.

When to Upgrade the Continuous Integration Process

Teams that choose to use a non-serialized continuous integration process may outgrow their initial (and hopefully simple) implementation of the process. There are many reasons to step up to a more advanced process. For example, the team may:

- Want to make the build machine more closely resemble production.
- Choose to configure the build machine to start automatically after someone has completed a check-in.
- Be ready to move to an open-source tool.

Regardless, the team faces the question of when to perform this upgrade because it will take some time. Try submitting this upgrade as a task, feature, or story (depending on your agile methodology preference). That way, the build machine upgrade will be weighed alongside all the other work the team needs to perform. When it becomes clear that other work will progress faster once the upgrade is performed, then it will be queued for completion.

Programmers Who Refuse to Perform Frequent Check-Ins

A single programmer who keeps a branch of code on his workstation and then jams it into the codebase after two weeks can be a serious danger to everyone. Just imagine a tractor-trailer rolling down a fast-moving highway at 20 miles an hour (this is why American highways have minimum speed limits). Approach this person and try to reason with him. Ultimately, though, if this individual will not change his ways, put him on a less critical assignment until you can roll him off of the team.

See Also

- Martin Fowler and Matthew Foemmel have a good and well-known article on continuous integration online at *http://martinfowler.com/articles/continuousIntegration.html*. [Fowler01]
- Anthill Build Server, available at *http://www.urbancode.com/projects/anthill/*.

AGILE PRACTICE: SIMPLE DESIGN

It is only natural for us to want to plan and prepare for tomorrow. If you need the CV joints replaced on your car and your mechanic tells you that the struts will also need replacing in the next six months, you are likely to have both jobs done at once. This way you save time and money because the car needs to go into the shop, be hoisted up, and get taken apart only once. A good mechanic will charge less to do both jobs together than he would charge to do them separately. Most everyone would agree that having both jobs done at once, even though the second job does not actually need to be done yet, is the best strategy for your automobile. But you should not necessarily apply a strategy that works on your $18,000 Honda Accord to your half-a-million-dollar project.

In the highly changeable world of agile development, doing less-important but planned work ahead of schedule may result in a setback instead of a benefit. This is because in an agile environment, the customers can swap out or drastically alter half the functionality planned for the next two months. Suddenly, the extra day that a programmer invested in writing a multi-function interface "because we will need it next release" results in negative ROI. The time is lost because the customer changed his mind. If your team is following an agile planning approach, then it is within the customer's right to do that. And even if you are not following an agile planning approach or an agile development process, what are you going to do about it? He's the customer.

In software development, it often does not make a lot of sense to design big plans for the future. Instead, we design to implement more simply for today. For a discussion of simplicity in planning, see Chapter 11, "Features and User Stories."

Purpose and Benefits

The benefits that arise from simple design can be significant. First, code can be modified and added to more quickly because, where there is no duplicate code, anything that requires a change needs to be changed in only one place. Second, clean code that is easy to understand and update facilitates a gentler learning curve for new team members. Third, that same clean and easy to use code engenders a more enjoyable and confident programming experience for the entire team. Finally, a well-implemented simple design practice drastically reduces the writing of code that gets deprecated before it is ever used.

Prerequisites

Simple design is an intermediate-level agile practice. To use this practice, programmers should have implemented build automation and automated testing. These practices will allow the programmer to write just enough code to complete a new task, compile the code, run the test to ensure that nothing has broken, and then repeat.

Implementation

Once implemented, simple design is a practice programmers should follow throughout their day. At its most basic, simple design means that all new code written by each programmer should [Beck99]:

- Compile and pass all the tests.
- Result in no duplicated logic across the system.
- Do everything it needs to do.
- Leave behind the fewest necessary classes and methods.

There are a couple of hurdles each programmer on the team may have to overcome when adopting simple design. First, teaching oneself to code for today and ignore tomorrow is not easy work. It forces us to squash a natural and nurtured urge to plan ahead and—falsely—makes us feel as though we are living dangerously. Second, simple design is not a challenge to devise the world's most parsimonious design. Simple design simply means to make the code work for today, keep it clean, and make sure it all tests. Ideally, simple design may also result in a discuss-more, code-less approach in which a solution is found prior to programming through collaboration with other programmers, rather than at the top of a heap of tangled code.

In order to keep everyone's mind focused on designing for today and not planning for the future, it may be useful to commit to memory (or post in an area of high visibility for the team) the three XP mantras of simple design [Martin02]:

- Consider the simplest thing that could possibly work.
- You aren't going to need it.
- Once and only once.

These are not hard rules, but they are serious rules. If a programmer wants to plan for tomorrow and has a compelling reason for it, then do it. If code duplication must be done, then so be it, but keep an eye on undoing this in the near future.

If the Project Has Yet to Write Any Code

This project team merely needs to start programming as simply as possible from day one. Like many other practices, learning in pairs may be best. A team that successfully adopts simple design may find its way into soft refactoring (discussed later in this chapter). That is, when a programmer is working in the code and sees a chance to make simpler something he did previously, he will likely do it on the spot. This is a good thing.

If the Project Has Code

Whenever the team is writing new code, everything in the previous section applies here. When programmers need to enter into legacy code, they will need to either respect its complexity (simply make the changes that need to be made and get out) or select refactoring as the team's next agile practice to adopt.

Opportunities and Obstacles

Here are a few other tips for adopting and maintaining a simple design practice.

Collaborate

Two heads can often devise a simpler solution than one. If you are working in code that someone else has written, and you are unsure of what to do, consult that person. If you are in code that you have written and are unsure of what to do, still consult someone. This will nearly always be more efficient that struggling to think up a solution.

Rolling New Programmers onto the Team

When bringing new programmers into a simple design environment, it is important to ensure that they are up to speed on the prerequisite practices. Otherwise, simple design may quickly be mistaken for easy design. Unit tests will go unwritten and unused, the build machine will throw a cylinder, and the whole team may have to get under the hood to fix the car.

Learn About Patterns

Think more and code less. Simple design can mean reusing someone else's solution instead of inventing your own. Pick up a pattern book and spend some time reviewing the tried, true, and simpler answers to many of software's common problems. However, be mindful that just because you have a hammer in hand, everything within reach does not magically become a nail. Do not refashion your problems to make them fit a desired solution.

See Also

- Kent Beck introduces simple design and provides more rationale for it in the "Design Strategy" chapter of his first book on XP [Beck99].
- There are several lively pages on simple design and the principles behind it on the Wiki. Start at *http://c2.com/cgi/wiki?SimpleDesign.*

AGILE PRACTICE: COLLECTIVE OWNERSHIP

Traditionally, some programmer gets assigned the invoicing system for the dapper new leasing application, bangs away at it in his cube for about six months, shoves it off to testing at 2 a.m., steps off a curb into the proverbial bus, and there goes the project. Okay, perhaps that is not entirely fair, but this extreme example highlights the issues many Agilists identify with assigning specific application areas to specific programmers: Nobody understands anybody else's code, it is difficult to shift programmers over to troubled areas halfway through the project, and turnover can really smart.

Collective code ownership repeals the implicit and explicit relationships between programmers and components. Instead, programmers are encouraged to work in areas they have not worked in before. Meanwhile, everyone on the team is allowed time to assist other members in areas that they know well. Ultimately, every programmer on the team is empowered to change any line of code.

Purpose and Benefits

The primary benefit of collective ownership is the reduction in both wasted time and duplicate code. With this practice in place, a programmer owns every bit of the code on the project, and he can change any piece of code as necessary. Practically speaking, this means that when the programmer needs changes to code he has not written, he does not need to locate the original writer of the code or its current owner and request or negotiate the change he requires. Further, collective ownership removes the temptation a programmer may have to simply copy and alter another programmer's code (again, avoiding the effort entailed in locating and negotiating with that person). With collective ownership, the programmer just makes the change, runs the other programmer's tests, and integrates. No mess. No hassle. Done.

The practice has many other benefits as well. It improves the quality of the system because most any line of code will be viewed by more than one set of eyes. It makes codes more consistent because programmers will begin to write code by standards common to the team (thus, we inch closer to a team-wide coding standard). It fosters communication among programmers, another big goal of agile. It encourages programmers to team up on tricky pieces of code, leading to a more optimal solution (and veering toward pair programming).

Now for the knockout punch. Collective ownership reduces the time that elapses between a show-stopper defect setting a user's hair ablaze and delivery of the emergency release that puts the fire out. Suddenly, the project manager does not need to find the right programmer and pull him up from the cafeteria to fix it. Since every programmer on the team can touch any part of the code, and since each of them has become comfortable with this concept, the closest programmer may be able to put out a sudden fire.

Prerequisites

Collective ownership is an intermediate-level agile practice. To get to this practice, the team at the very least should have implemented automated testing, build automation, and continuous integration. These are necessary practices because realistically no one programmer can know everything about the code. Therefore, every programmer will need to have the ability to test and integrate the code he has changed, thus confirming that his changes did not adversely affect the original purpose of that code.

Additionally, teams implementing collective ownership should consider employing regular stand up meetings to discuss who is working on what area of the code. This will minimize toe-smashing and encourage collaboration. Collocating the team also helps. More generally, consider reading Chapter 17, to learn more about communication and collaboration on agile projects.

Finally, in order to transition to collective ownership effectively, a team's programmers must be on good terms with one another and have some interest in working on a more collaborative basis. This is no foregone conclusion if your project was once grounded in a traditional development process.

Implementation

Collective ownership works best when everyone really feels like they all own the code. Programmers should not merely sit upon and complete tasks with their own components, making forays into the components of others only when they need something. The team's programmers need to be actively shifting between different areas of the code. The tasks they choose or are assigned should reflect this freedom of movement. At the same time, each programmer does not need to work throughout the entire application. If each programmer works regularly in half the code, the team will fare fine, and this becomes a necessity on larger projects.

Short iterations and small releases provide the easiest way to allow programmers to wander through the code base, because these timebox structures provide regular points in the project where programmers can pick up new tasks in different regions of the code (short iterations and small releases are discussed in Chapter 13, "Small Releases"). Projects that do not have an agile management approach may still operate on some form of an iterative basis such as multiple releases or functionality-based milestone dates that would provide similar points where programmers and responsibilities can be switched.

Finally, it is worth noting that FDD does not subscribe to collective ownership. Instead, it tackles feature requests that span multiple classes by forming a feature team of the owners of each of those classes. This feature team coordinates to design and implement the new functionality.

Opportunities and Obstacles

This section gives some important advice about resolving disagreements over collectively owned code and then closes with a quick chat on the crossover between collective code and text.

In Disagreements, the Right Answer Is Probably Option C

Disagreements, hurt feelings, and the occasional bar brawl may erupt when one programmer discovers that a particularly cherished bit of his code has been altered by another programmer. Worse yet, the change may not have been made to support any new functionality; the second programmer merely believed that his changes made the code cleaner and easier to understand. Does everyone see how fists could get mixed up in this?

The disagreement over options A and B may quickly devolve into a Bugs Bunny and Elmer Fudd dialogue, where each programmer simply restates his own view. Time to back out of the disagreement and ask the questions that really matter:

- Do all the tests still pass?
- Did the code integrate cleanly?

If the answer to both questions is yes, then there is little cause to continue the debate. In all likelihood, the correct answer is C, and some other programmer will wander by that patch of code in three months and make it so [Venners03]. Admittedly, it may take some time to for the proponents of options A and B to accept this.

Keep an Eye Toward Keeping the Code Clean

While the previous discussion notes what may happen if programmers too vigorously rewrite one another's code, there is also a peril that may arise from collective ownership when programmers use too light a touch on code that does not belong to them. To illustrate what may go wrong, Alistair Cockburn uses the example of the office refrigerator that keeps acquiring food that people have forgotten about [Cockburn04a]. Of course, the brown paper bags with the grease soaked through and the ketchup that appears to have hardened within the bottle should be thrown out, but because it no longer seems to belong to anyone, everyone in the office is afraid to pitch it in the trash.

The same situation can occur within code that is owned by the whole team. For example, a programmer may see something that looks odd in a patch of code but, instead of cleaning up the code, will leave it because the person who wrote the code must have written it like that for a good reason. Another programmer may add functionality by writing new lines of code to a class for much the same reason. Ultimately, as a result of such tentative touches, a de facto class ownership situation may result. This one, however, will not have ownership broken out by individual classes but instead will break classes out by areas of ownership (think marble cake), making it very difficult for programmers to make significant changes to the code.

Two things can help to mitigate this phenomenon, both of which should be good practices that the team is already following. First, a thorough suite of unit tests should give programmers a reasonable level of confidence about changing code that other programmers have written. When the tests pass, the changes are okay. If the tests fail, the changes are not. If the unit tests are not up to snuff, then the project team needs to take this into account when estimating tasks so that programmers have a sufficient amount of time to write additional unit tests before working with code they have not written.

Second, when a programmer hits a patch of code that is convoluted and confusing (especially when it is tied to an area in which he needs to work), he should consult the programmer who authored that code. What was the author thinking? Is there some reason behind the madness? Did he not have a better idea at the time of how to address his task? Did he intend to go back and clean up that area? Better still, the two programmers could pair together to clean up that swath of code.

Read a Taste of Collective Ownership

For a flavor of what collective ownership can accomplish, hop on a Web browser and scoot over to *www.wikipedia.org*. The Wikipedia is a free, wiki-based encyclopedia (we discuss wiki technology in Chapter 21, "Seeking Additional Assistance") that is editable and updateable by anyone who deems himself a contributor. Wikis are founded on the notion of collective ownership, and the Wikipedia should convey how a multitude of people (more than you will ever see on your project) can collaborate to create a consistent and coherent work product [Venners03].

AGILE PRACTICE: FEATURE TEAMS

This practice, built out of FDD, is founded on the concept of class ownership and represents the antithesis of collective ownership. Crystal is another agile methodology that calls for class ownership, but it has no specific practice built around it. In FDD, programmers own and develop specific classes within the application. As part of its iterative process, FDD pulls the owners of classes related to a specific feature together to complete that feature during a one-to-two week iteration. A project operating via feature teams is constantly breaking into subteams, completing customer-valued functionality, disbanding those subteams, and reconstituting itself as a new set of subteams specifically shaped to address the next set of functional requests.

The use of class ownership—and by implication, feature teams—can slow down the speed of a project because it imposes specific constraints, for instance, that only the owners of a class may write code in that class. Nonetheless, many will argue—as does David Anderson in "The Case for Class Ownership"—that on projects of more than a dozen programmers, where upfront modeling is already the norm, class ownership and feature teams can result in a system that is better designed and easier to maintain than one developed through collective ownership [Anderson02].

Purpose and Benefits

The proponents of feature teams argue that the practice makes the most of class ownership while providing many of the benefits of collective ownership.

First, when working within feature teams, programmers typically do not need to wait for other programmers to make changes to code. This is because under normal circumstances all the programmers with coding responsibilities related to a given feature are members of the team that has been assembled to complete that feature [Palmer03].

Second, feature teams distribute knowledge of the system across the entire project team. Programmers are constantly working within feature teams alongside other programmers who own other classes within the system. Because design sessions and code reviews are performed over every one of those classes (as explained in detail later in this section), each programmer becomes familiar with many parts of the system. Of course, for a team to see this benefit, these sessions must be focused on collaboration and mentoring and not merely serve as a sign-off process [Cockburn97].

Third, feature teams promote better overall design. Because classes are owned by individual programmers, a single individual is ultimately responsible for keeping the code within each class clean and maintainable. Unlike the collective ownership approach, where a less-than-diligent team may end up leaving code lying about in the same way food piles up in a communal refrigerator, there is never a question as to who is ultimately responsible for the state of any patch of code within the system. At the same time, low-level design is performed by the entire feature team, and the feature is considered complete only after the team has performed a design review for that feature, ensuring that design decisions are not being made by one individual in a vacuum [Palmer03].

Finally—and this should have already become apparent in this section—feature teams ensure that programmers collaborate on the design for every feature [Anderson02].

Prerequisites

Adopting the feature teams practice will take projects in a bit of a different direction than some of the other agile programming practices discussed in this chapter. While an automated build and unit tests (discussed in Chapter 8) would serve as a good complement to feature teams, some other practices in addition to collective ownership (namely, simple design and refactoring) cannot be adopted along with the use of feature teams. Finally, a team's use of continuous integration will need to be adjusted [Anderson02].

Implementation[3]

A project following the feature teams practice assigns specific roles and responsibilities to different programmers on the team. First, each programmer on the team becomes the owner of one or more classes within the system. Essentially, this is the enactment of class ownership. Depending upon what features are currently being developed, programmers may sometimes serve as class owners on two or three teams at one time.

Second, features are assigned to owners in a similar fashion. While nearly every programmer on the team will own one or more classes, feature owners (usually called chief programmers in FDD) should be more experienced programmers and will take on roles similar to that of team leads. Chief programmers typically receive an "inbox" of features that they need to work through in order to complete the project (typically, the chief programmer will establish a new team to complete each feature). While he personally will not complete the majority of the programming, the chief programmer—much like a team lead—is ultimately responsible for the correct design and completion of each of the features that have been assigned to him. Finally, chief programmers often are also class owners and members of feature teams run by other chief programmers.

Feature teams are dynamically assembled to complete a specific feature and then disbanded when that feature is complete. Each chief programmer, prior to setting out to complete a feature or a small group of related features that will all entail the involvement of similar class owners, will assemble a team based on the owners of the classes required to complete that feature. This means, of course, that the team should never be dependent upon the work of another individual outside of the team in order to complete its tasks. An example to illustrate the creation, makeup, and disbanding of feature teams within a project can be seen in Figure 7.2.

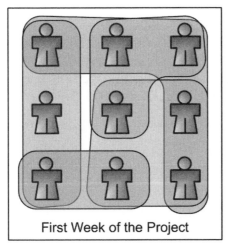
First Week of the Project

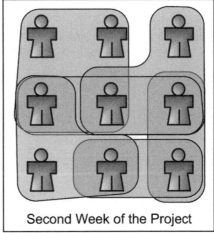
Second Week of the Project

Individual Programmer / Class Owner

FIGURE 7.2 Feature teams change with each iteration [Palmer02].

Because features on agile teams are kept small, each feature team is not very large, typically three to six programmers.

The life of a feature team begins with a walk-through of the domain and ends with the inclusion of the completed feature into the team build [Coad99]. The lifetime of a feature team in FDD is illustrated in Figure 7.3.

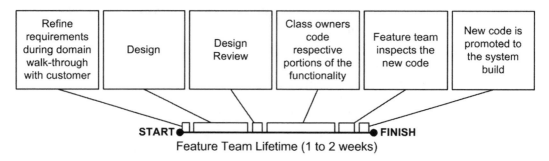

FIGURE 7.3   The lifetime of a feature team.

Although a project team not following FDD might want to alter the plan depicted in Figure 7.3, the general flow of events—requirements refinement, collaborative design, programming, and full feature team review—should be maintained.

If a chief programmer realizes that the feature currently being worked on extends into a class that he had not originally taken into account, he can attempt to bring that class owner into the feature team. If that class owner is too busy with other work to take on an additional feature team assignment, the feature owner may declare that progress on that feature has been blocked, temporarily disband the team, select a new feature for development, and return to the blocked feature when all the necessary class owners are available.

Opportunities and Obstacles

The following sections discuss a couple of things to keep in mind about working with feature teams.

Regular Integration

When two or more programmers are both working on code for the same feature, issues can arise that conflict with a continuous integration approach. For example, when a feature team has agreed on the interface between two objects (such as the parameters of a method call), one class owner might make those changes before the

end of a day and the class owner for the second object might not. ⌐
grammer, of course, will want to check his code into source contro
home, if for no other reason than to ensure that it is not lost to a hard ⌐
By doing so, however, the first programmer will cause the build to break. Even if
this were the beginning of the morning, the first programmer would have to check
in his code at some point in order for the other class owner to get hold of it. Unless
the two class owners arrange to check in their code simultaneously, there will be a
period where the code build is broken.

David Anderson details a solution for this problem called regular integration
[Anderson02]. The solution involves separating the team's source control system
(where code is checked in and versioned) from the process of integrating code. Programmers can check their code into version control at any time, and the team does
not care whether all the code pulled out of version control can compile. However,
every time a team satisfactorily completes a feature, the chief programmer checks
that code into version control with a specific label (such as build). Regular integration can be performed by checking out and compiling all the code under the build
label. This must be done every time a chief programmer promotes a feature, and at
this time the entire system must compile and all its tests must pass.

The upshot of a regular integration approach is that, although integration and
testing may occur only once every few days instead of a few times every day, it is just
as important that all the code compile and all the tests run clean.

Sharing Class Owners

One potential area for trouble in the feature teams practice is that a single programmer may on occasion be assigned to two or even three teams. At this point,
two or three chief programmers may need to have a discussion about how they will
divvy up this individual's time. This process can just as likely be pain free as not.
Anyone implementing this practice may benefit from reviewing the discussion on
working with shared resources in Chapter 14, "Executing Iterative Development."

See Also

- Palmer and Felsing describe the activities of feature teams in significant detail
in their book, *A Practical Guide to Feature-Driven Development* [Palmer02].
- David Anderson provides a compelling argument for code ownership and
feature teams in an issue of the *Coad Letter*. Browse to *http://bdn.borland.
com/article/0,1410,31957,00.html.*

AGILE PRACTICE: REFACTORING

Big design upfront (BDUF) is all about getting the system right the first time. This might work if the designers know the technology, the requirements for the system have been correctly captured, and the customer does not change his mind about what he wants you to deliver to him nine months from now. No sarcasm intended. If all three of these assumptions hold, then BDUF is your man. We all know how rarely all three of those assumptions will line up. It may not be as rare as Venus, Mars, and the moon getting together to do a Vegas-style kick line, but it might be close.

Maybe the system did not get put together quite as planned, but it works. As systems age and as enhancements and fixes are patched on to the code, things begin to grow cantankerous and hard to understand. The system gets drafty, the methods start to creak, and then there's that moldy smell. Perhaps the code will live on for decades, but after a few years many programmers would readily admit that BDUF code loses that new house look, feel, and smell.

Refactoring sets all of this on its head. What if the system code was actually fresher a year after it was first written? What if, even under the constant winds of use and footfall of enhancements the code stayed that fresh for several more years?

This is the promise of refactoring.

Purpose and Benefits

Refactoring makes other agile practices work better. For example, it enables a rigorous application of simple design, allowing programmers to implement a sufficient but less than optimal solution today and fathom and implement the right solution tomorrow. Additionally, and for much the same reason, refactoring helps facilitate iterations where whole features are defined in as little as one week.

As stated in the beginning of this discussion, the practice has several other benefits as well. First, it allows programmers to clarify the design of code after it has been written, reducing the need for BDUF. Second, it may be used in tandem with other agile practices to recover a poorly written system, even if that system is already in production [Fowler99]. Finally, refactoring can maintain that new code smell for years to come.

Prerequisites

Like collective ownership, refactoring is an intermediate-to-advanced level agile practice that requires automated testing, build automation, and continuous integration. These practices are necessary because without them the refactoring programmer will have little confidence that his refactorings did not adversely affect some portion of the system.

Additionally, a team implementing refactoring that has already adopted collective ownership should—if it has not already—institute regular stand up or daily Scrum meetings (see Chapter 17). Two programmers unknowingly refactoring the same piece of code at the same time is akin to two cooks trying to prepare two different soups in the same pot.

Implementation

At its essence, refactoring is the process of changing the design of a system without changing what it does [Fowler99]. There are three major activities performed when refactoring [Lyndvall02]:

- Simplifying complex chunks of code
- Replacing similar operations into reusable code
- Removing duplicate code

All of these activities require automated tests in the portion of the system that will be refactored. If there is not sufficient test coverage, then more tests should be written before refactoring. This makes refactoring old, pre-agile code a bit of a time commitment.

Refactoring is often not an endeavor in its own right. Rather, refactoring is something a programmer may do as he goes about doing other things. When changing a patch of code in one area, he may recall that there is another method in the application that does the same thing, and he will replace both methods with a single solution. Small refactorings can seem unconscious. A programmer may go about his business on one feature, spot a convoluted instruction, simplify it, and move on.

Finally, go slow. If you are on a team that has already implemented collective ownership, check in often. That last thing you want out of your first week of refactoring is programmers mad at one another for smashing each other's binary toes.

Opportunities and Obstacles

Refactoring can, unfortunately, cause contentious moments, both among team members and in the beginning with the business and management. Proceed with caution.

Refactoring Is Not Rework

One obstacle a team may encounter when discussing the merits with management or the business is that refactoring, from the point of view of the person who is paying for the work, may sound a lot like rework. Arguing that refactoring is not rework into a bit of a bind because, from at least a benign point of view, rework and really do result in the completion of the same task a second time.

are two directions to take this predicament. First, argue by analogy. , make the point that refactoring is more than rework in the same way mming is more than typing [Jeffries02]. In each case, the second term is merely an action with no specific purpose, whereas the first term has a specific and useful goal. Second, do not call it refactoring; instead, just call it maintenance. This has worked on several of my projects.

Be Wary of Large Refactoring Projects

Refactoring is meant to be a continuous activity and therefore should entail lots of small changes to the system and not a few big ones. Think in terms of the powerful but subtle movement of tectonic plates, not the Fire of San Francisco (which was started by a tremor measured at 7.9 on the Richter scale).

In a project experience of mine, previously documented in *IEEE Software,* two assistant team leads chose to do some refactoring on a system that was still in the stages of recovery (an automated build and an automated test suite had only recently been implemented). They chose to start by applying a constants pattern to the entire system. Because the constants were scattered throughout the application, the switch took them the better part of two weeks. They kept a separate branch of code on their workstations and integrated the main branch on a nightly basis. When they were done, they wrote the branch from their workstation over the code trunk and broke everything. While the implementation may have been solid, its introduction (a seismic shift to the codebase) cost over a day of time to every person on the team. [Schuh01a].

Consult Patterns

This may be a wonderful time to implement a design pattern. When you are at the point of refactoring, you can really focus on implementing an optimal solution, since you no longer need to worry about what the user really wants here and whether the code being written will satisfy that need. You are already certain of what the code is supposed to do because it is right there in front of you. Be mindful of the rest of the team. Patterns may sometime affect significant portions of the system, and as noted in the previous section, such activities need to be done with the awareness and buy-in of the entire team.

See Also

- Martin Fowler has written the definitive work on refactoring: *Refactoring: Improving the Design of Existing Code* [Fowler99].
- Also check out the refactoring Web site at *www.refactoring.com.*

AGILE PRACTICE: PAIR PROGRAMMING

Of all the practices agile has to offer, pair programming is the one that seems to cause the most consternation and unhappy sounds among the traditional development processes crowd. In some manifestations (particularly when not a scrap of code may be written if there are not two bodies in front of the monitor), pair programming can be thought of as radical. Pair programming is also the following:

- A new programmer on the team getting acquainted with the code by sitting with a programmer who has been on the team for more than a year.
- The team's two best programmers working together to track down a particularly heinous defect in the code.
- A junior programmer learning about design patterns while working with a senior programmer on a piece of new functionality.
- Two programmers learning to implement an agile programming practice by working together at the same computer [Kearns04].
- None of these examples sound too dreadful, do they? In fact, they look like the trappings of a healthy team environment.

Purpose and Benefits

There are quite a few benefits that a team may glean from pair programming. First, it has been all but proven that pairs produce better code quality and fewer defects [Williams00]. Second, pairing is an excellent means of mentoring junior programmers and training new team members, while both programmers remain productive. Third, regular pair programming spreads knowledge rapidly across the team. Frequent pair programming reduces the territory of code that is known by only one programmer, while constant pair programming obliterates it.

Finally, pair programming reduces the likelihood that people will shirk the rules. One might think of this as being similar to running with a partner. If you and your partner both agree to meet to run at a specific time, you are both much more likely to run because you made a commitment to one another and feel a responsibility to meet that commitment. Similarly, team members make commitments to one another about writing tests and simple design and all other manner of things. And, similarly, it is more difficult for two people to cheat on those rules together than it is for one to cheat on his own.

Prerequisites

Pair programming is an advanced agile practice. In theory, no other practices need to be implemented to start pair programming, because there is nothing to stop two programmers from sitting together and collaborating on the same task. However, because pair programming can be hard to sell, it may be better for most teams to start first with a few of the other practices discussed in this chapter and Chapter 8.

In order to pair, programmers require an amenable physical space. At the very least, this is a desk or table that will allow two programmers to sit comfortably next to one another.

Implementation

Pair programming starts as soon as two programmers sit in front of a workstation to collaborate on a piece of code. One programmer passively watching a second is not pair programming. The programmers regularly swap between the roles of driver and partner. The driver has the keyboard and mouse and writes the code. The partner points out things the driver fails to see, proposes ways of simplifying the code, and thinks ahead about how the next line, method, or object should be fashioned. When the partner wants to tackle something or gets bored or fidgety, he may ask the driver for the keyboard and take over [Beck99].

It is important to remember that pair programming may feel awkward and un-natural at first, and it can take time to get good at it. Ron Jeffries et al. offer a few tips [Jefferies00]:

- A partner should ask to drive when he sees the driver is stuck or when he has an idea he cannot verbally express.
- It is typically better to have the partner who is less sure about the task to do the driving. Otherwise, that programmer may not really understand when his partner is driving and not say much, and the benefit of pair programming will be lost.
- Use the pronouns "we" and "I" rather than "you."
- The partner should attempt to learn the driver's rhythm, so as not to prompt him at distracting moments.
- The driver should recognize that the partner may have the better idea more often because, while the driver is focused on coding specific statements, the partner has time to look around.

Gradual Adoption

Pair programming may be adopted slowly. It is probably not best to try to switch a team to it all at once (or at least have a first aid kit at the ready if you do). It may take plenty of time for programmers to get past their egos, to learn that they do not need to win every debate, and to learn to collaborate on such a close level.

The team may start with occasional pairing. Programmers may pair to solve a difficult problem, explore an unknown area of code, or hunt bugs. When this catches on, the team might start an iteration with half-time pairing, where everyone must spend 20 hours a week working in a pair. If this catches on, the team could move to an iteration with full-time pairing. If the team does not seem to operate well at a new tier, it can step back to a lower tier and try again in another couple of iterations. If either the full-time or even the half-time tier seems unattainable, the team may have met its limit with pair programming.

Side-by-Side Programming

In Crystal Clear, Alistair Cockburn proposes a practice that is less than pair programming but may induce many of its benefits within a small project team. The practice is side-by-side programming, and it may also work as a stepping stone to pair programming [Cockburn04].

Side-by-side programming entails two people with two computers and two separate tasks sitting right next to each other. These two individuals need to be close enough that they can easily view one another's screens while working on their own tasks. This way, one programmer can ask the other to take a look at a particular piece of code or test. The practice allows the two programmers to work on parallel activities, while each may add a second set of eyes to his work as required by varying levels of complexity. Side-by-side programming may be a good way to perform informal design and code review activity while a task is being completed, instead of having to perform a review as a separate process and without having to transition over to pair programming.

Opportunities and Obstacles

There are a lot of dimensions to pair programming and many places to find unexpected benefits.

Give New Team Members No Tasks of Their Own

Instead of assigning a new programmer tasks for the first couple of weeks, have him spend the whole time pairing with one or two other programmers on their tasks. This is a highly effective way for the new programmer to learn the system without breaking anything [Lyndvall02]. The new programmer will also learn many of the documented and undocumented team processes the easy way, as opposed to the more popular "flail away at it for an hour before going to ask anyone" method that, for some strange reason, we all seem to prefer. Finally, as long as the new programmer already knows the language the team is coding in, he should be an asset from day one. Even though the new programmer will not know the particulars of the system, by pairing with a knowledgeable programmer, he may still be able to provide general input on coding, think ahead of his pair, and be on the lookout for errors in the code.

Analysts, Testers, and Customers Can Pair, Too

Surprising results can come of an analyst or even a customer pairing alongside a programmer. It has been my good fortune to work on both sides of this equation. Some years ago, when implementing an ObjectMother test data framework (see Chapter 9, "Data and the Database"), my role was that of the programmer pairing alongside one of the project's analysts. The analyst provided the domain knowledge to build the creation and attach methods required to create viable test data structures, while my attention was focused on trapping his knowledge within the code. More recently, while managing a project at a large in-vehicle telematics client, my role switched to that of the analyst, sitting alongside one of the team's programmers while we devised and tested and he coded the logic for an algorithm that determined the date at which past due customer subscriptions should be cancelled.

Finally, it is worth noting that this approach can even be extended to include programmers who speak different programming languages. A reporting programmer, for example, who uses a proprietary language to perform ETL transformations—and spends a significant amount of his time coding templates—can still sit alongside a Java programmer to pass along schema- and performance-specific knowledge for the completion of a particular feature.

Remote Pairing

While it might seem surprising, programmers really do pair effectively from remote locations. Typically they use a phone line, a broadband connection, and a program like VNC or PCAnywhere™ to share a single computer. The practice is called remote pair programming or virtual pair programming. It seems not to be as efficient as pair programming but better than programming alone in some situations.

Remote pairing may work best when the programmers have paired together in the past and already have an established method of pairing together. Additionally, an instant messenger application, although alluring, may not provide an acceptable substitute for a voice line; it can just become too much typing. If a remote pair has the bandwidth but no phone, they should look into voice-over-IP [Meyer04].

Why Do I Need Two Programmers to Do the Work of One?

This is a question asked more than once by skeptical individuals with every right to have one eye focused on the bottom line. One might respond with a flurry of monosyllables (like, um, aw, uh, well) and a little tap dance. Better yet (and it is good to be prepared for this one), one could admit that studies have shown that there is a 15 percent reduction in productivity when programmers pair, but that those same studies show that the code generated by pairs has 15 percent fewer defects [Williams00]. Those defects will cost a lot more to fix than 15 percent of the overall project cost if even one of significant size makes it into production. Plus, if you act now, we'll throw in better knowledge sharing and unbeatable mentoring at no additional cost.

The Programmer No One Likes Pairing With

This will be a significant problem on teams where pairing is the norm. It can be (but does not have to be) a problem for teams where pairing is optional. Basically, if the individual otherwise gets along normally with everyone on the team, then it should not be a serious issue. However, even if pair programming is optional, if the individual is not gelling with the team on other fronts, there may be a larger problem that needs to be addressed. Dealing with it may go well beyond pair programming.

In the case of an individual who is not pairing well with others on a team where pairing is the norm, but that individual otherwise gets along with the team, the situation may still be stable and can be left alone. Such a situation does need to be monitored, because it is just as likely to resolve itself as it is to get worse. Worse could be when the team begins to resent the lone developer because they believe (correctly or not) that he is the source of too many defects in the system. Worse could also mean that the lone developer begins to disengage from the team in other areas. Worse could mean any number of things, but it means most that the problem will need to be addressed.

See Also

- For more information related to personal experiences and some empirical findings, browse to *http://alistair.cockburn.us/crystal/articles/ppcb/ pairprogrammingcostbene.html*.
- Laurie Williams and Robert Kessler's tells you everything you need to know [Williams02].
- You can find a good Web site dedicated to pair programming at *www.pairprogramming.com*.
- The Wiki page on pair programming also has a very thorough discussion of pair programming and lots of organized links to related topics. Browse to *http://www.c2.com/cgi/wiki?PairProgramming*.

STARTING MONDAY: GO SLOW

This "Starting Monday" section is a bit different from the rest . That is because this chapter, arguably, already has eight "Starting Monday" sections, each with the heading "Agile Practice." Therefore, it seems appropriate to hold up a handful of helpful caution signs.

It Takes Time to Make Time

Implementation of most of the practices in this chapter will initially slow down the progress of the team, but in every case the long-term benefits to team productivity and system flexibility will outweigh any upfront investment. Nonetheless, make sure everyone on the team and downstream from the team is prepared for the extra time and effort that may be required to incorporate an agile practice.

If given the choice between extra time and extra effort, take extra time.

When Refactoring, Most Surprises Are Not Welcome

Surprise birthday parties will win you brownie points. Surprise refactorings could get you lynched. Ultimately, any change to the way the team goes about doing things is more likely to be accepted and embraced if all the parties involved are consulted in advance and feel they have a hand in the process. A daily Scrum or stand up meeting may be a perfect time to bring up such topics.

Do Not Be Team Agile

This cannot be said often enough. There is no need to be secretive about adopting agile, but there is also no good reason to draw unnecessary attention to a team adopting agile development. The less the process of adopting an agile practice is interrupted and disturbed by outside individuals and events, the better.

Learn in Pairs

This was discussed in Chapter 6, but it is worth revisiting quickly. Two people working together will solve a problem more quickly than one. In the same way, two programmers working together will get the hang of a practice faster than one alone.

8 Testing

In This Chapter

- An Agile Approach to Testing
- The Good Enough Approach
- Testing as the Best Defense
- Agile Practice: Automated Unit Testing
- Agile Practice: Acceptance Tests
- Agile Practice: Test-Driven Development
- Starting Monday: Quick and Dirty Automated Testing

Inconsistent quality has been the bane of software development for four decades. It was almost that long ago (in the autumn of 1967) that the North Atlantic Treaty Organization (NATO) tried sorting out the mess [Shapiro97]. Suffice it to say, NATO had more success in other areas. They did, however, coin the term *software engineering*. This, it seems, was their attempt to challenge programmers to behave more like mechanical, electrical, and physical engineers, whose more mature sciences produced better estimates and higher quality deliverables.

AN AGILE APPROACH TO TESTING

The agile methodologies could be characterized as the Young Turks of software testing. From the late 1960s through the early 1990s, the solution to software's persistent quality issues was almost exclusively to build a better standard [Schuh02]. Two examples may best frame these standard-based solutions:

- The Institute of Electrical and Electronics Engineers' (IEEE) one XXXL size to fit everyone's standards
- The Capability Maturity Model's (CMM) "just pick a standard and stick to it" certification process

By 1996, there were over 50 recognized standards dedicated to quality assurance alone. Interestingly, by 1996, most aspiring standards writers seemed no longer to be writing new standards but instead were writing to discuss why so few people were following any of the existing ones.

What agile development (and perhaps most notably XP) brought to the party was not another standard but usable, ready-to-implement solutions. These solutions did not work in every situation—which Agilists readily admitted—but they tended to work extremely well for small, disciplined teams of like-minded individuals. Those initial processes have been expanded, improved upon, and made to fit larger and more diverse teams. Today, agile development has caused a shift in the discussion of software development testing from what should be done to control quality to how to control quality.

The fundamental difference between the standard and agile approaches to testing can be gleaned from Figure 8.1, which defines the unit test from both the IEEE and the XP perspectives.

One can easily see the difference in the direction of attack IEEE and XP take. While IEEE approaches the unit test as a term to be defined, XP sees the unit test as a tool to be put to use and then tells you how to use it. Going further, let's look at Figure 8.2 and see how each of the standard and agile approaches integrates testing into the development process.

Figure 8.2 illustrates the single biggest issue Agilists have with standard approach testing: Testing is not really integrated into the development process. Rather, it is appended onto the end as an afterthought.

Finally, the standard and agile approaches to development differ over who is ultimately responsible for ensuring software testing. For the standard approach, the plan is the most important part of software testing; as long as there is a good plan

IEEE Standard for Software Unit Testing	**Extreme Programming**
A Unit Test Is:	*The Unit Test:*
A set of one or more computer program modules together with associated control data, (for example, tables) usage procedures, and operating procedures that satisfy the following conditions:	The Programmers write tests method-by-method. A programmer writes a test under the following circumstances.
• All modules are from a single computer program	• If the interface for a method is at all unclear, you write a test before you write the method.
• At least one of the new or changed modules in the set that has not completed the unit test	• If the interface is clear, but you imagine the implementation will be the least bit complicated, you write a test before you write the method.
• The set of modules together with its associated data and procedures are the sole object of the testing process	

FIGURE 8.1   Defining the unit test: IEEE versus XP [IEEE86], [Beck99].

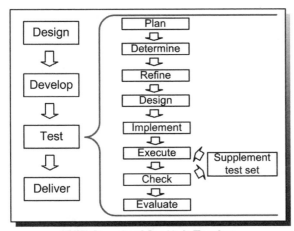 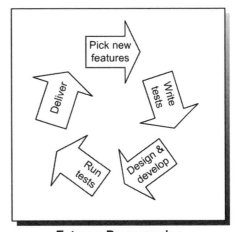

IEEE Standard for Unit Testing   **Extreme Programming**

FIGURE 8.2   Integrating testing into the development process: IEEE versus XP [IEEE86], [Beck99].

and people follow that plan, then the delivery will go without a hitch. The agile approach focuses on people following agreed-upon processes, evaluating the effectiveness of those processes, and making adjustments as necessary. The ultimate party in the agile approach is the people who constitute the project team.

THE GOOD ENOUGH APPROACH

A somewhat controversial concept that has been picked up and bandied about by Agilists is the notion that quality might not need to be paramount or sacrosanct in the development process; rather, quality should be applied at the discretion of the customer. Some refer to this as the delivery of good enough software. In the absence of a direction, of course the project team should assume that the customer wants a quality product (that is, one that adds value, has few defects, and is easy to use) to be delivered. However, there are times when quality may not be of primary concern. Obvious examples include spiking and prototyping and situations where code will be used once and then thrown away. More typically, quality needs to be balanced against delivery dates and additional functional requirements.

Absolute quality is something that can never be guaranteed, and the closer a project team attempts to get toward absolute quality the more effort it will take to make a single step forward. Testing is an activity that will benefit nearly every project, but at some point, testing becomes a bet. Then, the more time spent testing will come at the expense of productivity. The sweet spot of quality for a project is the point where it would actually cost more to notch up one more level of quality than it would to identify and fix all the defects that would be caught at that higher level of quality. Admittedly, identifying and keeping a project in a space such as this is no simple matter.

Speaking more practically, factors that indicate the level of testing required on a project may include:

- The criticality of the system (as defined by Cockburn and discussed in Chapter 3, "The Agile Methodologies")
- The desired level of system maintainability
- The customer's tolerance for error
- The ease or difficulty entailed in redeploying the system

Of these three factors, the first may be the most obvious. Who would disagree that more quality is required for a system where defects may result in the loss of life or essential money than a system where defects risk comfort and discretionary money? For projects with low criticality, the last three factors may be more important.

Often the customer dictates the level of maintainability of a system, and the team needs to develop at a level of quality that meets the requested level of maintainability. DSDM, for example, recognizes three distinct levels of maintainability: first, that the system is maintainable from its first day in operation; second, that maintainability is not guaranteed from day one but will be added later; third, that maintainability is not a requirement because—typically—the system will be used for only a short period of time [Stapleton03]. Each level of maintainability will require a different level of quality in the development process.

The final two factors are not driven by system requirements but rather by the environment in which the system will be constructed. Even on a low-criticality project, such as an internal content management system for a medium-size company, a customer with insufficient patience for mistakes and rework may cause a team to employ a higher quality standard than demanded by the system's level of criticality. Similarly, a low-criticality project may have to meet a higher quality standard when rework and redeployment are arduous tasks, such as when the technology a project employs makes rework and redeployment especially difficult or in a heavy-process environment where deployment points are fixed, and redeployment takes a significant amount of political cost from a project.

TESTING AS THE BEST DEFENSE

In a perfect world, every project team not only builds the right system with clean code, every project team behaves like a responsible citizen when sharing interfaces and (more impotantly) the code base. With regard to other projects that share or rely upon its code, the project team that practices responsible citizenship may:

- Advise those project teams in advance of making changes to interfaces and the expected behavior of code
- Provide those teams with access to updated code in a timely manner
- Perform some minimal testing activities to reduce the chance of adversely affecting the operation of the systems owned by those projects

Some projects do attempt to act like responsible citizens. Many projects with which we share code or on whom our code is dependent make life hell. At least this has been my experience.

Imagine sharing a code base and common components with a project team that does not write automated tests, a team that integrates all its code only days before a release and in which not all of the programmers truly comprehend object-oriented programming. How does your team work with these guys? This is where the art of testing as a defense comes in.

A project team should already be writing automated unit tests. Its next action, therefore, will depend on its specific situation.

Sharing a Code Base with Another Project Team

This situation may arise whenever two teams share common components within a system. A solution should be based on a continuous integration system that is fully automated and supports simultaneous check-ins (see Chapter 7, "Design and Programming," for more information on establishing this type of system).

The continuous integration environment should cover all the code on both projects and run automatically after a check-in has occurred. It must compile and test the code quickly so that no programmer can get very far if his check-in causes a test to fail. In the event of a test failure, the continuous integration machine should e-mail everyone on both projects, including the management of both teams. It does not matter whether the other team is writing unit tests, although you should encourage them to do so and offer assistance. What makes this system work is your team writing a comprehensive set of tests over your area of the code. If the other team changes something that affects the behavior of your code, the tests your project team has written should sound the alarm.

This solution will likely not stop the programmers on the other project team from continuing to maintain separate branches of code on their workstations for an extended period of time. However, every programmer on that project team will eventually have to check-in his code in order to release. Knowing that your side of the system will squeal if it is adversely affected by a check-in, they may give themselves extra time to integrate their code. If nothing else, everyone will know within half an hour of a check-in that something has gone wrong, the programmer who tripped the alarm should be easy to identify, and he may still be in the building.

Sharing Common Components with Another Project Team

This approach applies to shared components that exist in another code base but are updated by both teams. Here you can take a very similar approach to the one recommended for sharing a code base, but instead of putting the continuous integration environment on the shared code base, place it on top of the code base for the shared components. The effect will be the same.

Depending upon Code or Components Produced by Another Project Team

This is a frustrating situation that affects many project teams. The solution entails building an automated process that:

- Deploys, installs, or otherwise obtains access to the latest build of the other project's system
- Compiles and tests your team's code against the other project's system
- Promptly provides the results of the tests

Once you have built this system, make it available to the other project. Encourage them to use it as part of their testing process. Be gracious and provide them prompt support if any is requested.

If this first step does not fix the problem (that is, if the other project does not use the system as you have requested), then attempt to get access to a stable build of the other project's code as often as you can. If possible, set up a schedule to receive the code on a regular and predictable basis. Notify them of the results of your test runs. If they will only give you the code days before they intend to release it, then the process you have built should be optimized to get the test results back to you and the other project as quickly as possible.

If in the end the other project is allowed to act with impunity and your project is forced to react to any refuse they let downstream, this solution may still prove useful. The ability to automatically, regularly, and with minimal effort pull new builds from the other project and test them against your team's code will, at the very least, act as an early warning system. This way, you will be able to anticipate and plan for changes in the other project's system that will affect your code.

Do your absolute best to engage the other project team when implementing these solutions. Make a big to-do about how the solution you have built will help verify the quality of everyone's code. Consider talking up the benefits of the solution to the business. There is, of course, a trap associated with all this effort. If the quality of the software they produce does not improve, you now have an accepted mechanism for determining the acceptability of code, and assuming you are writing and maintaining your own tests, you will have secured the high ground in the next exchange over whose code has broken the system.

Bad intentions tend to beget more of the same, so it really is best if you are sincere about helping the other team help itself. The point is not to throw their code back at them and cry, "Fix it!" Instead, politely hand it back to them and say, "Can you correct this? Maybe a couple more unit tests would help." or even "Would you like someone from our team to pair with you to get this right?"

Finally, for projects that share components or where one is dependent on the other, these approaches can be beneficial even when both projects are producing quality code and interacting well together. Projects under my management have established such systems with other responsible projects. At one time we had three distinct projects all depending upon and actively developing the same set of common components. We set a rigorous continuous integration process on top of the common code base. The arrangement benefited everyone.

AGILE PRACTICE: AUTOMATED UNIT TESTING[1]

It would be hard to overstate the importance of testing in agile development, and automated unit tests are where the majority of teams get their first taste of what agile testing practices can do for a project. It is a bit like getting your first chemistry set. Stuff some early agile matter into a beaker, add a slow drip of testing automation, crank up the Jeffries Burner, and then ponder whether dad will believe it was a meteorite that hit the garage.

Automated testing takes more investment than build automation and can necessitate some serious cajoling to get skeptical programmers (and perhaps management) on board, but its benefits are well worth the effort. Automated testing is the cornerstone of most successful agile teams. At its most basic, the practice requires a suite of tests (ideally, the complement to an automated build) that rely on restorable data and can be run at the push of a button.

Purpose and Benefits

Just as an automated build reduces the time a team spends on compilation and convergence issues, so too will automated testing reduce the time spent identifying and correcting defects. Similarly, automated testing will increase the team's turnaround and confidence when performing small, quick changes to code. Finally, a correctly implemented and cared for testing framework will improve code quality and save time over the long haul, as automated tests written for one release become the regression tests for future releases.

A rational programmer will be inclined to use the testing framework frequently for the same reason he will use an automated build process—to save himself from the pestering and calls at home he would otherwise get from checking in code that inadvertently breaks other functionality. Taking a more positive view of human nature, the programmer will gain additional confidence and motivation from seeing all his tests run successfully in the midst and at the end of a coding session.

The team, as a whole, will most likely sense the benefits of a testing framework in one of two ways. Hopefully, there will be a gradual realization that everyone is spending less time reacting to critical defects. One way to encourage this outcome might be to track and graph in a public place the number of defects reported per week. Conversely—and something one may prefer to avoid—the team may realize how good they had it only after they fall off the testing wagon and get run down by the Defect Express. Therefore, in all seriousness, once on board, do not let your team fall off the testing wagon.

Prerequisites

Automated testing could be implemented without a single agile practice to support it. However, an automated build is recommended.

Implementation

Tests should validate meaningful functionality, not getters and setters. To avoid devastating team morale the first time someone wipes the database, each unit test should rely solely on restorable data. (Test data maintenance will be addressed in Chapter 9, "Data and the Database.") Automated tests can be both unit and system level. Typically, teams just starting on this practice will cut their teeth on unit tests. System tests can come later, either when the team determines they need them or when the team chooses to institute acceptance tests (a practice to be discussed later in this chapter).

There are unit testing frameworks—xUnits—available for a wide variety of programming, scripting, and even markup languages. In xUnits, test cases are typically aggregated into test suites with names such as AllTests. The automated test paradigm, made famous by JUnit, is based on redbars and greenbars. When running a test suite, a programmer is presented with a progress bar that ratchets its way across the screen as each test case is completed. The bar is green as long as every test has passed; if a single test fails, the entire bar goes red. Below the bar is a numerical reckoning of tests that passed and failed. The developer may know from these numbers that only one in 40 test cases failed. The message is simple and clear, and you get no credit for almost getting it right. A failing test is tantamount to a broken build.

Zero Tolerance for Broken Windows

Sometimes a test starts failing for some reason beyond the control of the team, such as when an external system that the application must interface with has gone down. There is no problem with this situation if it lasts a few hours, but if it carries on into days then the test should be pulled. A failing test suite—even if everyone knows it's just that one test—has a psychological effect on individuals and on a team. After a couple of days, when the team has gotten used to the acceptability of failing tests, that original test on the failure list will likely no longer be alone. This logic follows the same logic as the Broken Window Theory, where police in big cities have found that cracking down on minor crimes has actually reduced the incidence of major crimes [Hunt99].

On occasion, someone makes the case that failing tests should be left to fail because, ultimately, they serve as reminders that some actions need to be performed by the team. But every team should have a task list, a pile of stories, or at least an issue log, and these mechanisms are much better suited for tracking the problem.

If the Project Has Not Written Any Code

At first blush, this is probably a scarier prospect than having a bunch of legacy code that requires automated testing. For a team of programmers who have no hands-on experience writing automated unit tests and have, therefore, never experienced the benefits of it, the thought of writing tests for every line of code can feel like a lot of extra work, not to mention downright daunting.

The team can start with an empty AllTests suite that is plugged into the automated build process. The greenbar that pops up at the end of the build will help make programmers comfortable with the test framework and remind them (perhaps even encourage them) to write tests as they code.

In a situation where no one on the team has experience with automated testing, it is recommend that the team find someone who has experience to work with them for a few weeks. Ideally, this individual would spend several sessions working individually with each programmer. Pairing is a good idea as well, but pairing is a good idea in any situation where a lot of learning and thinking is involved.

If the Project Has Code

A team does not need to stop and write tests for existing code to benefit from automated testing. In fact, a team adopting automating testing should not do this, because it might well burn out and drop the practice before it has gotten any benefit. Instead, the team needs to implement a rule that all new and modified code will be covered by unit tests, and the comprehensiveness of the testing framework will grow over time. If the team has a handful of useful tests already written, they should be included in AllTests—as long as they pass.

The approach of cordoning off old code and writing tests for everything new might not work for every team. Some teams may not be actively writing new code because they are in maintenance mode, they have realized their application is too unstable to move forward, or they otherwise have spare time on their hands. In these cases, there are two other options for starting to build robust test suites.

First, programmers can identify the manual tests they perform frequently and automate them [Clark04]. These manual tests are the steps each programmer runs the application through after he has worked in a particular section of the code, thereby satisfying himself that everything works. Since the programmer values these steps enough to perform them manually, he should value them even more when he can watch them happen faster and automatically.

The team may also devise a way to implement some quick-and-dirty system-level testing. The focus here is breadth, not depth. The team needs to come up with a way to quickly and cheaply make the system do a lot of things and then see if it breaks in the process. See the final section in this chapter, "Starting Monday: Quick and Dirty Automated Testing" for more on this approach.

Opportunities and Obstacles

Implementing automated testing will take some real forethought and a lot of teamwork and can entail some difficult conversations and tough decisions.

Embed Test Suites Within Suites

Test cases should be grouped into component- or package-level AllTests that are then grouped into a hierarchical structure with a single AllTests test suite at the top. This allows programmers to run the test related to the portion of code they are working within frequently and then easily run all the tests to verify that no other area of the code was inadvertently affected.

What If a Failing Test Suite Has Become the Norm?

This is a red flag that a project team is in clear danger of falling off the testing wagon. It must be addressed with the utmost urgency. The following are two possible approaches. Adjust or invent as necessary.

> **The Daily Test Calendar:** One simple technique that can be employed to reverse this trend is to print a calendar, place it in a public place, and start sticking on colored post-it notes to reflect the status of the last test run of each day. If the test fails, the day goes red. If the test passes, the day goes green. This helps to remind the team that a passing test suite is a project priority. At the same time, if the team pushes back and says the tests are failing because they do not have time to fix them, then they must be given that time. The calendar will no doubt start with a swath of red, but if the team is given the appropriate encouragement and time, the days will turn green. When the calendar has gone green for some time and people have forgotten to update it, then it has served its purpose and should be taken down.

> This approach could, of course, be automated so that something, somewhere gets updated on a daily basis with the status of the final test run. For any team that considers this approach, there are two things to keep in mind. First, the approach is effective only when the calendar is in a highly visible place so that no one can ignore the appearance of a string of red days. Second, it is not the failure of the tests on any single day that matters; rather, it is an apparent pattern of patterns. This, too, would need to be conveyed in any automated approach.

Pull the Emergency Brake: A programmer who has little authority on the team, is watching the test suite fail repeatedly, and has found that no one wants to listen or seems to care can still pull the emergency brake.

One programmer, several years back, was on a team that was cutting its teeth on XP. The team had been doing automated testing for only about three months, and for the last month the test suite failed regularly. No programmer would take responsibility for a failing test, and the number kept going up. The programmer lobbied the team lead but to no success. The problem had become serious enough that the team was promoting builds with breaking tests to UAT. Finally, the programmer authored an e-mail plea to the team, restating the situation and urging that they make fixing the tests a priority, and used an e-mail group that included the project manager. Yes, he played the snitch and was none too happy about doing it, but it worked. The project manager, who had no knowledge of the situation, immediately came down on the team lead, who came down on the team. The tests were fixed and stayed fixed.

For anyone who is curious, that programmer never received any flak for his action, perhaps because using the list gave a defense of plausible deniability.

Mind the Duration of the Test Run

Just as with builds, the longer it takes for a test suite to run, the less often programmers will run it. Cleaner tests run faster, but this will not solve every problem, especially with larger teams. One option is to run a performance profiler against both the tests and the code. This should help to identify both tests that are more active than necessary (such as testing the same thing two or three times) and areas in the code where performance could be improved.

If the system has simply become too big and the tests too numerous, memory upgrades for developer workstations may also provide a cheap solution. Finally, some of the projects under my management, after throwing the kitchen sink at the problem, have split their tests into two groups: the quick ones that get run on a regular basis and the slow ones that must be run before a programmer checks in his code.

Programmers Who Refuse to Write Tests

This can be a real and significant issue because it is possible for only one bad apple to spoil the whole bunch. Programmers who write and run tests can begin to resent other programmers on the team who do not, because of a perception that those non-testers are shirking their responsibilities and leaving a mess for others to clean up. A team lead or project manager will need to ask the programmers why they are not writing and running tests. Perhaps the non-tester needs extra slack in his workload to get up to speed with testing. Perhaps some other compromise can be struck. If the failure to test persists, ultimately and unfortunately some difficult decisions may need to be made.

See Also

- *www.JUnit.org* provides easy access to both the latest version of JUnit and many extensions. It is also has a good inventory of testing-related articles and links to other resources.
- Ron Jeffries maintains a list of xUnits for a wide variety of languages on his site at *http://www.xprogramming.com/software.htm*. Most of these are ready-to-use open source tools.
- A good article focused on implementing testing, written by Mike Clark, can be found at *http://today.java.net/pub/a/today/2004/01/22/DozenWays.html*. It discusses test-driven development as well, but it has a lot of good tips for the beginning agile tester [Clark04].

AGILE PRACTICE: ACCEPTANCE TESTS

In the first release of a small system, it may be relatively straightforward to write some functional test scripts a month before deployment, assign a couple of testers to sit in front of the system for a day or two, send the results back to the programmers, wait a week for the development team to clean up the code, and repeat the process. But what about a larger project that shoves out a good-size system on its first release? Suddenly you may have a significant number of tests to write all at once.

Worse, yet, what happens—even with a small team—when you get several releases down the road? The number of programmers on the team has not changed, and the volume of functionality they deliver with each release has not changed, but the number of functional tests that need to be run every release keeps doubling (as illustrated in Figure 8.3).

Two years ago, there were eight programmers and two testers on the team. Now the number of testers equals the number of programmers, and those testers still are not getting through all the functional tests before each release. Management has balked at the idea of having more testers on the team than programmers. And, by the way, where exactly do you plan to find time to write tests for the new functionality?

Any successful project team with several releases under its belt could find itself facing this problem.

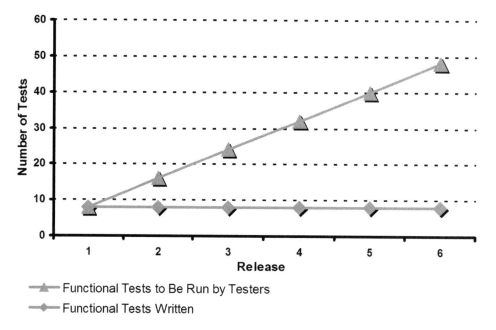

FIGURE 8.3   Functional tests written, versus number of tests that must be executed, by release.

Purpose and Benefits

Acceptance tests are typically used in tandem with features, user stories, or use cases as well (see Chapter 11, "Features and User Stories"). As opposed to unit tests that ensure the appropriate functioning of methods and other small bits of functionality, acceptance tests cover and are associated with features. They may also be called functional or system tests. As much as is possible, they should be automated.

The first purpose of acceptance tests is not to snag random defects. Rather, they first serve as a mechanism for the customer to accept a feature (by being convinced that it works) that has been programmed by the team. Acceptance tests may also be thought of as a means of capturing and documenting requirements (this more "extreme" interpretation is discussed in the "Bare Minimum Documentation" section of Chapter 17, "Communication and Collaboration").

In addition to assuring the acceptability of features as they are completed, correctly implemented acceptance tests have two additional benefits. First, with automated acceptance tests, the amount of effort expended on testing activities holds steady over time, instead of increasing with every new test (as depicted in Figure 8.3). Second, the number of defects that make it out of development should be significantly reduced, because with automated acceptance tests, programmers cannot consider their work complete if the associated acceptance tests do not pass.

Implementation

Acceptance tests are of the greatest benefit when they are specified (and written) by the project team's customer (see Chapter 14, "Executing Iterative Development"). They may, however, be written by an analyst or domain expert assigned to the team. The acceptance tests for a given user story should test everything that the test writer would want verified in order to feel comfortable about signing off on the implementation of that story [Beck99]. Acceptance tests do not need to be written until a user story is queued up for development, but then they need to be completed early enough to be useful to the programmers completing the user story.

The test writers (such as the customer, analyst, or domain expert) cannot be expected to automate the tests on their own. One or more members of the team should work with the test writers to build the automation framework that will run the tests. All manner of methods have been used by teams to store instructions for and to execute acceptance tests, including spreadsheets applications, Microsoft Access®, and even customized scripting languages. Also, consider employing the project's test data management system (if you have one, and to be discussed later in this chapter) for the creation of data structures to be used when automating the tests.

Finally, unlike unit tests and like functional tests, acceptance tests should not be expected to pass 100 percent of the time [Jeffries00].

Opportunities and Obstacles

This section details one opportunity and one obstacle.

Programmers Complete a User Story with Acceptance Tests That Do Not Pass

To be clear, this is different from one or more of the acceptance tests just up and failing. This is an observable pattern where one or more programmers release features to QA, and the newly written acceptance tests for those features do not pass.

The first thing to do is investigate whether the test writers are delivering the acceptance tests to the programmers with a sufficient amount of time for them to be put to good use. If this is the problem, then work with the test writers to keep the problem from repeating. Second, give the programmers the benefit of the doubt and see if some other mix-up or odd set of events can explain what is happening.

Finally, if this is simply the fault of one or more programmers not bothering to run through all the acceptance tests related to the feature they are coding, then this is absolutely unacceptable. At the same time, and unfortunately, it does happen. One might try to communicate to the programmer or programmers that, while it is okay not to complete all the work for a given iteration, it is not okay to fail acceptance tests on completed functionality. Pair programming might help in a situation like this, since it is more difficult for a pair of programmers to shirk the rules. If none of these tactics work, it may be time to apply some tough love.

Include Other Types of Tests with the Acceptance Tests

A project team's acceptance test framework may include most or all of the elements necessary to write and execute load, failure, and parallel tests. If so, the team should consider taking advantage of this obvious opportunity.

AGILE PRACTICE: TEST-DRIVEN DEVELOPMENT

Here is a mental exercise that a programmer (or someone acquainted with programming) may use to understand the usefulness of test-driven development (TDD). Think of a method that you may need to write in the near future. Assume that the method is written, and in your mind write the code that you would use to test that method. If you cannot write the test because you do not know how you would use the code you have already mentally written, then TDD may have just benefited you for the first time. Advocates of TDD argue that writing tests before writing code ensures that the programmer knows what code he wants to write, how he wants to use it, and how he will be able to test it.

This practice (a.k.a. test first development) could have been included in Chapter 7, but it is discussed in this chapter because of its grounding in and reliance upon the implementation of disciplined and thorough testing.

Purpose and Benefits

Some people will be honestly skeptical about the promise of TDD. Nonetheless, its benefits are quite impressive. First, followed diligently, TDD can ensure a test suite so exhaustive that no code will make it into production that is not covered by a test [Coad03]. Second, the very act of writing code before tests ensures that the code that has been written is testable [Martin02]. Third, with such a thorough set of tests, programmers can alter and update code almost without fear. Finally, code that is fashioned through TDD (where every object in the code was written from the point of view of another object that needed to access and test it) will have a cleaner and simpler design.

Like many other agile practices, learning TDD will initially slow a team's productivity. However, once the programmers have gotten up to speed on the approach, practicing TDD (on top of unit testing) should add no upfront cost to the development of new functionality.

Prerequisites

TDD is an intermediate-level practice that relies upon build automation and automated testing. Continuous integration is also highly recommended. TDD follows many of the principles associated with simple design and refactoring. Reading up on these practices is recommended. Finally, agile practitioners have reported that TDD can be a difficult practice to introduce to teams new to agile. Unless it is specifically excited about TDD, a team relatively new to agile may wish to focus on some of the entry-level practices first [Fraunhofer02b].

Implementation

The actual steps to follow when writing tests before functional code are surprisingly straightforward. Programmers using TDD adhere to the following steps when adding a new feature to the system:

1. Write a test (and ensure that it fails).
2. Write just enough code so that test and all other tests pass (applying a simple design that does not plan for any future coding).
3. Repeat (and refactor as necessary) until the feature has been completed.

While somewhat minimalist, these steps should help illustrate the simple discipline and power behind the practice of TDD. This is the easy part of TDD. Getting individuals and teams to adopt TDD, however, can be more of a struggle [Fraunhofer02b].

The difficulties many encounter in learning TDD may stem most directly from the fact that TDD requires a change in mindset for those who choose to learn it. Programmers who have always seen value in business code will feel awkward putting so much thought and upfront effort into the design and implementation of test code. This will be the case especially with individuals who are already skeptical about the value of testing in the first place. Someone who has yet to see the advantages of automated unit testing, for example, is not likely—at least initially—to be very amenable to TDD.

Experience has shown that once programmers get accustomed TDD they tend to like it [Fraunhofer02b]. So the challenge for many teams may be to reduce the slope of the learning curve so that the practice may be more easily picked up. Build and test frameworks that the programmers are well acquainted and comfortable with, for example, can ease the transition to TDD. Other tips to adopting TDD include:

- Start by tackling something very simple. Make sure that the requirements are well understood before beginning.
- If after an hour or so of trying a test first approach to a specific chunk of functionality seems elusive, then quit. Throw away the test-in-progress, select a smaller slice of functionality, and try again.
- TDD is definitely a practice that could benefit from being learned by pairs (as described in Chapter 6, "Agile Practices") [Kearns04].

While this approach may feel awkward at first, a programmer who keeps going will find himself falling into a test-code-refactor rhythm [Clark04].

See Also

- A good Web portal for information and tools related to TDD can be found at *www.testdriven.com*.
- Peter Coad has a healthy selection of columns on TDD available at *http://www.coadletter.com/coadletter/testdrivendevelopment/*.
- Take a look at David Astels' *Test Driven Development: A Practical Guide* [Astels03].
- Another recommended book is Kent Beck's *Test Driven Development: By Example* [Beck02].

STARTING MONDAY: QUICK AND DIRTY AUTOMATED TESTING

If your project has determined that a lack of automated testing is its current worst problem, then even after reading through this chapter you are probably asking yourself how you could possibly throw enough testing coverage over the system with little enough effort to make the whole endeavor worthwhile. You may have already considered building a comprehensive test suite at the unit level but dismissed the idea because it would be too time consuming and even turn off the programmers to automated testing. And in this case, you would be right. But what else can you do?

Consider a means of fashioning a coarsely woven net of tests over the entire application. Can you quickly implement a solution that may not catch the small defects but will still snag the big ones? Such a solution might give the team confidence to move forward with development while simultaneously getting serious about testing. Is there anything your project has at the system level that may facilitate some form of quick-and-dirty testing? Are there artifacts such as testing scripts that could with some effort be automated? Is there anything about the architecture of the system that you might be able to take advantage of to throw together a rough net of tests?

There is no generic answer to these questions, but here are two examples of projects that faced a similar dilemma and how each went about solving it. The first example comes from my own experience and the second from the experience of a former colleague.

Page-Level Tests for an Online System

One day while working on a Web-based project, our team was surprised to discover that a dozen pages in the system (comprising two complete sections of functionality) were broken and had been broken for several days. Such a situation was possible because no automated testing had been done for the first six months of the project, and we were in month eight. Because the system was only weeks away from going to UAT for its second release, a couple of programmers put their heads together to try to keep such a gross malfunction from occurring again.

The pair devised and programmed a simple component, dubbed HttpTestRunner, that operated as a series of independent JUnit test cases. HttpTestRunner worked its way though a list of URLs, making an HTTP request and then reporting whether that request returned a complete page of HTML. HttpTestRunner loaded its own data into the database and then extracted that data after it was done, ensuring that the framework could run in multiple environments and that other tests would not monkey with its data and cause false alarms. All 50 pages of the system were fed through a text file as URLs, ensuring that each page was live. HttpTestRunner did have its limits. It could not determine whether a page was returning correct data, but by flagging pages that were only partially rendered or not delivered at all, HttpTestRunner kept an embarrassingly defective build from ever making its way out of the development environment [Schuh01].

This, of course, was not a final testing solution for the team. It took time after the release as new functionality was coded and old code was refactored (with tests) for a full testing suite to be built around the system. However, a solution such as this may serve to be the perfect stopgap measure.

Test Scripts Rewritten in XML

This example involves a project team at a financial services company that came to work one day to discover they had adopted a partially implemented C++ application and all its heavy documentation accoutrements but no real word from the project's former parents. Their assignment was to patch up the system and get it into production (apparently, running away screaming was not an option). The team spent some time investigating the system and its documentation. Eventually, they landed on a viable (and very useful) solution.

The purpose of the system was to manipulate and transform data. Put most simply, it was XML in and XML out. The system documentation also included a thorough list of test cases that entailed feeding data through the system and verifying the result. The team realized that not only did they have a system that could easily fit within an end-to-end test framework, they also had the very data that needed to be fed into the tests that would be fed through the framework.

The team started with the simplest test cases first and then added new test cases by feature. At first the team focused on rehabilitating the system (ensuring it worked, feature by feature) and then followed the same approach to implement the system's remaining required features. In the end, faster than anyone had imagined and in the face of many expectations of failure, the team delivered a finished, fully tested, and reliable system.

9 Data and the Database

Nearly every system does something with data. Financial systems track money in its numerous forms, e-commerce systems track customers and orders through the online shopping experience, and medical systems track us in our varying states of health and health care coverage. In every case, data must be collected, stored, retrieved, and referenced. Without places to put and get data, these systems could not exist.

Good data management is often neglected or considered unattainable even by agile teams. Databases may be viewed as a necessary evil, XML definitions can be written without any thought toward good data modeling practices, and database administrators (DBAs) can administer the project data sources with a need-to-know approach that hinders a project team from doing anything but the most basic development-related activities.

Data management can enhance or hamper the progress of an agile team. If the project's data sources creak and moan at every change to the data model and if the programmers' data sandbox resembles a litter-strewn shoreline, the team will be less agile. If the data sources flex in tune with changing requirements and allow for the existence and maintenance of multiple datasets for programming and testing activities, the project will be two steps closer to true agility.

WHY WORKING WITH DATA IS TOUGHER THAN WORKING WITH CODE

Many project teams treat the database (or other forms of data storage) as a necessary evil, but they have not taken the time to examine why managing the database can be more complicated than managing code. A project team must understand the factors that make managing data so complex (both technical and cultural) before it can learn to make data more agile.

Context Adds Complexity

On most projects, source control is the place of record for all code. Therefore, if a team were in its fourth iteration and wanted to see the code at the end of iteration two, a programmer could easily check out the code—as it was on the last day of iteration two—from the source control tool. Because source control is typically deemed the system of record, a team knows there will always be only one version of the codebase at any given time during a project. Even when a team branches the code, there is always only one version of code available across time for each branch of the system. Figure 9.1 illustrates a main line of code and its branch.

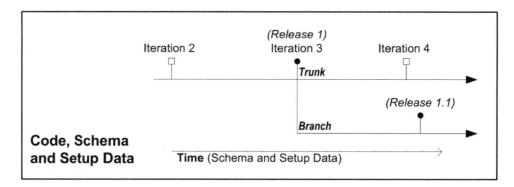

FIGURE 9.1   The code, schema, and setup data for a branched system.

A portion of the system database—that is, its schema and setup data—can be drawn out and traversed on a timeline in exactly the same manner as application code. This applies to all data sources for an application, but only the database is discussed here for the sake of simplicity. Setup data includes all the reference (such as drop-down lists and status codes) and configuration data (such as user preference settings).

If a development team were to use scripts to build its database schema and maintain setup data and source control those scripts in the same tool that keeps its code, the team would be able to re-create a functional database instance at any point in time (in a remarkably similar fashion to the way this can be handled with code). Therefore, the illustration in Figure 9.1 applies not only to the system codebase but also to the schema and setup data. Locating the exact structure and initial data state of the system in time is not difficult, even with branching.

What about all the other non-setup data that various team members and subteams need loaded into the database for reasons including (but not limited to) general programming activity, acceptance testing, regression testing, automated testing, and deployment? A medium-size project working on a data-intensive application can have a dozen different sets of data that it needs to maintain to perform these and other activities.

This is where data context comes into play. Each different set of data just mentioned exists for a different purpose in a different context. Unlike the development timeline (which can be traversed forward and backward), context is a non-linear and noncontinuous dimension. As illustrated in Figure 9.2, a new data set merely adds a new and distinct line (also called a lineage) that may be traversed back and forth in time [Schuh02b].

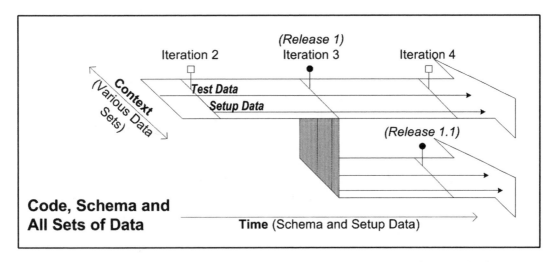

FIGURE 9.2 Adding context: the code, schema, and all data associated with a branched system.

When you branch with lineages of data, you suddenly have four distinct data lines (each at a different point in context) that must be maintained.

Look at Figure 9.2 again, and imagine adding just one more lineage (such as user testing) or having to perform one more branching operation. Either way, the total number of data sets that need to be tracked or maintained will increase (or even double). Data context makes managing and maintaining data a complex activity even on relatively straightforward systems. A failure to acknowledge and address the effect of context can make data on even a medium-size project unmanageable.

Later in this chapter we will discuss different ways to either mitigate or manage this complexity.

Cultural Differences Between Object People and Data People

In addition to the technical issues, there are cultural reasons why data can complicate software development. At its most basic, this is a cultural divide between programmers (object people) and data professionals (data people) [Ambler04]. Programmers often argue that relational database mappings do not adequately fit their world of objects. Database administrators (DBAs) and data modelers, meanwhile, often claim that programmers simply do not know how to lay out data structures [Cockburn97]. Much of this disconnect has to do with the two different worlds in which these individuals work.

Programmers can—somewhat understandably—forget that they are not the only users of databases. For example, while programmers may work best with highly normalized data structures, reporting systems often rely on highly denormalized structures—that is, the exact opposite. Another example is financial and billings systems that must maintain certain data for anywhere between two and seven years. In addition, some critical systems may require enhanced auditing capabilities. Programmers often forget that, when designing and maintaining databases, a DBA is often thinking in much larger terms than simple, well-designed objects.

DBAs (along with other data people such as report designers) often do not sufficiently engage and support programmers in a way that would help them most.

The larger the system a DBA supports, the more activities he becomes responsible for beyond that of supporting any specific programming team. In addition to attending to the project teams, a DBA is typically attending to or supporting reporting activity, tuning databases to increase average user and batch job performance, and otherwise maintaining the hardware on which all the databases run. Data modelers, similarly, must answer to other parties and attend to other duties in addition to supporting any one programming team. In other words, DBAs and data modelers often are not given sufficient time to understand the tasks and problems of the average project team, limiting the amount of truly constructive input and assistance they can deliver.

As will be discussed in this chapter, there are ways to bridge this divide and bring these individuals into a more communicative and collaborative relationship.

THE AGILE DBA

Agile projects, in order to do many of the things that they do—including the ability to respond to change through constant testing, simple design, and refactoring—need data and data sources that are willing to flex and adjust to the activities of the team. Of course, data and the structures that hold data are only as nimble as the person who directs them. Therefore, projects need an individual who can help bridge the chasm between code and data, writing tools, developing techniques, and otherwise working toward a more amicable relationship between the two worlds. Agile projects need an agile DBA.

An agile DBA is an individual who:

- Performs the traditional development-related duties for a project team, including the creation and modification of new data sources, structures, queries, and procedures.
- Provides an additional level of assistance to the project team, including collaborating with the relevant team members on the design of new data structures and the management of test data sets.
- Has a good understanding of the software development process in order to respond quickly to the changing needs of the team.
- Serves as an emissary between the development team and other parties within a large project or users of a shared data source, such as members of other development teams, report writers, and even power users.
- Is a full-fledged (if not full-time) member of the project team so that he is encouraged to consider more than simply the immediate needs of the team (that is, be forward thinking), so that he focuses on improving the team's development environment by devising processes and tools that simplify the sometimes arduous task of working with data, and so that he is able to recognize and communicate potential data-related issues and pitfalls before the team has the opportunity to stumble upon them.
- Does not need to know much about production database issues because a real production DBA can be brought in to assist with performance issues and maintain the system data source after deployment.

An agile DBA does not need to be an actual DBA, nor does he need to have any formal DBA training. Much like the team buildmaster of years gone by, the DBA may be a team programmer (or even an analyst or tester) who takes on the task of managing the team data sources. This individual, of course, will need time to learn a sufficient amount about whatever database product or data source the system is using to be of real use to the project. This training may be gained through self-instruction or by working closely alongside a real DBA. The agile DBA also does not need to remain the same person on a project but may be a hat that is passed about in much the same way that teams sometimes regularly transfer the duties of the buildmaster.

START WITH SOMETHING SIMPLER THAN A DATABASE

One proposal regularly discussed in XP circles is simply to start without a database. The idea is that the application should not be hooked up to a database until it needs to be. In the place of a database, programmers at the beginning of the project may use flat files, XML, or anything else they can think of that allows speedy implementation, does not involve connecting to an external system, and can ease the creation and management of test data. This approach enables the team to work its way into appropriate data structures, since it can quickly and easily alter data structures in a way that conventional database systems would not allow. Additionally, a project team may actually deliver early releases with such a system in place, thereby meeting an aggressive production schedule and converting to a real database at a later date [Jeffries01].

Similar approaches resulting in similar benefits might begin with an object-oriented database or even an embedded relational database (such as Hypersonic-SQL for Java and SQLite for C++). Ultimately, the approach requires an eye for simple design and an ability to refactor (each practice is discussed in Chapter 7, "Design and Programming"). The data access layer must be defined and developed in a way that makes it straightforward halfway through the project to shift over to an actual database. (Of course, one might argue that another benefit of this approach is that it necessitates a simple yet well-thought design of the system's persistence layer.)

LEGACY DATA CONVERSION

Many software projects involve replacing an old system, which means converting data. Two standard approaches have been to build the system first and convert the data and to spin off a separate team that will handle data conversion. Both approaches pose significant perils.

A separate team tackling the conversion process while the main team builds the application can face multiple problems based on its nature and positioning as a subteam. First, the conversion team may find itself in a constantly reactive mode, as the main team enhances, tweaks, and corrects the structure and contents of a system's data sources. Second, when tough decisions need to be made, conversion may be seen as a less critical activity, and the team may lose out on the number and skills of its members. Finally, because of its situation relative to the main team, the conversion team may not follow the same rigorous management and programming approach as the main team. Ultimately, none of these issues will spell good fortune for the entire project.

During my year-long participation on one large, agile-minded project, the project's conversion subteam, staffed with less-experienced programmers, fell behind schedule due to a faulty technical approach and unsteady management. The team manager was replaced, more experienced programmers were assigned to conversion, and the subteam was brought back on track. Then, as the main team headed for critical releases, the more experienced programmers were pulled from the conversion team to meet project milestones. The conversion was again staffed with less-experienced individuals, and after six months, we were bailing it out again.

Converting data after the system has been (or is nearly) completed may avoid the problems related to a separate conversion team—an ever shifting target and second class status—but will create another potential hurdle. Data conversion activity can be very tough to estimate in advance because it is often hindered by unknowns such as insufficient or incorrect documentation for legacy data, limited access to domain experts, and significant quality issues. Data reconciliation, when it is required, further complicates the conversion activity because it involves writing a whole new mini-system for comparing the legacy data in its original and new states. Such unknowns, in combination with the general optimism, are likely to lead to the serious underestimation of the actual effort entailed in conversion.

There is another option for project teams to consider. Legacy data can be converted as it is required by the application. In this scenario, the entire project team takes on the responsibility of converting legacy data and tackles the task gradually over the course of the project. The rules behind delivering a release may include converting to the new system all the data that the new functionality covers. Further still, in order to call a feature complete, the individual or team that owns the feature may have to ensure that the data associated with it is being converted successfully, providing an easy way to add gradual reconciliation to this gradual conversion process.

Converting legacy data as the system grows provides major benefits. The moving target problem is mitigated because conversion activity is performed by the same programmers who design and code the system. Instead of being reactive to the movements of another team as relationships within the system change, conversion processes will simply need to be updated in the same manner that unit tests are kept passing.

Converted legacy data can be used in system testing. Real data will be readily available, increasing both the speed and effectiveness of testing.

The conversion process itself will be thoroughly tested. Because conversion activity becomes part of the development process (and may be executed on a daily or even more frequent basis), most or all of the unknowable surprises associated with conversion will be found before they have the opportunity to wreak havoc on the project's schedule.

TEST DATA MANAGEMENT

We touched on restorable data when we discussed automated testing. If a team already has a test framework in place that is being actively used and augmented, this may be the next step to adding some agility to the project.

The traditional approach to test data, even for teams that write repeatable tests, is to use whatever data is hanging around the database. This approach works great until two tests alter the same bit of data, the database is cleaned, someone does some manual testing, or one of a dozen other things goes wrong. Basically, test data—if not managed correctly—can be the Achilles heel of a testing framework. Most agile teams, because they live by their tests, need to develop a mechanism to ensure the availability and maintainability of the data those tests rely upon.

Agile Projects Need Good Test Data Management

Test data management is not explicitly addressed by any of the named agile methodologies. This makes it no less important. Test data management gives teams flexibility. They can run their test framework in a UAT environment and load the latest and greatest production data into the development database. A project team that is diligently writing data structures one-off in each test can still benefit by moving to a real system that reduces the time spent on rework, both in terms of writing duplicate data structures and updating test data when the relationships between objects change. Finally, the availability of ready-to-use and ready-to-extend data leads to more tests and better tests.

Managing test data guards against development snafus. On the project where the term ObjectMother was coined and before we had coined it, for example, the programmers noticed one day that the application's address lookup screen would time out intermittently and fail. This seemed a particularly odd mystery because no one had been working in that area of the application for weeks. After several days the failures became rather consistent, and someone had to go nosing around in the code to see what had gone wrong. The cause of the timeouts, it turned out, was that someone on the team, when writing the functionality to attach a new address to a lessee, wrote a test for the functionality (good) that consisted of creating a new address, calling the attach functionality, verifying the functionality, and leaving the address behind on the lessee as junk in the database (bad). Every time a programmer or the continuous integration machine ran the unit tests, another address was added to the lessee. By the time the problem was identified there were 6,000 addresses attached to the lessee (we were, after all, diligently writing and running our tests). Even though such a snafu could conceivably have occurred in the presence of a data management framework, the likelihood of such a situation would be greatly reduced because the programmer would no longer have had to commit a venal sin of not cleaning up after his tests but the more serious sin of writing a test outside the framework.

Test data management also guards against test data atrophy. This situation occurs when test data is simply created as necessary within test cases and even individual methods. This type of test data too often simply gets stacked upon itself and becomes more and more brittle with time until one significant change to the system causes the team to have to fix data creation statements in two dozen different places. Any test data maintenance framework should reduce the likelihood of such an event and, when such an unlikely event does occur, reduce the cost of addressing it.

A Number of Approaches

Agile programmers have cooked up myriad ways to implement test data management solutions. The simplest solution is to mandate that each test instantiate and delete its own data. Another common place teams start is with reloadable data sets (contained in spreadsheets, SQL scripts, and the like) chock full of data that is loaded into the database before the tests run. These are relatively straightforward systems to understand and not complicated to establish, but they can become difficult to maintain as data relationships shift and (in the case of the reloadable data set solution) new tests affect the data that old tests rely upon. It is, however, better than nothing.

A project may roll out a test data management framework the same way it would a testing framework. This project would use the framework in all its new tests and any tests that have broken or otherwise need updating. Unfortunately, if the team is aware of an impending disaster (for instance, the development database is going to be cleaned because the quantity of corrupted data has rendered it all but useless), days may be needed to convert old tests to the new system. At least it is the last time this action will need to be taken.

Spreadsheet-Based Solutions

Many agile (and non-agile) teams turn to spreadsheet-based tools to manage test data for acceptance and even unit testing. These tools can be relatively generic and focus simply on getting data into and out of the database. They can also be very specialized, containing knowledge of the system and even allowing test cases to be scripted directly from a spreadsheet or other graphical user interface.

The benefits of such systems are that they are relatively simple to use, allow for quicker entry of test data than would be possible either with a system's frontend or with simple SQL scripts, and can be navigated more quickly to find and alter the data they contain. They can be a more useful method for programmers to manage test data, and they may be essential if the project wants to enable analysts and users to do the same.

The downsides related to a spreadsheet-based solution typically stem from the fact that the data is managed apart from the database. The most common problems arise when the structure in the spreadsheet falls out of sync with the system database. Another common problem is primary key collision, when the spreadsheet and the database are both using the same set of primary keys. The latter problem, given forethought, is easily surmountable; for example, development teams can use negative values for all spreadsheet-based data. As discussed in the following examples, the earlier problem may be overcome as well. The first example is of a general nature, and the second is specific to a particular situation.

All-Purpose Example

At one site, we used a spreadsheet-based solution to manage test data over the lifetime of several projects. The tool was built over a couple of years, and its capabilities were augmented as each project found new and valuable uses for the tool. The tool itself fit into a single Microsoft Excel workbook. Each worksheet within the workbook represented a database table. The workbook could connect directly to an Oracle database. Its features included the capability to:

- Create a new workbook populated from a target database. The tool could obtain only schema or schema with data and could read all the tables from the database or work from a user-defined list of tables.
- Insert the contents of a single spreadsheet or the entire workbook into a target database.
- Delete the contents of a workbook from a target database.

■ Update the schema within the workbook based on the changes in the target database.

■ Allow the use of meaningful primary and foreign key data instead of meaningless numeric keys. The key labels were replaced with numbers when the tool inserted data into the database.

■ Verify the accuracy of user-entered data. This included the correctness of column types and lengths.

The tool allowed analysts to enter data into a clean copy of a system's database via that system's user interface, extract that data into a workbook, create new data scenarios within the workbook, insert the data back into the database, delete it again in order to run the same tests repeatedly, and keep the workbook up to date as the system grew through the development process.

Situation-Specific Example

On another site, the testing team on a large project took a situation-specific approach to testing a system that had been in development (and delivering releases) for more than a year. The team was faced with hundreds of frontend-driven regression test cases and an ever-changing user interface that refused to be tamed by any frontend testing tools.

Each spreadsheet represented a meaningful bit of the system, typically mapping out to two or more database tables. The testers piled these bits together to automate much of the grunt work required to run each test case. All the logic that handled foreign key relationships and uninteresting data (that is, not screen based) was encapsulated in the tool that chewed through the spreadsheets and injected data into the tester's databases. This meant that the system could be relatively easily updated as the system's data model continued to develop.

Embedded Databases

Another approach that can address some or all of a project team's issues with managing test data and even finding a dependable method of testing some data-related functionality entails the use of a small, language-specific database that can be manipulated completely (from instantiation to full tear-down) from within code. Such embedded databases (which were mentioned briefly earlier in this chapter) include HypersonicSQL, SQLite, and Cloudscape.

Embedded databases can enable a programmer to generate a test database with a few lines of code and populate that database with any data that is required for either one or an entire suite of tests. This approach has three major benefits. First, embedded databases can typically be run entirely in memory, which is an ideal situation for testing, where no data needs to be persisted at the end of the run. This will significantly reduce the time it takes to run tests.

Second, an embedded database helps to fully encapsulate the testing environment. Similar to the spreadsheet-based approaches described earlier, test data does not linger in a shared database where it may be corrupted by other programmers or atrophy with time. Moreover, two programmers may run tests on embedded databases simultaneously with no fear of data collision because each will be operating on an entirely separate data space.

Third, an embedded database can help in those difficult-to-test areas, such as certain select and update queries. Some queries—for example, search queries that scan the contents of one or more tables—can be difficult to test because there is no capability to make them look for something unique. Take the following query:

```
SELECT * FROM address a, customer c
WHERE a.customer_id = c.customer_id
AND c.status = "DELETED"
AND a.status = "ACTIVE"
```

This query (which may be used to identify any active address hanging around after its customer has been deleted) may be run on a nightly basis to verify users of a system that have been closing out accounts correctly. But writing an automated test for such a simple query in a common development database would be near to impossible. The programmer may insert data into the database to ensure that there will be data for the query to snag during the test, but who knows how much flotsam he might net as well? The average development database is chock full of all manner of illogical and abandoned data and accumulates new data at nearly the same rate that Earth accumulates space dust (estimated at 40,000 tons a year). Using an embedded database, a programmer can instantiate a new copy of the database, insert the required data, execute his tests, and leave that unit test in the test suite to continue to run through the life of the project without fear.

It should be noted that there can be a bit of extra work associated with designing a system for testing with embedded databases. Obviously, data access should be designed in a way that it is easy to switch between database connection types, but this is just good programming. Less obvious but more tricky can be differing interpretations of SQL and the use of vendor-specific operations and functions. Often, project teams can get around the majority of these issues by sticking to the accepted realm of the SQL standard. Other times, embedded databases may accept add-ins that can be coded to replicate the vendor-specific functions of the system's production database.

Other Approaches

In the remainder of this chapter, two additional approaches to test data management will be presented as agile practices. ObjectMother is addressed first because it builds on the topics discussed here—that is, constructing a system to provide reliable and robust test data. Mock Objects, a more popular approach that attacks the data problem in unit testing from a different perspective, is addressed second.

AGILE PRACTICE: OBJECTMOTHER[1]

The ObjectMother pattern details a simple, scalable, and project-wide approach to creating data for unit tests. Like the spreadsheet and XML-based solutions discussed earlier, ObjectMother removes the responsibility for test data creation from the individual test case. Instead, the responsibility for creating test data is assigned to a code object or set of objects, the sole purpose of which is to serve as a fabrication plant for customizable test data. ObjectMother delivers test data to order via only a handful of method calls, ensures that each test case receives new and reliable testable data, and removes the data from the database once testing activity has been completed.

Purpose and Benefits

ObjectMother starts with the abstract factory pattern and adds a couple of elements essential to testing. In total, an ObjectMother class or framework provides five services:

- Produces a fully formed data structure, typically in the form of an object and all its associated attribute objects
- Delivers a requested data structure at any point in its lifecycle
- Customizes the delivered data structure, as requested
- Updates the data structure during the testing process, when needed
- Terminates the data structure and all its related objects at the end of the test process

These activities should provide a programmer with everything he needs to grab data for a unit test, run the new functionality through its paces, and move on to the next task.

ObjectMother simplifies and standardizes the creation of test data while easing maintenance activity because test data creation is entrusted to a specific class or group of classes that must adhere to the rules of simple design. The approach provides two other benefits. First, after an initial investment of programming activity, the approach saves time that would otherwise be spent coding test data and fixing broken test cases as data relationships evolve with the system. Second, by reducing the activity required to obtain reliable test data to a handful of method calls, a mature ObjectMother will encourage programmers to write more tests.

Detail

Writing an ObjectMother is a lot like building with Legos™. The pattern relies largely on two distinct types of methods: creation methods that return all manner of data structures and attachment methods that serve as glue. With these two types of methods, smaller, simpler bits of data are locked together to create larger, more complex objects. An ObjectMother creation method might look something like this:

```
public static Invoice createNewInvoice() {
    Invoice invoice = new Invoice();
    invoice.setInvoiceNumber("InvTest001");
    Address address = createAddress();
                        // Point-of-interest #1
    invoice.setBillToAddress(address);
    attachInvoiceLineAsCharge(invoice,
                        new Money("4999.95","USD"));
                        // Point-of-interest #2
    invoice.setStatus(InvoiceStatus.NEW);
    return invoice;
}
```

Point-of-interest #1 in the above sample is the `createAddress()` method call, which demonstrates how ObjectMother's creation methods are designed both to be accessible by unit tests and to be employed by one another to create ever-more complex test objects. Therefore, creation objects should be made public and accessible by any test.

Point-of-interest #2 is the `attachInvoiceLineAsCharge()` method call, which demonstrates both how an attachment method is employed and how it might take certain parameters (in this case `Invoice` and `Money` objects) in order to add a customized attribute object to the data structure. The attachment method being called might look something like this:

```
public static void attachInvoiceLineAsCharge (Invoice invoice,
                        Money money) {
    InvoiceLine invoiceLine = createInvoiceLineAsCharge(money);
    invoiceLine.setInvoice(invoice);
}
```

There are two things to note from this code sample. First, the attachment method performs the work necessary to associate the two objects it has been handed. Second, the attachment method itself does little more than call another creation method. Why push this small bit of code out into its own method? Because the primary role of attachment methods should be to resolve relationships between objects. Therefore, if the application that this ObjectMother supports was updated with a many-to-many relationship between `Invoice` and `InvoiceLine`, possibly the only change that one would need to make to ObjectMother would be to retool the above method to look something like this:

```
public static void attachInvoiceLineAsCharge(Invoice invoice,
                                             Money money) {
    InvoiceToInvoiceLine invToInvLine = new InvoiceToInvoiceLine();
    InvoiceLine invLine = getInvoiceLineAsCharge(money);
    invToInvLine.setInvoiceLine(invoiceLine);
    invToInvLine.setInvoice(invoice);
}
```

Admittedly, other changes might need to be made; nonetheless, ObjectMother has begun to take on the look, feel, and advantages of well-rendered object-oriented code.

We are through with the basics. Now, on to a few more detailed points.

First, whenever possible, ObjectMother should return a valid, test-ready data structure. This should be common sense, since running tests against incomplete or invalid data is simply an invitation for disaster. However, this principle is worth noting because there are times it may actually have to be broken. On occasion, in order to avoid code duplication, incomplete objects may need to be built by one creation method for use by other creation or attachment methods. When possible, these methods should be made private; however, if an ObjectMother has been built as a framework of nodes spread across numerous test packages, one is forced to rely on good documentation and competent developers. Either way, such instances should be kept to a minimum.

Second, ObjectMother should provide any given business object in any of the various incarnations or statuses in which it may be found. Therefore, building on the last code sample, ObjectMother might contain a gaggle of the following methods:

```
public static Address createAddress(String city,
                                    String state,
                                    String zip) {
    Address address = new Address();
    address.setAddressLine1("1011 Bit Lane");
    address.setCity(city);
```

```
        address.setState(state);
        address.setZip(zip);
        address.setStatus(AddressStatus.ACTIVE);
        return address;
    }
    public static Address createAddress() {
        Address address = createAddress("Chicago","IL","60647");
        return address;
    }
    public static Address createInactiveAddress() {
        Address address = createAddress();
        address.setStatus(AddressStatus.INACTIVE);
        return address;
    }
```

Notice how each creation method builds on the one above it in order to generate its result. This way, any given object may be returned in a variety of formats any
number of times, in order to provide a wide array of easily accessible test objects.
Ideally, the constructor call to any given object will appear within ObjectMother
only once—or, in reality, as few times as is absolutely necessary. This will lead to a
straightforward design and simplify maintenance.

Third, when they return valid business objects, ObjectMother's attachment
methods should be made public so that tests may customize objects received via
creation methods. For example, a test that requires an invoice with four lines might
contain code something like this:

```
public void testInvoice() throws Exception {
    Invoice invoice = ObjectMother.createNewInvoice();
                    // Remember that createNewInvoice()
                    // returns an Invoice with one
                    // InvoiceLine already attached
    ObjectMother.attachInvoiceLineAsCharge(invoice,
                                    new Money("19.95","USD"));
    ObjectMother.attachInvoiceLineAsCharge(invoice,
                                    new Money("10","USD"));
    ObjectMother.attachInvoiceLineAsCharge(invoice,
                                    new Money("20","USD"));
... //And on with the test
}
```

By making attachment methods public, test writers may customize the objects
they receive however they see fit. When several tests are found to be customizing a

test object in the same fashion, that code may be pushed up into ObjectMother as either a creation or attachment method.

Fourth, and similar to the above point, tests should be able to update Object-Mother-provided objects as necessary in the middle of the test process. Often this will mean nothing more than running a test on a created object, calling an attachment method to alter the object, and then performing another test. Sometimes, however, this requirement may involve more complex procedures, such as altering a business object's status. Procedures of this type might involve the implementation of new types of ObjectMother methods. For example, to alter a test object's status, a development team may implement a `makeStatus()` method. The ObjectMother code for such a method might look something like this:

```
public static void makeGenerated(Invoice invoice) {
    invoice.setGeneratedDate(new Date("10 Jan 2001"));
    invoice.setDueDate(new Date("10 Feb 2001"));
    invoice.setStatus(InvoiceStatus.GENERATED);
                    //Invoice status has been updated
    Iterator it = invoice.getAllInvoiceLines().iterator();
    while (it.hasNext()) {
        InvoiceLine invoiceLine = (InvoiceLine) it.next();
        invoiceLine.setStatus
        (InvoiceLineStatus.GENERATED);
    }
                    //All the InvoiceLines are also updated
}
```

The key point here is that, however it is done, ObjectMother must allow for changes to its created objects that emulate how those objects are manipulated within the application itself.

Fifth, ObjectMother must be configured to track and delete every piece of data it creates. This is most easily handled by having ObjectMother keep track of all the bits of data it creates and employing a special test case class that includes a call in its tear-down routine to tell ObjectMother to purge its list of generated objects.

Implementation

Rolling out an ObjectMother framework is very simple to do at the onset of coding and is most effective if included as an iteration zero activity (as described in Chapter 5, "Going Agile"). Then, from the beginning of the project, all data required for unit testing should be obtained from existing or newly written ObjectMother methods.

Implementing ObjectMother on a project that has already been in development for several months can be more difficult because of the time that will be involved in building the class or framework. There will be a small upfront cost just to write an initial ObjectMother class with registry and purge methods and to tie that functionality into an xUnit test case class. Then the process of writing creation and attachment methods may be undertaken gradually and be driven by the requirements of new tests.

As noted earlier in regard to rolling out any test data framework, preexisting tests can be left alone and converted over only as they fail or need to be updated.

Opportunities and Obstacles

There are a couple of additional twists that may be taken with an implementation of ObjectMother.

Use ObjectMother for Other Testing Activities

ObjectMother was initially conceived to support unit-testing activities, but the same framework that serves unit tests could also be employed to support acceptance and system testing activities. The code used to transform the rows of spreadsheets into test data scenarios could engage the ObjectMother framework to do the construction and demolition of data structures. But why stop here? ObjectMother may also be used to assist other testing activities, including performance and load testing.

Disconnect from the Database and Gain Speed

A well-designed application can be configured so that during testing it holds data in memory and never needs to make calls to the database. This will add two benefits to an ObjectMother implementation. First, the tests will run faster because of the time savings from not having to write to the database. Second, because the data constructed by ObjectMother is never written to the database, there will be no need to track and delete that data.

AGILE PRACTICE: MOCK OBJECTS

Mock Objects is another approach to the problem of test data management, but it approaches a solution from the inside out. Instead of providing a superior method of creating test data, the Mock Objects approach attempts to remove the need to generate test data altogether. The approach entails building tests that "mock" real objects, passing them into the application as though they were real objects, and then querying them as to whether they were mistreated in any way.

Mock Objects can also be used as an overall approach to testing. Some project teams write the vast majority of their tests with the technique, using Mock Object to ferret their way into portions of the system that are typically difficult to reach, isolate, and test. Mock Objects is also a technique that has been embraced by many advocates of test-driven development (this agile practice is described in Chapter 8, "Testing").

Purpose and Benefit

A single Mock Object takes on the roles of both the test subject and the test observer. In this way, a Mock Object may be coded to resemble an MP3 file (dubbed MockMP3), dropped into the cart of an online MP3 store, and wheeled through different steps of the checkout process. In each test, the system will poke and prod MockMP3, asking questions about its price, the album to which it belongs, and its recording label. Meanwhile, MockMP3 will record the interactions it has with the system, noting whether it had been asked certain things and giving answers that will keep the test going. In the end, a test case may review the things MockMP3 recorded to make certain the system performed the correct actions and not any unexpected ones.

Mock Objects may be used for a variety of reasons:

- To isolate and test very specific behavior within a system.
- To reach and test functionality that is buried within the application and cannot be reached by a conventional unit-testing approach.
- To tackle tests that might otherwise require difficult-to-construct or large quantities of fabricated data, thereby potentially reducing time both in writing and executing the test.
- To test functionality that is nondeterministic, where test results cannot be made predictable, such as the output of a random number generator.
- To test a condition that is hard to reproduce, such as a connection failure [Wiki].
- To serve as a stub; that is, to take the place of an actual object or component that has yet to be developed.

Like many other agile practices, Mock Objects may initially increase development time, both in terms of an initial learning curve and when writing some (but not all) new tests. Of course, this investment will pay for itself with easier maintainability. One other noteworthy item about Mock Objects is that the practice causes some changes in the way an application is structured. This is discussed further later in this section.

Prerequisites

Mock Objects should be built upon an automated unit testing framework. Additionally, an automated build process is highly recommended.

Implementation

Mock Objects complete their tasks by mimicking the interfaces or objects within a system. They are built with a sufficient number of methods to give sensible input to the objects they are testing and then, typically, passed in as parameters within the method call to a real object. This leads to the one significant effect Mock Objects has on the design of a system. Everywhere a Mock Object will be used, an interface must be used to allow either the production object or the Mock Object to be run. This need to write interfaces can also become a benefit by forcing programmers to think consciously about how the objects within a system should and will interact with one another.

Mock Objects can be built and used in several different ways. Some objects may be built to act as recorders (such as in the MockMP3 example previously), where they simply get passed in as parameters and are then examined by the tests that instantiate them. These implementations may have variables that can be set to induce different activities within the system. For example, one may have a promotional code set to it, while another may point to a non-existent MP3 file to test how the system will react in a failure scenario. Mock Objects are typically reusable and can be made to run in a variety of test scenarios.

Other Mock Objects may resemble MockMP3 but be targeted to complete only specific test scenarios. This object will contain logic to assess how the system interacts with it and will know by the end of its test whether the system functioned correctly. In this case, the test is essentially coded within the object. Such targeted objects may be used to replicate complex scenarios within a system and to collect very specific information when a test failure does occur [Meyer04].

The Mock Objects method may also be used to mock entire components within the system or entire applications external to the system. A `DatabaseConnection` object, for example, may be configured to hand over either an actual database connection or a Mock Object that receives and feeds data based upon whatever test scenario has been coded into it. Instead of being acted upon during the test, the Mock Object may also become the driver of the test, feeding test scenarios into the system. Conversely, the Mock Object can take on the role of a stub so that some other testing activity can occur in the absence of the component or system being mocked, either for speed or to simplify the test. Extending our example of an online MP3 shopping system at the beginning of this discussion, Mock Objects could be used to replicate UI-based interactions with the system, the MP3 file manager, the download controller, the credit card billing system, and any other components or external interfaces.

If the Project Already Has Code with Unit Tests

The difficulty of transitioning to Mock Objects on systems that already have code written depends upon whether or not the system has an operational suite of unit tests. If so, the team can easily transition to using Mock Objects, leaving the old tests be. If the old tests are trustworthy, then the team may never need to worry about them and, even when they need to be updated (due to changes within the system), can merely update the legacy unit tests as opposed to replacing them with mock tests. If an existing suite of units tests is not trustworthy (perhaps it is based on the data hanging about in the development database), then the team will want to convert the legacy tests over to Mock Object tests as they break or need updating.

If the Project Already Has Code but No Unit Tests

If the legacy code is not covered by unit tests, then the team will need to take a two-pronged approach (similar to the one it would take if it was merely transitioning to automated unit tests). First, the team should use Mock Objects in all applicable testing situations moving forward. Second (and here's where the pragmatic bit comes in), the team needs to determine whether it will use mock or more standard unit tests to cover the patches of legacy code that either break or need updating. As discussed earlier in this section, the use of Mock Objects involves a change in the design of the system. In places where legacy code is very tangled and brittle, the team will want to throw down a cordon of unit tests prior to doing any rework. When doing so, it will need to make a judgment call between using standard unit tests or mildly intrusive Mock Object tests. Ultimately, the team will want to avoid breaking the code in its attempt to safeguard the code [Meyer04].

Complement Mock Object Tests with Real Tests

A potential failing of a testing approach that relies too heavily on Mock Objects is that it can lead a project team to a false sense of security. While a team may do the vast majority of its unit tests with Mock Objects, it should ensure that it has tests that exercise the system's functionality in the way it will actually be used in production. At the unit-test level this should entail a set of tests that focus on the interfaces with other systems (such as writing to and retrieving from data sources and interacting with any external systems or components) [Kearns04]. At the system level, this will include functional or acceptance tests (see the use of acceptance tests as an agile practice in Chapter 8) [Mackinnon01].

Finally, TDD is definitely a practice that could benefit from being learned in pairs [Kearns04]. This approach is described in Chapter 6, "Agile Practices."

Opportunities and Obstacles

The following sections discuss a couple of additional tips regarding the use of Mock Objects.

Standalone and Portable Development

One somewhat unintended benefit of Mock Objects derives from their tendency to behave like stubs—that is, their ability to interface with a system and act in place of another component. A system with a full complement of Mock Objects often can be run through its entire suite of unit tests without ever needing to be connected to an external system such as a database, an LDAP authentication server, or other third-party systems.

This approach can be extremely useful on projects where an entire team is not located on the same development network (as opposed to simply the same physical space) or where a team is comprised of individuals who often work remotely (such as traveling consultants or people who work one or more days from home). A complete set of Mock Objects that stubs out all external systems enables a programmer to complete work at the office, at home, or even on the plane. When the programmer does have network access, he can then run all the interface-dependent tests to confirm his code is ready for integration.

A second benefit from a full set of mock tests may be more rare but is a Godsend when it does occur: to insulate the programmers from issues within the development network itself.

On one project team working within a 200-person development organization, the development servers simply were not available when the team arrived to work one morning. Upon further investigation, our team discovered that the servers were being moved and would not be available for a week. While the infrastructure and maintenance teams had planned this move a month in advance, no one ever notified the project teams. A dozen teams were affected by the move. Most of them could not work without the network-based systems to test against. Our team already had a full complement of mock tests and had been backing up our source control server on a daily basis. Each programmer simply turned off the tests that hit the network system, and we sailed through the outage with individual workstations and a back-up CVS server. The Blackout of 2003 did, however, bring that project team to a screeching halt.

Tools

There are several tools now becoming available to simplify the use of Mock Objects. The Mock Object folks themselves created and made available a Mock Objects framework consisting of commonly needed mocks (available at *www.mockobjects.com*). Other groups have gone farther, writing tools that either automate the generation of

Mock Objects or increase their reusability. These tools include jMock, MockCreator, MockMaker, and EasyMock, which has versions available in both Java and .NET.

Like any other form of automation, these tools can reduce repetitive and mundane work, speed development time, and even lead toward a better overall design for the application. However, as mentioned in Chapter 6, it really may be best for a project team to cut its teeth on the approach without the interference, predisposition, and additional learning curve introduced by a tool. The team should at least get up to speed on Mock Objects before transitioning to one of these tools.

See Also

- Andrew Hut and Dave Thomas, the Pragmatic Programmers, have made the chapter on Mock Objects from their book *Pragmatic Unit Testing in Java with JUnit* freely available at *http://www.pragmaticprogrammer.com/starter_kit/ utj/mockobjects.pdf.*
- The Mock Objects Web site contains many articles and tools, at *www.mockobjects.com.*
- The original paper on Mock Objects is available at *http://www.connextra.com/ aboutUs/mockobjects.pdf.*

AGILE PRACTICE: AGILE DATA MANAGEMENT[2]

On many projects today, a programmer or tester may create a standalone copy of the system being developed from a workstation or centralized server and may code and test against that live instance without fear of disrupting the activities of other team members who are all working on their own instances of the system. While this approach is typically employed only with executable code, it can also be applied to the system's database (or other data sources) through the use of a data instance.

The agile data management approach allows the whole team to continue programming and testing activity as the database evolves with the application. In an agile data management environment, changes such as new tables, data updates and even column renames are automatically propagated to every data instance without disrupting the individuals currently relying on those instances to do their work. Agile data management will also enable a project team to load a copy of the production database into the development sandbox and run all the updates necessary to make it compliant with the current version of the application so that the programmers can design, develop, and test with real data.

An extended example (as illustrated in Figure 9.3) may best demonstrate the usefulness and versatility enabled by this practice.

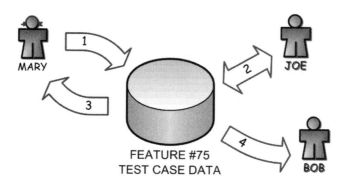

FIGURE 9.3   An example of the benefits of a data instance.

In step one, an analyst (Mary) creates a new data instance named `test_data_75` and uses the system being developed to enter the data needed to run the acceptance tests she has written for feature #75. Mary communicates the information for feature #75, including the location of `test_data_75`, to the programmer who owns the feature (Joe). In step two, when Joe has finished writing the feature, he creates a copy of `test_data_75`, runs the acceptance tests, and finds a defect. Joe corrects the defect, restores his copy of the test data from `test_data_75`, and runs the test again. In step three, when Joe communicates to Mary that he is finished with the feature, Mary creates a copy of `test_data_75`, runs the acceptance tests on her own, and follows up with some ad hoc testing. In step four, two iterations later, the team tester (Bob) is performing regression testing for the next release. He pulls up the acceptance tests for card #75, makes a copy of `test_data_75`, and runs the test script as part of his regression testing.

These examples could be a reality only on a project team with a data management approach that:

- Supports easy creation and access to multiple instances of the application database.
- Has a mechanism in place to keep each of those instances up to date as changes are made to the system in development. On an agile project, changes will include the addition and refactoring of data structures, such as the creation of tables, altering of data relationships, or the deletion of columns.
- Simplifies the manipulation of data instances through an agile DBA and tools pushed out to the team, so that analysts and testers are comfortable and confident with the process.
- Agile data management provides the foundation for such an approach.

Purpose and Benefits

An agile data management approach enables a team to work with the system's database in a way that both increases productivity and makes the entire application more flexible. More specifically, the approach enables every member of the team to code, test, and work safely in his own instance of the system database. Second, it enables a project team to easily manage and maintain multiple datasets for the system, including application setup, development sandbox, acceptance testing, and datasets for any branches. Third, it makes the database portable and restorable, enabling team members to share datasets during development activities, test rigorously without fear of data corruption or loss, and store datasets for future use. Fourth, the standalone nature of the data instance increases the ability of the team to prototype, perform spikes, and otherwise experiment with the applications data sources—again, without fear of adversely affecting other members of the team.

Prerequisites

Possibly most essential to the agile data management approach is the availability of an agile DBA. Summarizing a discussion earlier in this chapter, this is an individual on the team who has some appreciation for both the programming and data sides of software development and who actively uses that knowledge to enable everyone on the team to work in a more efficient and productive manner. Additionally, an agile data management approach is best suited to augment and improve a team that is already following several other agile practices and processes, such as automated unit testing, continuous integration, agile planning, and iterative development. It will likely provide less benefit and be harder to implement in environments that have not already begun a transition toward agile development.

Detail

Describing the inner workings of agile data management is most easily approached by discussing the individual parts of the approach.

The Data Instance

The data instance (a.k.a. the database instance [Schuh02]) is no more and no less than an easy to obtain and maintain copy of the data source required for the system to operate. The data instance is an analog to the development instance of a system or application. It will include all the structure (such as tables, views and triggers for a database) and data (both setup and use-specific) necessary to fully support the system under development. The data instance is a single concept, but its manifestation depends upon the database product in use. Figure 9.4 provides examples of data instances in three different data source technologies.

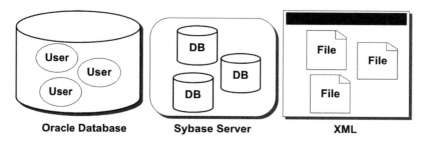

FIGURE 9.4   Three examples of data instances.

These examples should help to define the database instance as a concrete concept. In each of these technologies, the data instance corresponds to a standalone unit that may contain all the required data for a system. This unit may be an Oracle™ user, a Sybase™ database, or an XML file.

Depending on a system's size, complexity, and lack of architectural clarity, a data instance may be much more than a single unit of structured data. For example, an XML-based system might rely on an entire directory or even a directory tree of files, or a system that connects to Oracle may store data in two or more users. Trickier still, a system may employ a mix of technologies (such as both an Oracle user and several XML files) to maintain and access all the data it needs to operate. In this case, a data instance will be an aggregation of data storage units.

The Data Lineage

A data lineage represents the progression of a particular dataset over time [Schuh02]. The lineage was illustrated in Figure 9.4 and can be seen in more detail in Figure 9.5, where it is represented by the development, acceptance testing, and production datasets.

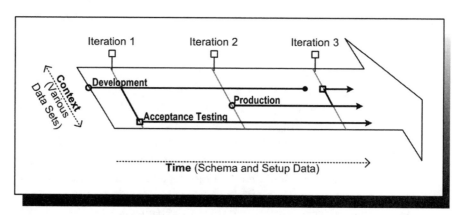

FIGURE 9.5   Sample data lineages across three iterations of a project.

The first lineage of any application is the one that supports the application itself (the primary lineage) and contains only schema and setup data. While the primary lineage is not depicted in Figure 9.5, it is the common base shared by the three lineages that are shown.

New lineages should be created every time an application is branched or when a portion of the team (such as development, QA, or reporting) requires a new, unique, and maintainable dataset. However, it is worth remembering that each new lineage adds a degree of complexity to the DBA's workload (as demonstrated earlier in this chapter). Lineages should not be created for frivolous reasons or, worse, to encourage bad habits. For example, a valid reason to add a new lineage is to maintain a specialized dataset for acceptance testing. Conversely, an invalid reason for a new baseline is to support a unit test suite that breaks on the latest run of converted data. In the latter case, the suite should be made to run on the new batch of data, and the team should seriously consider adopting one of the test data maintenance practices discussed earlier in this chapter.

While the DBA should readily create new lineages as necessary, he should also be forever vigilant about decommissioning unnecessary lineages. Even with a significant amount of automation, additional lineages can take time to administer. Furthermore, depending on the presence and quantity of setup or legacy data, unnecessary lineages can soak up spare disk space.

Finally, each lineage has a master instance, a change log, and an update list.

The Master Instance

Each lineage has one master instance. The master instance is the gold standard for a lineage. It is the data instance from which all new instances of that lineage are created and all existing instances of that lineage are restored. A master instance should never be directly accessed for programming or testing activity because it is the dataset of record for each lineage. All work should be performed on copies of the master instance.

The Update List

Update lists are used to update all the data instances for a system as it wends its way through development. Each lineage has an update list, which is the mechanism by which updates are communicated to all the instances derived from that lineage (including the master instance). Depending on the data sources employed by a given team, the update list for each lineage may be very simple. For example, the update lists for a small project may look like those in Figure 9.6.

In Figure 9.6 (intended for an Oracle database), the schema and data updates are written in a file at `c:\dbSCRIPTS\changes.sql`. The update is performed as the script in the `all_update.sql` file connects to each data instance, executes the changes, and

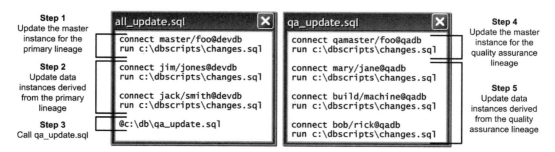

FIGURE 9.6   Sample update lists for a small project.

moves on to the next data instance. Note how the main update list, `all_update.sql`, calls the update list for the quality assurance (QA) lineage in order to propagate the changes. The QA team may have two reasons for maintaining a separate lineage. First, the QA team may wish to keep a set of data specific to the acceptance and system tests they need to run. Second, the QA team may want to "freeze" its lineage so that it can have additional time to test a specific build prior to its release. Freezing for QA is now a simple matter of commenting its update call out of the `all_update.sql` script.

New instances derived from a given lineage will need to be added to that lineage's update list in order to be kept up to date and may be frozen simply by being removed from the list. If an instance is being created and used for only a few hours, it may not need to be added to the list. Finally, frozen instances will need to be updated with the lineage's change log before they can be added back to the update list.

The Change Log

The change log is a compilation of all the changes, ordered in time, made to a given lineage. If the system is using a relational database, the change log may look something like the sample in Figure 9.7.

Maintaining change logs is necessary for two reasons. First, change logs are used to migrate out-of-date instances (as discussed earlier with regards to QA). Second, change logs allow for a lineage to be reconstructed at any point in time. This is useful both as an analog to the code rollback and as a supplement to database backups. While database backups are necessary, they are not always sufficient. For example, an acquaintance of mine once worked on a project team where the client's database server crashed, taking the hard drive with it. When the backup tapes were pulled, they turned out to be blank. The team then discovered that the backup script for that server had not been working correctly for more than a year. The team had nothing resembling a change log and was set back several weeks.

```
Change Log - Primary                                          [X]

--feature 39
--2004.05.18
CREATE TABLE customer
(        code            VARCHAR2(10) NOT NULL,
         name            VARCHAR2(40) NOT NULL,
         dunsnumber      VARCHAR2(40) NOT NULL,
         website         VARCHAR2(255) NULL,
         status          VARCHAR2(5) NOT NULL,
         createdBy       VARCHAR2(10) NOT NULL,
         createdDate     DATE NOT NULL,
         modifiedBy      VARCHAR2(10) NOT NULL,
         modifiedDate    DATE NOT NULL,
         CONSTRAINT pk_customer PRIMARY KEY (code))
TABLESPACE usertables;

--feature 21
--2004.05.19
ALTER TABLE address ADD countrycode VARCHAR2(3);
UPDATE address SET countrycode = 'USA';
```

FIGURE 9.7   Sample change log.

Deprecation for Data Changes

Except in the case of very small teams, changes to data and code typically need to be handled in some fashion so that they do not adversely affect programmers who are not up to date with the very latest code. The DBA must be mindful to identify and time any actions such as deletions or renames. If handled incorrectly, these activities cause data and code to fall out of sync, result in failing unit tests, and force programmers to check and merge the latest code with their own incomplete work.

A good practice is for the DBA to perform any immediate changes required for new code to work and then wait some amount of time (depending on how often programmers check in) before performing any actions that may result in the deletion of columns, tables, or data integral to the operation of the system. Figure 9.8 provides an example of how this approach may be taken to rename a column.

Occasionally, changes must be made to the data model that do not allow for reverse compatibility. In these cases, team members should be warned of the upcoming change and be given the ability to check out new and working code at the same time the change is made to the database.

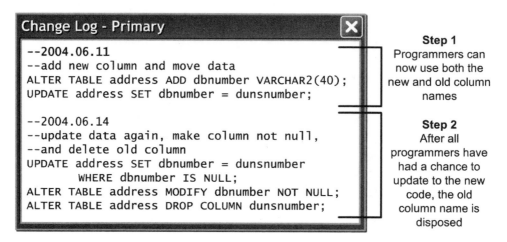

FIGURE 9.8 Example of a column rename (from dunsnumber to dbnumber) in a programmer-friendly manner.

Implementation

An agile data management approach can be implemented regardless of whether the project is just starting or a year into development. In either case, it may be implemented in much the same manner. The one significant advantage for a project that has not begun building its system—and that has control over the nature of its data source—is that it can select and design that data source and the system with an agile data management approach in mind.

A Manageable Data Instance

As discussed earlier, the data instance must contain all the structure and data required to support a functioning system. For many systems, this may be as simple as a single user (Oracle), a single database (such as for Sybase or Microsoft SQL Server™), or a folder full of XML. For more complex systems, a data instance may include two different data components, such as two users, or a database and a handful of XML scripts. This will add a bit of complexity to the administration of master instances, update lists, and change logs, but it should be manageable.

Sometimes, a larger, less-well-designed, or otherwise special system may have four or more data components. This situation may pose more of a challenge for an agile data management approach and will need to be handled with some ingenuity. There are two questions to ask in such a scenario. Why are the data sources for the system so complex? Can anything be done to simplify the situation?

Automation

Automation is a principle that has quietly underpinned most of the discussion in this section. Instances must be easily created, copied, updated, and restored. This can be done with a gaggle of batch scripts or a more sophisticated and custom-built toolset. The whole system must be something that one DBA can manage while supporting the team in other areas, such as advising on the data model and writing SQL scripts.

Nonetheless, automation itself is not sufficient. These automated tasks should be pushed out to programmers and other team members, allowing them to queue up and switch between database instances in much the same manner as they might create and maintain their own instances of the system. This kind of automation should be set in place both to spare team members the hassle of having to hunt down a DBA and to spare the DBA the hassle of having to perform such menial tasks.

A sticking point project teams may encounter regarding task automation and the database is the perceived danger of handing to the average programmer tools that would allow him to alter schema, drop databases, corrupt data, and otherwise inflict misery upon the rest of the team. This includes analysts and testers as well. Regrettably, some programmer will sooner or later bring down a database through the incorrect or inappropriate use of a DBA-provided tool. That is what backups are for. In the end, it should become apparent to everyone on the project team that the time spent mopping up the occasional mess is a worthwhile investment that, by removing unnecessary obstacles and processes, returns a higher team velocity. This does not mean that safeguards should not be put in place. Master instances may be hidden away from the rest of the team, tools may log their activity, and data modeling decisions that affect an entire project should not be made by an individual in a vacuum.

STARTING MONDAY: CULTIVATE AN AGILE DBA

DBAs are often a bottlenecked resource within an organization. Truly good DBAs, who understand the needs of and are attentive to the team, are almost a rarity. However, as discussed earlier in this chapter, an agile DBA can be a significant asset to a team without having a formal data background. Cultivating an agile DBA may be a lot simpler than one may initially believe.

Only two things are required to cultivate an agile DBA: a bit of slack time on the project and a willing candidate. That individual may read this chapter, book up on SQL and the database (or other data source) being used on the project, identify the team's worst data-related problem, and attack it. The slack time that was initially used to cultivate the agile DBA may be quickly paid back in increased team performance or system quality.

Once a project has one agile DBA, it should concentrate on cultivating another. This is a prudent move for several reasons. First, the programmer or analyst who initially volunteered for the job will at some point likely tire of its novelty and want to get back to his chosen line of work. Second, and even if the first candidate is perfectly happy in his new assignment, while only one agile DBA has been cultivated, he will remain a bottleneck and a scarce resource. If the first candidate has really taken to the job and there is not enough need for two agile DBAs on the team, this may still be the ideal situation for the project's organization. In this case, the first candidate may take some time to train a replacement on his project and then move to assist a new project team (particularly one that may be struggling with data issues).

10 Agile Management

In This Chapter

Several common concepts underpin an agile approach to project management. All of these concepts are shared by some or all of the agile methodologies. As often has been repeated regarding other topics within this book, none of these concepts is unique to agile development; what is essential, however, is the emphasis that agile methodologies put on them.

This chapter includes a discussion of the place of the project manager on an agile project.

CONTRASTING AGILE AND TRADITIONAL MANAGEMENT

Before we move on to the concepts behind an agile and iterative approach, it is worth noting a thought-provoking irony that may be seen in comparing the traditional waterfall approach and an agile management approach. The traditional approach begins with a very detailed plan that typically falls out of date only days after the project begins work. Usually the project manager on this project will spend a few months chasing after ad hoc changes to the plan and trying to input them into whatever tool is being used to manage the plan, thereby keeping it up to date. Eventually, as emergencies arise and reality diverges ever further from the original plan, the project manager stops inputting new information into the tool. Months pass, and when the waterfall project completes its work, it is left with a plan that hardly resembles the actual activities performed during the project.

Meanwhile, at the onset of an agile project, there might only be a vague plan in place, such as one set of features being flagged for the first release and the rest set off to the side. Then before each iteration, the team determines how much effort it can put into that iteration, and the customer identifies one or more features that equal that level of effort—and that he finds most valuable—for the team to complete. Over time, as the project queues up features for each iteration, develops them, records them as completed or not, and moves on to the next iteration, the team builds up a detailed history of how it has gone about completing project work. Months pass, and when the agile project completes its work, it is left with a history that closely details the actual activities performed during the project.

The irony here is this. The team that invests heavily in a plan ends up not being able to say what it did during the project, while the team that does not invest in a plan can. This is because the agile team invests in planning gradually throughout the project, paying for planning only when it can get the most for its dollar.

TIMEBOXING

Timeboxing is a tool that, like any other, can be used for both good and bad purposes. An inappropriate use—from an agile point of view—is to timebox an entire project, that is, to provide a drop-dead completion date for the entire project. This sort of strategy, combined with a fixed amount of scope, too often lends itself to the 70-hour workweek, burnout, and failed projects. Even when a timeboxed project allows scope to be reduced, this single timebox does not provide the team with any additional support to ensure that it will deliver anything by the fixed delivery date. For example, a team working toward a delivery at the end of a six-month timebox may give itself the final month to integrate code and perform user testing. What happens if the team completely misestimates the time and complexity of integrating all its code because it will not have integrated even once prior to the beginning the sixth month of the project? If the integration activities go horribly awry (which has certainly been known to happen), and integration takes all of month six to complete, the team has blown its timebox. At best, the project-level timebox is an ineffectual instrument; at worst, it can wreck a project team.

Agile projects perform timeboxing at the release and iteration levels, so a single agile project contains multiple timeboxes. Each timebox (or iteration) contains most to all of the activity that is typically performed during a project, including integration and user testing. Therefore, an agile project can make an absolute mess out of the first iteration, reflect on the iteration to determine what went wrong, adjust the plan for future iterations based on what they now know, and—most important—recover.

There are three other major reasons why agile projects use timeboxes. First, timeboxes force the customer to make decisions on the short-term direction of the project. Second, they always provide a near-term goal, which can keep the entire team from wandering off target. When an individual knows he needs to deliver something in the near term (such as two weeks), he is much more likely to spend the majority of his time on concrete steps that will achieve that goal. Conversely, when a team starts working toward a deliverable that is four months away, with no near-term goal in sight, the individuals on the team will be much more likely to act as though they have all the time in the world and explore and experiment with all manner of things that may or may not provide any true benefit to the goal of the project.

Finally, timeboxes ensure that the team delivers something useful within a short and defined period. The customer may not get everything he thinks he needs within a single iteration, and the team may not complete every feature that has been requested, but there will be working functionality that provides some value at the end of that iteration. The benefits of timeboxing are that it forces tradeoffs and tough decisions to a point at which they cannot be put off. The customer may claim he needs a certain bare minimum number of features built at the end of the third iteration, but the limited amount of programming time afforded by each timebox will help him to recognize the scarcity of resources early enough so that he can reduce that bare minimum and get something instead of asking for everything and get nothing. For the development team, timeboxing combined with binary status reporting forces each programmer to make a conscious decision about what he can have done by the end of the iteration. Two features completed today are nearly always more valuable than five features that have been started and will all be done sometime next month.

CONTINUOUS PLANNING

Recently, a client was having a discussion with two consultants regarding the future of his company's core business application—a Web-enabled exchange that allows health insurance customers and vendors to trade information and services. One of the consultants depicted the application's structure and code in a dire state (which it was) and recommended the client set out on a concerted analysis and design initiative and then rebuild the application from scratch. The client agreed that the application's situation had to be addressed and then pointed to a large box that had been delivered to his office during the meeting. "But the forms in that box," he said, "could change the entire focus of our company" [Schuh02a].

Complicated and well thought out plans too often fail because by the time they are executed, the present planned for has become the past, and the current present is something different. This can be applied just as readily to the "big picture" of project management as it can to the developer who takes two extra days to write the "universal interface" on a piece of code that business decisions render obsolete the following week.

Project teams cannot work every day expecting the future to be different the next day; they would lose all sense of continuity. This is one reason why agile methodologies and practices employ timeboxing: to ensure both that tough decisions are made and that once work has been started on something, it gets completed.

Additionally—and unlike traditional projects—agile projects are always planning. As described by Boehm and Turner in *Balancing Agility and Discipline,* in contrast to traditional development processes that are plan driven, agile projects are planning driven [Boehm04]. The change in language is subtle, but the change in meaning is tremendous and has a literal ripple effect through agile projects. Agile planning continuously takes into account changing business conditions, discoveries regarding the technologies and systems being used, and the customer's evolving understanding of what he wants and most needs from the project.

As illustrated in Figure 10.1, projects following a traditional approach will be very busy in their early phases performing planning activities and, once clear of those phases, will spend very little time on planning activities through the rest of the project. In an agile process, however, this planning activity occurs throughout the project, beating like a steady pulse at the beginning of each iteration and release. The goal is both to delay decision-making (especially decisions that may be costly to undo) until the very last reasonable moment, while laying a planning process that ensures that those decisions will be made when they have to be made and in a timely manner [Poppendieck03]. This is the driving force behind an agile and iterative process, and it is one of the major reasons why an agile project can steer itself in the midst of the project toward changing goals and shifting requirements.

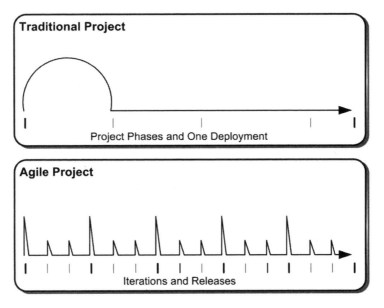

FIGURE 10.1   Traditional versus agile planning activity across the lifetime of a project.

In several agile methodologies, the planning meeting is the steering wheel of the project. Various types of planning meetings (or other activities that typically take no more than a day) are employed prior to the outset of both iterations and releases. For any given timebox, the planning meeting is used to direct either or both the functional and technical directions of the system. The planning meeting is typically held either the day before or the first day of an iteration or release, so it also serves to kick off each new timebox.

CONTINUOUS EVALUATION

Agile project teams use simple metrics and constant feedback to detect issues before they grow into significant problems. This can happen only when a team is dedicated to regularly evaluating the input coming from people and work products, identifying issues that require immediate attention, finding solutions acceptable to all affected parties, and implementing those solutions. Figure 10.2 illustrates how metrics, feedback, and evaluation interact to detect and address a project issue.

As suggested in Figure 10.2, a smart agile team will use a mix of feedback and metrics when tackling the issues that arise on the project. A team is not agile if the

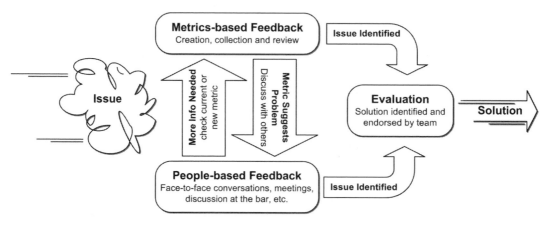

FIGURE 10.2   The relationship between feedback, metrics, and evaluation.

majority of its feedback loops can be measured in months. Feedback loops are built into many agile practices (as illustrated in Figure 10.3). At the development level, for example, short feedback loops can emerge from practices like automated testing and continuous integration. For development and management activities, it is important to ensure that the correct feedback is being received and evaluated by the right people and that the appropriate changes are being implemented as a result.

FIGURE 10.3   The duration of the feedback loop provided by three different agile practices.

Management must encourage and support an environment where short feedback loops are used and valued. Additionally, the project also needs someone leading the team who is sensitive to the information coming from both metrics and the individuals on the team, who tends not to underreact or overreact to the information he receives, and who works with the entire team to produce a workable solution that resolves the issue.

BINARY STATUS REPORTING

Asking programmers and team members to give status by estimating the percentage of completeness of each of their tasks is a profoundly imperfect mechanism of tracking and reporting progress. It is an opaque and varied process (known only to each individual providing each percentage) and encourages both runaway optimism and resolute pessimism. Most often, tasks are 80 percent done in a matter of days and then take a couple of weeks to finish the last 20 percent. On the other hand, programmers who have been burned one too many times by their own optimism will provide wildly conservative estimates of progress or even refuse to play the percent-complete game at all.

Agile projects base status reporting on binary feedback: what is done and what is not done. In other words, they measure accomplished goals such as completed features and not estimated progress. This is one reason why agile methodologies call for features that are sized to fit within a single iteration. First, while it is easy to fib (either intentionally or not) about progress when estimating percent complete, programmers are much less likely to incorrectly report whether something verifiable (like a feature) is complete. If there is a real user or tester who validates all the completed features at the end of an iteration, this becomes nearly impossible.

Agile projects still report progress in terms of percent complete, but it is important to remember that such status reporting always rolls up from a list of "done" and "not done" features or feature equivalents. This non-subjective approach provides a reliable means to roll up and report progress. Nonetheless, agile projects must and do recognize that this approach is not perfect. All the "not done" tasks are only estimates that on occasion can be wildly off the mark, and there is no guarantee that a forgotten must-have feature will not be remembered by the customer two-thirds of the way into the release. These are the known unknowns of agile projects.

Finally, two agile methodologies employ approaches to progress reporting that, at first glimpse, do resemble estimated percent-complete strategies. They are worth discussing, both to establish why they do not follow an estimated percent-complete approach and to further differentiate the traditional and agile approaches.

First, the Scrum approach to managing within a sprint is based on a daily update of work remaining measured in hours. During the sprint, a programmer appears to receive credit for having labored on but not completed a feature, because the following day that programmer can reduce the hours remaining on the feature. Nonetheless, Scrum teams are not responsible to management and users for their progress during a sprint; they are only evaluated based on what is delivered at the end of the sprint. Therefore, while a programmer may gain a measure of credit during the sprint by reporting a lower level of work remaining for a given feature, the true evaluation of the completeness of the feature comes at the end of the sprint, when it will be either done or not done. Why work remaining is a useful progress reporting technique during the sprint will be explained in Chapter 14, "Executing Iterative Development," when we discuss the burndown chart and other methods of monitoring progress during the iteration.

Second, the FDD approach reports the percent-complete of each feature set as it wends its way through a DBF/BBF cycle. However, the programmers on an FDD team do not estimate how complete the feature set is; rather, they merely state what milestones (preset in the development cycle) have been reached. These are hard milestones, including completion of design, passage of a design review, completion of coding, and so forth. Percent-complete is based solely on the milestone that the team has reached for each feature set, so the process of assessing the percentage of work completed remains free of subjectivity. This approach will be discussed in detail in Chapter 16, "Reviewing and Reporting Progress."

VELOCITY

Velocity is simply the amount of work (measured in some form of ideal time) that a single programmer or project team can complete within a given timebox (such as an iteration or release). The team's velocity is required in order to adjust the plan at the onset of each iteration.

Agilists recognize that it is impossible to know, either at the beginning of a project or even halfway through, how much work a project team will be able to complete during a given iteration or release. Numerous and unforeseen factors determine the velocity of the team. Technologies turn out to be more stubborn than thought, an organization starts to pile on the meetings, people roll off the project, domain experts become less available. In short, things constantly change. Velocity enables a project team to acknowledge changes in its carrying capacity and factor them into an iterative approach.

Velocity is a concept introduced by XP. Other agile methodologies use similar approaches, but potentially not to a similar level of detail or not down to the individual programmer. Scrum, for example, authorizes the team to choose the number of features it can complete in each sprint. (To be clear, the team does not select what features it will complete; this is the responsibility of the product owner.) In this way, Scrum enables the team to select a velocity it is comfortable with at the beginning of each sprint. Scrum does not, however, specify how the team should go about determining its velocity. Teams may do so passively, by allowing an amount of work in each sprint that does not exceed its collective comfort level, or actively, by adopting a process such as the one about to be described.

An example of how to compute velocity is provided in Figure 10.4. Velocity should be tracked first at the programmer level. This is because each programmer—due to his individual skills, abilities, experience, work habits, and other duties—will work at a slightly different pace. An experienced programmer with a long history on the project, for example, may average six ideal days per iteration, while another, junior programmer who is new both to the company and the team may complete only three-and-a-half ideal days in the same time period. There is nothing wrong with this difference in productivity because each programmer is coding to the best of his abilities given his experience level and history with the project. However, over time, one would expect the junior programmer to graduate to a higher velocity.

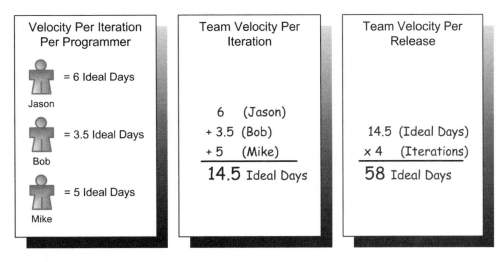

FIGURE 10.4   A practical example of velocity.

Agile teams typically look to their most recent performance to determine a programmer's or team's velocity for an iteration or release (XP refers to this practice as *yesterday's weather*). The approach is not intended to be dead-on accurate, but it does not need to be. Since projects run through multiple iterations in a release and multiple releases in a project, there are plenty of opportunities to make up for velocities that are estimated at too high or too low.

One final note about velocity. Teams should be wary of adjusting their velocity too quickly when a new member joins the team. Programmers new to a team should start with a low velocity, and if the iteration is two weeks or less, consider zero velocity. The reality is that in his first iteration a programmer new to the team will spend a significant amount of time learning and a lot less time being productive. In some cases, especially on small teams, a new member may actually bring the velocity down for an iteration, as other members take time training the new guy and possibly helping him get up to speed on things only tangential to the activities of the project, such as completing timesheets, installing software, establishing an e-mail account, completing HR forms, and so on.

SUSTAINABLE PACE

Many Agilists put a high premium on maintaining a regular pace of work and keeping overtime at a bearable minimum. This is because at its simplest, overwork results in fatigue and harried actions, which beget shortcuts and bad decisions, engendering rework and corrective actions, fomenting collective burnout and free-falling morale, occasionally resulting in ruined projects and loss of prized employees.

A sustainable pace does not necessarily mean 40 hours a week. It may be 38 or 45, depending on a variety of factors, not the least of which is the capability of each individual, but it is not 60, and it should not include weekends. The point is that people start work when they are fresh and full of juice and quit when they are tired. And people need to quit before fatigue begins to affect their work.

Short iterations and a sustainable pace can reinforce one another. The iteration timebox can be used to effectively meter the amount of work doled out to teams and individuals, enabling them to state every one or few weeks the level of work they believe they can take on and restricting the introduction of new work that would push a team beyond its normal carrying capacity. Maintaining a sustainable pace, meanwhile, makes the amount of work a team can do over a given period—and into the future—very predictable, which is a huge asset when planning iterations and releases. It also enables the team to spin up for the occasional week when really necessary, providing projects with an actual boost of extra production on the rare occasion that it is truly necessary.

Regarding the occasional deployment of overtime, Kent Beck provides a good rule of thumb in *Extreme Programming Explained:* An individual should never work overtime two weeks in a row. Having to work two consecutive weeks of overtime, he argues, is a symptom of a more serious problem that needs to be addressed in another manner [Beck99].

Finally, shorter iterations may be more effective at maintaining a sustainable pace than longer ones. This topic will be elaborated upon in Chapter 14, when we discuss one-week iterations.

INDIVIDUAL EMPOWERMENT

Unlike some of the other concepts just discussed, this is a rather soft issue. Agile management is about letting everyone do what they are best at doing and trusting that they can do it right. Programmers know how to design and develop. The customer knows how to identify and prioritize what he wants. Managers know best how to foment communication, encourage decisions, direct activities, monitor status, and report progress.

Of course, trust should not be blind. Things go wrong when people are not doing their jobs correctly. We have all met programmers who cannot program, managers who cannot manage (too many of those), and customers who just cannot figure out what they want. Everyone still needs to be on the lookout for such individuals. When identified, such individuals need to be put on a quick improvement program, removed from the project, or marginalized, if nothing else can be done.

Things seem to go wrong more often when people start doing the job of someone else. When programmers and managers start making decisions for the customer. When the customer starts telling the manager and programmer how he thinks the application should be designed instead of what he needs done. When the manager starts telling the programmers how long something should take. When the programmers start telling the customer how much or how little testing they are willing to do. These are all signs that a project is barreling headlong into a heap of trouble. They are indications that mutual trust, respect, or team morale (all significant foundations of an agile approach) has broken down.

THE AGILE PROJECT MANAGER

Somebody, whether officially or not, has to play the role of project manager on any team that is building software. Typically, this individual is called a project manager or a team lead. Sometimes, this individual is a senior programmer or analyst, and sometimes, this ends up being more that one person. Whoever the project manager ends up being, that person is an integral component of the success of the project. While it is too much to say that the success of any project relies solely on its project manager, it can be said that under normal operating parameters, the actions of a project manager can make or break a project.

Managing an agile project is, without doubt, different from managing a traditional software process. In general, agile projects require a manager who is more engaged in the everyday activities of the project, who is aware of what work each individual is performing (instead of the mere status of that work), and who is actively involved in promoting and maintaining a project environment where team members are both productive and able to enjoy their work.

There are, of course, duties that both the traditional and agile project manager share. Each project manager, for example, is still ultimately responsible for the relationship with the customer and must ensure that news (both good and bad) is relayed between the customer and the team. Similarly, each project manager is also responsible for the overall progress and health of the project. Nonetheless, the roles of these two individuals differ in some significant ways.

First, instead of agreeing to deliver on a detailed contract, the agile project manager strives to build a collaborative relationship with the customer [Stapleton03]. In so doing, the agile manager de-emphasizes the client-vendor relationship between the customer and the project team and instead focuses on constant communication, regular input and feedback, and win-win solutions.

Second, instead of focusing on the completion of individual tasks, the agile project manager zeros in on the progress of entire iterations. The agile project manager will not be looking at the task lines in a work schedule and continuously asking programmers what is complete and what is not. Instead, the agile project manager will want to be sure that features are being completed in their entirety. If it is clear that not all the work will be completed within the iteration, then the project manager will want to remove work from the iteration in whole feature chunks, so that the code that is delivered at the end of the iteration contains completed features that provide new and valued functionality to the customer.

Third, the agile project manager acts more like a facilitator and less like a foreman. Instead of telling each programmer what to do and how much time there is to do it, the agile manager fosters an environment where members of the team are able to make such decisions and base them on the best information available. The agile manager does this by establishing and maintaining a healthy and predictable iterative process where programmers regularly estimate work and collaborate among themselves to determine who will complete each bit of work and how.

The agile project manager also has some duties that may be performed by a traditional project manager. However, in the case of the agile manager, performing these duties is not optional but required. First, the agile project manager acts as a constraint elevator. Whenever engaging with members of the team (and specifically during daily and iteration meetings), the project manager needs to be on the lookout for obstacles that may be in the way of the team. Acting as a constraint elevator, the project manager will escalate any significant obstacle to the appropriate individual (such as the customer, a stakeholder, or upper management) in order to see that it is out of the team's way in a timely fashion. By providing this service, the manager leaves the other members of the team with more time to complete the activities they have been trained and commissioned to do.

Finally, the agile project manager must work to maintain a culture of communication and collaboration on the project, both between members of the project team and between the team members and outside parties (and especially with the customer). There must be an atmosphere of mutual respect, a sense that it is both sanctioned and expected that individuals speak their minds, and a general openness in the flow of ideas, knowledge, and constructive commentary. The project manager, by his actions and inactions, can have a tremendous influence on the culture of a project team.

THE CHAPTERS ON AGILE MANAGEMENT

While the last several chapters have focused on agile programming, the remainder of the chapters in this book speak more directly to the concerns of agile managers. The most readily identifiable of these will be Chapters 11 through 14, which anyone who is not well versed in iterative development may choose to read straight through.

Other chapters that are no less important include:

Chapter 15, "The Customer": The customer is an integral participant in any truly agile project. This chapter introduces the agile perspective on the customer and explores many of the issues associated with identifying, engaging, and working with a customer in an agile development environment. Readers who are not familiar with the role of the customer in an agile project or readers with projects that suffer from a lack of customer involvement (or a lack of healthy interaction with the customer) will want to skip ahead to this chapter and then return to Chapter 11, "Features and User Stories."

Chapter 16, "Reviewing and Reporting Progress": Obtaining feedback, both from targeted metrics and observant team members, is an essential activity on an agile project. As mentioned earlier in this chapter, feedback needs to be derived from short loops and is best when it comes from both objective and subjective sources.

Chapters 17, "Communication and Collaboration," and Chapter 19, "People": Agile projects require the involvement of skilled and empowered individuals working in an environment of open communication and collaboration. These chapters focus on the identification of these individuals, the establishment of such environments, and methods of keeping both individuals and teams healthy and happy as the project progresses.

Chapter 18, "Documentation": Non-code work products must be produced on nearly every project, although less so on some than others. Readers who are dealing with large amounts of documentation on a new or relatively new project (and who already know a thing or two about features and user stories) may want to skip to Chapter 12, "Project Initiation," and then proceed to Chapter 18. Readers may also find the "Solution Sheets" section in Chapter 11 relevant.

Chapter 20, "Real-World Environments": The chapter is one of the last in the book because so much of the content in this book already addresses real-world environments. However, readers working in a heavy process, waterfall, large project, fixed cost, or recovery environment might wish to skip to this chapter to review the section on their particular environment.

11 Features and User Stories

A gile projects build systems in small blocks of functionality that provide a new and valuable experience to the user. These bits of functionality are typically called features or user stories, depending on the agile methodology in use. Features are functionality-based and sized so that they can be completed within either an iteration or (in some cases) a small release. Features are not detailed specifications, but rather just enough information so that the customer can effectively communicate to the project team what he wants and so that the programmers can estimate it. This allows for detailed analysis to be delayed until it is certain that a feature will be developed, which saves time on two fronts. First, features that go undeveloped also go unanalyzed. Second, there is no need to spend time updating an analysis document that may have been written months or even years in the past.

Finally, gathering a list of features is discussed in Chapter 12, "Project Initiation."

FEATURES

The word *feature* is used frequently throughout this book. It is meant to specify something that is shared across agile methodologies, although it does not have exactly the same meaning in every agile methodology. A feature (as it is intended in this book) is the concept of a piece of functionality that:

- Represents a customer experience within the system
- Once completed, will be accessible to and usable by the customer (notwithstanding the completion of any other features that it might be dependent upon)
- Can be estimated by the project team
- Does not take more than a few weeks to complete

Features help the customer prioritize, the team develop, and everyone plan in little bits of functionality that will constantly add value to the system. Features need to be small enough to be completed within a single iteration. Small features and short iterations help to ensure that the system is regularly being returned to a deployable state.

Features are not requirement documents or use cases, although FDD argues that use cases may be used to find features [Palmer02]. Features do not need to be well defined or documented at the beginning of the project. Rather, they are merely an agreement between the customer and the project team on a high-level definition (typically no more than a few sentences) of what will be built and are based on an understanding that the project team and the customer will work together to define the finer points once the feature is queued for development.

Features may be considered a grouping of requirements, but in this case these requirements must lead to the completion of a whole user experience. User stories are features, but features are not always user stories.

Organization

Features and user stories are typically collected in a list that may or may not have an additional level of organization. This list-based approach is necessary if customers are to be allowed to regularly reprioritize and select functionality at the beginning of each iteration. Different methodologies have different names for this list. Scrum, for example, calls it a *feature backlog,* and FDD calls it a *features list.* Small projects may have no other organization besides a pool of features. Medium-size projects might group features, for example, by assigning each to a specific area or component of the system. Larger projects may follow a more hierarchical approach. In FDD, for example, all features belong to a feature set, and all feature sets may belong to a major feature set. It is important to keep in mind, however, that even on a project such as that, the entire pool of work to be performed is represented as a features list and not a hierarchy-based Gant chart.

Prioritization

One added value of features is how they lend themselves to easy prioritization. Because each feature represents an individual bit of functionality, prioritization can be based on the value of a feature, as opposed to what other parts of the system need to be built before the programmers have done enough to get around to it. This is not to say that features can be prioritized and queued for development apart from any dependencies they may have, notwithstanding the fact that some XP advocates argue that they can. Rather, it is simply that value to the customer can usually take the driver's seat in planning discussions.

Agile projects use many different prioritization schemes. First, there is the typical and rather simple prioritization scheme:

1. Must have
2. Nice to have
3. Add if possible
4. Not important

There are many flavors to this approach. DSDM, for example, has its MoSCoW Rules, which translates to **M**ust have, **S**hould have, **C**ould have, and **W**on't have [Stapleton03]. The advantage to this approach is that there is no misunderstanding of the importance associated with each category.

A second approach is similar to the first but may seem less dangerous to the customer who fears that anything besides "must have" translates to "won't get done." This approach has the customer flag features that should be done first, second, and so on. This can be done as a pure hypothetical or within a first draft (but not committed to) release schedule.

A third approach (employed by Scrum) is to have the customer keep all the features for development in a list ranked sequentially by priority. There's no agreement or even suggestion in this approach regarding what will be done and not done. The customer may reprioritize the entire list as much as he likes. The essential moment is during the planning meeting for each iteration, when the customer and the project team agree on a chunk of features from the top of the list that will be developed in the upcoming iteration.

Non-Functional Requirements

While they focus on defining and delivering functionality that is useful to the customer, agile projects do not ignore non-functional requirements. Rather, whenever possible, they turn them into something that can be valued alongside functional requirements and planned within an iteration. Therefore, the first approach to working with a non-functional requirement is typically to try to capture it as a separate feature. Then this non-functional piece of work may be subjected to the same cost-benefit analysis as the rest of the system. So, for example, multithreading (one requirement for small online systems) may be slated as a feature that the customer may queue for a release after more important, functionality based features have already been put into production. This approach works well only when the team is adhering to the practices of simple design, refactoring, and automated unit tests. This way, changes to the code can be made relatively easily since code is not duplicated across the systems, and the tests can confirm that any changes to code do not adversely affect the functionality that has been coded so far.

Second, some agile projects may also express some non-functional requirements as tests at either the unit or system level [Fraunhofer02a]. Finally, some teams may perform an extra upfront architecture or programming activity to address non-functional (or quasi-functional) requirements that are necessary from day one, such as those that may be required to support sophisticated security or multi-language operations.

Technical Tasks

Tasks are an essential aspect of some agile projects, but not in the same way that tasks are used on projects following a traditional approach to software development. On traditional projects, tasks become entries in a project plan. They may represent meetings that need to be held, weeks of development activity, or small checklist-like items that should not be forgotten. They may be baselines at the beginning of the project and may exist in some form until the bitter end.

The agile projects that use tasks (such as those employing XP and Scrum) use tasks in quite a different manner. First, tasks are not identified at the beginning of the project but instead only after a feature has been planned for development, sometimes as little as an hour before development. Second, tasks are typically discarded after the feature is complete.

Tasks and how they are used are discussed more in Chapter 14, "Executing Iterative Development."

Naming

The common convention to naming features is that the names should be meaningful to the customer; preferably, the customer provides them. This requirement ensures that the customer understands the functionality being discussed during planning sessions so that he can prioritize and queue work for each iteration and release in a knowledgeable manner.

FDD goes beyond this simple convention by providing a straightforward and useful scheme for naming features [Palmer02]:

<action><result><object>

For example, a feature might be named *add a new item to an invoice* or *calculate state tax on an invoice.* This convention, or any other, may not work in every situation (creating and deleting business objects, for example) but, especially on teams of a dozen or more people where more than one individual is writing features, it can help to make feature names both easier to decipher and more informative.

USER STORIES

User stories are features, but features might not be user stories. Like features, user stories describe functionality that is considered valuable by the user of a system, are estimated to take between two days and two weeks to be developed, and are planned and executed by iteration.

User stories are a practice advocated by XP that is sometimes adopted by other agile teams. A user story is composed of three essential aspects [Jeffries01]:

The Card: XP teams often work with user stories on index cards. This card may be the true record of the user story, or it may have been generated from or otherwise represent a line in a spreadsheet, database, or other software-based management system. The tangible nature of a user story is important because it aids in and simplifies the planning process (as depicted in the planning game agile practice, discussed in Chapter 13, "Small Releases"). In addition, story cards may be used as tokens that can be handed to a programmer, who hands it back when it is completed, or hung on a wall, where its status can be displayed to all members of the team.

The Conversation: Even more than the creation of a feature, the act of writing a user story is merely an agreement for a future discussion to be held between the customer and the programmers who are ultimately responsible for programming the card. Therefore, the card is written in terms that the customer understands and does not go into technical or even functional detail. When the card is first written, programmers may ask questions of the customer to determine an estimate for the card, but even this information will typically not be recorded on the card.

Confirmation: The last essential component of the user story is the acceptance tests that it will both engender and require. Any testable requirements that the customer has for the feature may be jotted down on the user story while it awaits development. Prior to (or sometimes in tandem with) the actual development of a story, the customer must write out the acceptance tests for that story. These tests serve as confirmation that the user story was in fact communicated and programmed correctly.

The point behind stories is that they are straightforward and simple. Customers do not have to write long documents in advance or approve long documents written by business analysts. Programmers do not have to interpret such documents or guess at the gaps. Even more than the features employed by non-XP projects, XP teams rely on communication and collaboration between the customer and the programmers to flesh out the facets of a user story almost as it is being programmed. Therefore, XP requires only three items of information in a user story: its name, the story itself, and the programmers' estimate. Ultimately, XP requires only two artifacts from a user story: working code and acceptance tests.

In XP, the customer writes user stories for two reasons. First, each story must be written in the language of the business so that the customer recognizes the stories and understands them enough to prioritize them. Second, the customer, typically being a user of the system, is most capable and suited to describe the intended functionality [Cohn04].

CONVERTING FROM USE CASES AND REQUIREMENT DOCUMENTS

Unless it simply did not document anything (which happens), a team transitioning mid-project from a traditional to an agile approach will likely have existing requirements or analysis-related documentation that it will need to determine what to do with. Depending upon the nature and quality of these work products, the project team typically can pursue one of three strategies:

- Throw out all the existing documentation and start over.
- Mine the existing work products in order to create a list of features.
- Split the existing documentation into smaller chucks that can be treated as features.

The first approach would likely be based only on the merit of the existing documentation. In some cases, the documentation may simply be too shoddy or untrustworthy for future use. In other cases, the goals or objectives of the project may have shifted to a degree that the analysis, no matter how good, is simply no longer on target. Either way, the powers that be may have to make the correct-albeit-lamentable decision to throw out the existing documentation.

Often the best strategy (and the one stipulated by several agile methodologies, including FDD and XP) is simply to use the existing documentation as fodder for a more agile features list [Palmer02]. Depending upon the size of the existing documentation and the mindset of the customer, this can be done in a very easygoing or methodical fashion. In many cases, for example, the customer, analysts, and other members of the team simply reference portions of the existing documentation that they know apply to the features they are working on. In other cases, when existing documentation is extensive and the team is required to do so, requirements within the existing documentation may be mapped to the new features to ensure that everything has been captured (this technique is discussed in more detail in Chapter 13 in the "Requirements Tracing" section).

Finally, splitting existing use cases (or other documents) into smaller bits that can be planned and completed by iteration or release is a strategy that might feel less than perfect but can still produce results. Such an approach may be taken due to either a perceived lack of time (regardless of the reality) or an unwillingness on the part of the business or customer to part with the current documentation set. The strategy is simple. Break each existing document into a set of feature-like bits. Plan and execute releases and iterations on the bits. Complete and deliver useable and complete functionality as much as possible. Roll up the status of the bits to provide progress reports on each of the preexisting use cases or the entire project.

SOLUTION SHEETS

Up to now, our discussions in this chapter have been based on the notion that features and user stories are little more than lines in a spreadsheet, index cards, or any other place marker in a project tool that says "This is more-or-less what the customer wants, this is the programmers' best guess of how long it will take, and we will sort out the rest in the iteration."

In many project environments, for a variety of reasons, some upfront analysis, design, or documentation may be necessary. Solution sheets can be used to bridge the gap between an agile and fast-paced project team and a traditional and change-adverse development organization. The strategy has been used on several of my projects to satisfy documentation requirements, ensure buy-in from a less-than-engaged customer, and forestall incorrect but still damaging accusations of code-first-design-later behavior from non-project architects.

A solution sheet may provide the answer to an actual problem or merely state the strategy the project team will take to implement a particular feature. Typically it will be one to three pages in an easily readable font (with big headings and a simple structure). Plain English and pictures are best. A solution sheet's goal is to communicate in as few words and in as little time as necessary the essential information about a feature or features. It does this by providing the following information:

Summary of the proposed development activity: This should be short but adequate.

Discussion of points integral to the functionality: This should cover only the important and situation-relevant aspects, such as a logic flow or an object model.

Statement of unknowns: This is perhaps the most important element of a solution sheet. The business or development organization needs to be made aware of any risks or wrinkles that may impede the team's progress, such as technology issues or requirements that have yet to be nailed down.

Clarification of boundaries: This is also very important because it is the team's opportunity to state clearly what it will and will not do (such as multithreading or field validation). In environments that are not always friendly to a project team, a clear statement of boundaries that has been reviewed and agreed to by all parties can forestall more than a few late-stage disagreements and emergencies.

A solution sheet may be necessary for members of the business, members of an organization-wide architecture team, or both. A single sheet can typically be generated to satisfy both parties. Such a solution sheet may, for example, explain both the business logic that a given feature will follow and the schema it will use to record the results of its activity. What is essential is that a solution sheet be created with input from its target audience.

Solution sheets have almost no value if they are not reviewed by their intended audience. The whole purpose of the solution sheet is to receive buy-in from individuals who could derail the project if they suddenly determine that their needs are not being met. In my experience, solution sheets are best used as the basis for a 45-minute meeting. During this meeting, someone from the team (typically the project manager) will talk through the solution sheet with the business people or architects for whom it was written. The goal of the meeting is to get buy-in from those individuals so that the team can proceed with the proposed solution (plus any changes that the team may agree to during the meeting).

Solution sheets can have other uses throughout the life of the project. For example, solution sheets can serve as the basis for the documentation to be delivered at the end of the project. At a client where all work was performed on a fixed-cost basis, my teams actually wrote and used these solution sheets as the basis for our responses to RFPs (Requests for Proposal).

ESTIMATION

Planning cannot be done without estimating the amount of work that will need to be done and estimating how long it will take to complete that work. Since planning on agile projects is typically performed at both the release and iteration levels, estimates are typically required for both tasks and features.

Who Should Estimate

Estimates for features should be performed by the team as a whole because the programmers who will write the features are not yet selected. This is important because, when only one or two programmers do the estimates for the entire team, the results likely will be skewed based on the areas of the system that those individuals know or do not know well and the overall aptitude of those individuals. Senior-level programmers may not always take into account the slower pace of the junior members of the team.

Estimates for tasks should be done by the programmers who will actually complete them. By the time features are broken down into tasks, this should be relatively clear. If for whatever reason a programmer has not done the estimate for a task that he owns, he should be able to estimate that task based on his knowledge of it or his experience level.

On agile projects, people who do not have a hand in doing the work do not take part in the estimation process—especially not project managers, analysts, or the customer. To do otherwise is a recipe for disaster, because no matter how unintentionally, those individuals' estimates will be on the low side. They will not take into account everything that a programmer has to do in terms of testing, integrating, setting up an infrastructure, and so forth. The programming team will likely not come anywhere close to meeting the estimates, and a failed project will result.

One final note on who should do estimates. Team leads and technically savvy project managers must be careful about making comments that unduly influence estimates. At one time or another, each of us may look at an estimate that we know is unrealistically high, but we do not want to give programmers the impression that we are trying to make them pad their estimates or work beyond a sustainable pace. Some leads and managers may just let the clear misestimates slide, figuring the programmer will catch on after some time. This is a good approach when the programmers do catch on. A practice of mine when working with a project team that is comfortable with me and vice versa is to make sure that I am challenging the programmers in both directions. If I think they are too high, I tell them, but I also make sure to tell them when I think they are too low. This makes it clear that I am only trying to lend my own expertise and knowledge to the discussion and not simply beat down estimates. And a favorite response of mine in such cases is that the programmer should come back and let me know when he needs more time.

Estimating Uncertainty

Often, estimates not only reflect the amount of time a programmer or team believes it will take to complete a task but also the level of certainty the individual or group has in the estimate. If the level of certainty is low and there is a fear among the estimators that a blown estimate will result in penalties, an individual or group is likely to provide a worst case estimate. Even after programmers have moved to an environment where estimate is not a loaded term, they often fall back on the instinctive habit of ratcheting up an estimate to account for a lack of certainty.

On small teams it may not be necessary for the uncertainty of estimates to be tracked separately as long as there are few enough features for programmers to keep in mind which estimates they are guessing at. For this to happen, however, the project needs to value and use this information. Features and tasks with highly uncertain estimates may, for example, be queued earlier than other items with a similar level of priority but better estimates. This will help teams flush out surprises earlier in the project, when it has a greater amount of time and flexibility to deal with them.

Larger teams may not be able to track such information effectively without writing it down. Uncertainty may be factored into a risk rating for features so that it is measured along with bigger questions, such as whether a task is actually feasible with the current technology. Teams that choose to be more specific about risk may rank uncertainty apart from feasibility—which is, after all, still a greater risk.

Ultimately and ironically, by no longer setting made-up values (a.k.a. worst case scenario estimates) in place of uncertainty in an attempt to control things that cannot be controlled, teams may be better able to plan for that same uncertainty.

Ideal Time

Many agile projects often estimate in (or based on) a quantity known as *ideal time*. This measure is based on the concept of the programmer being able to work within an ideal, interruption-free environment. The following question, which may be asked of programmers who are new to ideal time estimation, may help illustrate its precise meaning. The question is this: How long would it take you to complete this work if:

- You were allowed to work without interruption until the work was complete.
- You had access to the people and resources you needed when you needed them.

■ There were the typical number of technical issues along the way but nothing went horribly wrong.

Ideal time allows programmers to give realistic estimates without having to fear that they will be held unfairly accountable to them. No one should ever expect that an ideal day estimate will translate into the same amount of real time. There are too many meetings, e-mails, questions to be answered, and non-project work to attend to in the average day for anyone to reasonably expect that a programmer will typically work in ideal time.

Ideal time assists planning because it allows the project to easily understand how long it could (though not will) take any member of the team to complete a given amount of work, estimated in ideal days. Since each programmer on the team should know the velocity at which he can work (the number of ideal days he can complete in a given period of time, as discussed in Chapter 10, "Agile Management"), it is straightforward for a team to understand how long a junior, senior, or part-time programmer needs to complete a given amount of work.

In the last few years, some Agilists have turned away from the term ideal day because they have found that some customers and managers simply cannot make a firm enough distinction between ideal days and calendar days. We can all imagine the response one might receive from a customer who does not understand the difference when it is three business days into a task that he was told would take two ideal days. Therefore, some teams use other terms, such as story points, that might equal a specific amount of ideal time to mask the relationship.

Defining Done

For estimates to have real meaning, the team must agree upon what "done" means. Does it include analysis and design? Does it need to be unit tested? Does it need to be done in a deployable fashion? What about documentation? Such questions are not trivial.

On one project team, we had a programmer who completed a feature that e-mailed the support group when a failure occurred. However, it did so by bouncing off an e-mail server located on another machine in the development environment. While his code included unit tests that did pass, the feature would have failed the moment it was deployed outside the development environment. Luckily, that project team had collective ownership in place, and another programmer came across the hack only a week later and brought the issue to my attention. The story for that functionality was reissued, and the programmer who coded the functionality received a reminder about the definition of done.

The definition for done must be consistent and understood not only by programmers and the project manager but by the customer as well. Important considerations include:

- Updating documentation
- Writing unit tests
- Whether the completed feature will be ready for customer review, system integration, user-acceptance testing, or some other activity

How We Estimate and When to Guess

Intuitively, we often estimate based on experience and comparison. Since it took me two and a half hours to drive from Chicago to Kalamazoo, and since Kalamazoo is about 15 miles closer to Detroit than it is to Chicago, it should take me a bit under five hours to drive from Chicago to Detroit. Of course, estimation in software development is not so straightforward, but we typically use the same process, which is:

1. Identify the most similar thing we have done before.
2. Gauge the difference between what we have done before and what we are now estimating.
3. Come up with an estimate that takes into account both steps one and two.
4. If we have no experience to rely upon, guess.

Sometimes, however, there is no experience available to base an estimate on. When any reasonable estimate is still reasonably uncertain, a guess is appropriate and sometimes the only thing that can be done—as long as that uncertainty is noted and addressed as was discussed earlier in this section. Especially at the beginning of a project, it is worth remembering that estimates do not always need to be dependable, they just need to improve dependably as the team comes to know the technology and domain better.

Finally, there are ways to improve a guess prior to queuing up the work. XP encourages the use of programmer spikes (quick, throwaway investigations) to help ensure feasibility and refine estimates [Jeffries00]. DSDM, similarly, recommends the use of prototypes [Stapleton03]. Unless the work to be performed is of the utmost urgency, a spike or prototype may be queued for on iteration so that one or more features may be better understood when planning future iterations.

12 ▪ Project Initiation

This chapter discusses many of the activities that a project may perform before it begins executing iterations. Some agile methodologies have specific names for this period. Crystal Clear uses *project chartering*, ASD calls it *speculation*, and FDD devotes three of its five phases to the activity (though the lion's share of project activity is spent in the last two phases).

Different levels and types of initiation activities will need to be undertaken for different project environments. In addition to discussing the agile approach to project initiation, this chapter will discuss the different types of activities and provide a selection of approaches from the different agile methodologies. Projects with no initiation strategy may find the simple approaches that will help set the team off in the right direction. Projects operating in environments that do not specifically suit agile development or their methodology of choice may find alternative approaches to planning here that may be integrated into environments where the look and feel of a more traditional planning approach may be required.

This chapter is titled "Project Initiation" instead of "Project Planning" to distinguish between the one-time activities performed by projects in order to set them in motion and the release- and iteration-level planning that is ongoing within a more agile project. In a traditional process, a project will do most of the planning activities discussed in Chapters 13, "Small Releases," and 14, "Executing Iterative Development," at the beginning of the project. Since this book is about agile projects and implementing agile development in less-than-agile environments, release and iteration planning are discussed in Chapters 13 and 14 instead of here.

AN AGILE APPROACH TO PROJECT INITIATION

Traditional development processes attack project planning as an essential set of activities that must be performed before a project is given the authority to begin designing and building software. These activities include the creation of a business case, missioning the project, any number of approval gates, organizing a team, collecting requirements, selecting a technology, drawing up a plan, and defining architecture and a high-level design. The goal of all this effort is to ensure that, once set in motion, the project knows where it is headed, knows how to get there, and has what it needs along the way. Managers, stakeholders, and customers often focus on this activity—trying to stuff all the important decisions into the project while it is still in its infancy—because they have been burned by projects that appear not to have done sufficient upfront planning, labored for months or even years, and delivered little of value.

Often, the people on a newly formed project are full of the type of energy that comes from being on a new assignment and starting something new. Additionally, and also often, an unfortunate side effect of all the planning activities listed is that these same individuals have completely lost that startup energy by the time they get to the beginning of design and development.

Just as with traditional development strategies, the agile methodologies take the time to ensure that everyone on the project is headed off in the correct direction, that they know what is expected of them, and that they have the necessary tools and knowledge at their disposal. At the same time, the agile methodologies do not want to dwell on this activity. Besides snuffing the energy of the team, too much upfront planning can risk efficiency and even introduces the potential for project failure by analysis paralysis. Therefore, the agile methodologies try to strike a balance between investing enough effort to head in the right direction and moving forward soon enough to maintain the initial energy and momentum of the project.

Figure 12.1 illustrates the results after a fixed time period of three different approaches to planning for a project, where the goal is a near-term deliverable such as a beta release.

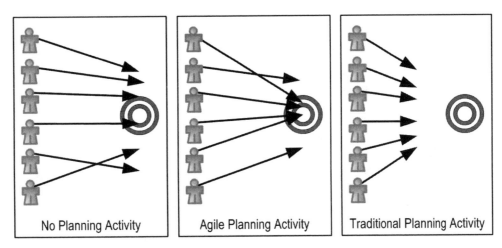

FIGURE 12.1   Progress over a fixed duration toward a target of demonstrable value.

In the first scenario, where no planning activity was performed, only one-third of the team was on target with their efforts, and about half the team did not work on or complete products that were ultimately required for the project. In the second scenario, the agile planning approach, the team takes a minimum amount of time for planning activities and completes work just as quickly as if they had done no planning at all, but the majority of the team completes work products that are ultimately required for the success of the project. In the final scenario, the traditional planning activity, the team only makes it halfway to the same goal in the same amount of time, due to the amount of time spent completing upfront planning activities. The figure illustrates a project team whose every member is working toward a product that fits the project's success requirements, but it may take this project team twice as long to hit its target. Notwithstanding the accuracy gained from the traditional project's heavier approach to planning, two outcomes cannot be ignored. First, the traditional approach has actually accomplished less in the same time period as the agile project. Second, the traditional approach will succeed only if its target does not significantly shift before the work products are completed. Suppose the target for the beta release shifts during the time period, as in Figure 12.2.

In the first scenario of Figure 12.2, the project that did no planning, some members of the team recognized the shifting target and adapted to meet it. This will likely happen for teams that do not plan because it is not difficult for them to break

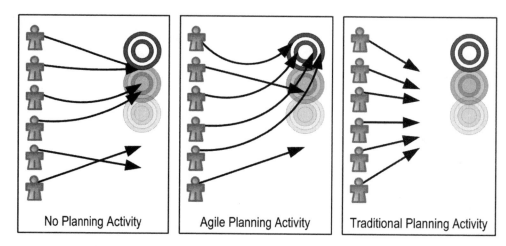

FIGURE 12.2   Progress over a fixed duration toward a moving target of demonstrable value.

away from a project initiation process that had little or no investment in it. The agile project, meanwhile, adapts quite well to the moving target, first because its small amount of planning has not locked it into a specific direction, and second because it will assess and adjust its heading at the onset of each new iteration, of which there should be several before the project reaches a beta release. Finally, the traditional project will adjust only slightly or not at all to the shifting target because it has invested so much into planning that it has locked itself into a specific direction and mindset about the nature of its deliverable, regardless of changing events. Worse yet, the project is only halfway to its goal, and who knows how far its shifting target has yet to go.

In short, agile projects typically try to apply just enough planning activity at the beginning of the project. The most useful activities performed by agile teams at the beginning of the project, and those discussed in this chapter, are defining the project mission, gathering a list of features, drawing up a plan, and upfront architecture and design.

However (as discussed in greater detail in Chapters 10, "Agile Management," and 15, "The Customer"), an agile project does not stop planning once design and development activities have begun. The project keeps on planning prior to the onset of each iteration. In contrast to a traditional project that spends a significant period of time planning and the rest of its life tracking and managing deviations from the plan, an agile project is constantly planning and doing so based on the latest and best information it can get as it wends its way from one release to the next.

DEFINE THE PROJECT MISSION

A very common beginning step that can be simple to perform and go a long way toward setting the whole team in the correct direction is the formalization of the project mission. This is most commonly done through the creation of a mission statement, but it can also be done through the institution of an XP practice called *metaphor.*

Explicitly stated or not, every project has a mission, whether it is to build a company-wide knowledge portal, replace a legacy invoicing system, or upgrade a call center application from Java 1.17 to 1.44. Codifying that mission in a short, lucid, and powerful statement will help keep the entire team from drifting into activities that are not central to that mission. Arguably, for agile teams, the need for such a guiding light may be all the more pressing as planning is done in small increments throughout the project. A mission or metaphor agreed to by the entire project can serve to keep an agile team, its customer, and stakeholders on the right track and away from pretty-looking but ultimately dead-end side issues.

A project mission should not be written and saved to a network hard drive where it is only visited as a project artifact, and this does happen all too often. The project will need to devise a method that ensures that the mission is in the mind of the project when it needs it the most, such as during release and iteration planning. One solution may be to post the mission in a highly visible place, such as the area where planning meetings are held. Another solution may be to review, revise, and reaffirm the mission on a regular basis, such as at the beginning of the release planning meeting.

Mission Statement

A project's mission, when it is clearly stated, is most commonly kept in the form of a mission statement or statement of purpose. The well-crafted mission statement should include three characteristics [Highsmith00]. First, it should set a clear sense of direction. That is, it should communicate to the reader a vision of what the project has set out to accomplish and a general strategy for getting there. Second, the mission statement should serve to inspire the members of the project. It should convey a reason to care and put commitment toward the endeavor. Third, the mission statement should, as appropriate, serve as a guide to implement the project. That is, at a high level, it should provide a framework for decision-making and steering the development process, for example, that the project should pay close attention to the changing business climate and be prepared to make rapid alterations to planned features to ensure that the delivered application is competitive in the current market conditions.

Metaphor

Metaphor is an XP practice that has had no real exposure to the greater world of agile development. One reason for this may be that it works only for smaller projects, but this is only speculation. A metaphor is meant to provide a simple, concise, but powerful picture of the system envisioned. It may be landed upon during one or more brainstorming activities. The ultimate goal is to have a short bit of prose that says what the system is, what it does, and how its parts fit together. One example of a metaphor, used in the first XP project, is this [Jeffries00]:

> C3 payroll . . . is like a manufacturing line building paychecks by taking hour parts and converting them to dollar parts, assembling all the various parts until you get a paycheck.

The example clearly states, from a high view, what the system does and how it does it. It should also make the difference between a mission statement and a metaphor readily apparent. Mission statements focus on objectives and sometimes what a system actually does. Mission statements do not discuss how a system goes about doing its business. The simple description contained in the metaphor can remind a team how the system goes about its work, as well as its purpose. Having the metaphor in mind while discussing and designing the system can keep a programmer or customer from wandering too far from it.

Statement Workshop

Palmer and Felsing propose a way to structure a workshop designed to produce the statement of purpose for an FDD project that may also be used to produce the mission statement or metaphor for any agile team [Palmer02]. The workshop attendees should include the users, stakeholders, and managers associated with a given project.

Start the process by breaking the workshop into groups of three and asking each group to take 10 minutes to write a concise statement (either mission or metaphor) for the system. In either case, the statement should not be more than 25 words in length and should be written in the language of the business. Palmer and Felsing, for example, recommend avoiding words that have no real meaning outside of a technology environment, such as scalable.

Next, each small group should read its result aloud. The entire group should note the words and phrases it most likes from each statement and then agree on two or three individuals who will merge the various statements into one while the rest of the group takes a break or moves on to another activity. The resulting statement then may be reviewed and approved by the entire group.

GATHER A LIST OF FEATURES

In agile development, the features list, with each item prioritized and estimated, is actually more important than any work schedule or drawn-out plan. Agile projects do not require a work breakdown structure (WBS), although agile projects can be documented within a WBS (discussed in Chapter 18, "Documentation") and can be executed from a WBS (discussed in Chapter 14). The bare minimum plan that an agile team requires is a features list.

The details of a features list differ, depending upon the agile methodology being used. FDD, for example, actually uses the term features list, while Scrum has a product backlog and a pure XP project uses a stack of user stories. The use of the features list is the same. It is the place where the customer records and prioritizes all features that may be developed for the system. Furthermore, it is the place the customer draws from to provide the project team with the work it will complete during the planning meeting of each iteration.

Customers may require assistance in identifying features for an agile project, especially the first time around. One approach, the story-writing workshop, is discussed next. Another approach can be found in the first portion of the blitz planning agile practice, discussed at the end of this chapter.

The Story-Writing Workshop

Mike Cohn, in *User Stories Applied,* proposes a simple group activity to quickly produce a large number of user stories (or features) for a project, called the story-writing workshop [Cohn04]. The workshop may be done in a single meeting and should include programmers, users, domain experts, and possibly stakeholders and managers. It can be held at the beginning of a project as well as at the beginning of every release.

The workshop is begun by asking all the participants to write as many stories as they can think of, regardless of priority, in a reasonable period of time. The facilitator then draws a box on a whiteboard or flipchart to represent the main screen of the system. He asks one of the participants to state what actions could be taken from that main screen. Each answer given by the participant may result in a line being drawn to a new box that represents another screen or component within the system. At each new component, the facilitator may ask questions to stir up additional thoughts and other stories. These could pertain to the additional action a user might take, typical mistakes that might be made, potential places of confusion, and any other information that might be helpful to the user. When one participant has run out of ideas, the facilitator moves onto the next. As this process continues, the group will begin to construct a simple representation of the system.

Cohn stresses that this workshop should be used to collect a large quantity of stories and should not be focused on quality. Further, the workshop should not get into a significant level of detail, such as the fields that may appear on a screen. Finally, the representation of the system drawn during this workshop should not be retained as an artifact. Doing so is dangerous because it could lock individuals into an immature conception of the system and hinder further progress on the project.

Did Everything Make It into the List of Work?

Of course not. Of course the customer and the team missed something. This happens on every project no matter the methodology, but in agile development it is okay. Because agile projects typically avoid committing to combinations of scope, time, cost, and quality, something will simply have to adjust.

Nonetheless, the previous paragraph is not meant to be a cop-out. It only helps to be thorough, and the goal for any agile project team and its customer should be to miss less as the team gets better at completing user stories. Here is a short list, based on experience, of often-forgotten items:

- An external SIT or UAT process that the team must perform before releasing
- Performing or automating the deployment
- Documentation or code reviews required of the project by parties outside the team
- Time spent with DBAs and data-modelers, who are not part of the team, to get database tables and other structures designed, approved, and put in place
- Integration with a third-party tool or system

DRAW UP A PLAN

Producing the first plan on an agile project is much less arduous than a project following a traditional development process. The first thing a project manager may notice when writing an agile plan is that there is a lot less guessing to be done. In agile development, there is no need to open a project planning tool, grab a company-approved project template (or worse, cobble something together from scratch), and start guessing at how long it will take to complete such tasks as "introduce programmers to the domain experts," "perform weekly design review," and "baseline the project plan." Once an agile plan is complete, the project manager may be both startled and somewhat unnerved by its simplicity. Figure 12.3 illustrates a sample project plan, based on a plan developed by an agile team working within a large, process-oriented development environment.

Feature	Estimate	Iteration	Release
Create and automate development environment, including "hello world" program that can be deployed through testing environments into production	5 days	1	1
Create a simple work queue where multiple users can assign generic tasks to one another	5 days	1	1
Allow work queue users to mark tasks as completed, escalated, deferred or deleted	2 days	2	1
Define and create a set of specific work queue task types that users can select from when creating a task	3 days	2	1
Create an admin access area where task types can be managed	4 days	2	1
Write a log-in screen and provide secure access to the work queue	4 days	3	2
Provide admin access to user and role settings	2 days	3	2
Allow administrators to add, rename and delete task types through an admin screen	4 days	3	2
Add functionality to track and store user activity	6 days	4	2
Write an audit report that can be executed and viewed by any administrator	4 days	4	2

FIGURE 12.3   The project's list of features, sorted to resemble a release plan.

At its most basic, the creation of an agile plan entails the arrangement of the feature list in each of the project's planned release points. What a project manager new to agile needs to remember at this stage is that, as discussed earlier in this chapter and in greater detail in Chapter 10, agile projects are not light on planning; they merely distribute the planning activity across the entire project.

Sometimes an agile plan as depicted in Figure 12.3 simply is not good enough. In that case, a customer, the business, or upper management may be willing to allow the project to pursue an agile approach but demand to see artifacts similar to the ones it has seen from other projects. Such plans can be built while the team continues to pursue an agile approach (to learn more, consult the "An Agile WBS" section in Chapter 18).

UPFRONT ARCHITECTURE AND MODELING

While the majority of Agilists avoid it when possible, some upfront modeling can still be a requirement for an agile project working within a heavy process environment or even simply within an enterprise system, where lots of teams and lots of shared components can translate into additional risk. FDD is the one agile methodology to both stipulate some upfront design and specify what this activity should entail. This approach may help agile teams otherwise following other methodologies to adapt to an upfront modeling requirement.

At the onset of any project, a team following FDD will bring the programmers and domain experts together under the direction of a chief architect to develop a model of the overall system, down to the "shape" of objects. In medium-size and large applications, the project members will split up into teams that model sections of the system. The individual models are merged on a regular basis to keep them working together as a cohesive whole [Palmer02]. This whole process should not be confused with heavy design because little or no design is actually performed. This activity is meant simply to produce an overall roadmap of the system. Like all other agile methodologies, FDD teams return to complete analysis and design activities on a feature only after it has been queued for development.

Developing an overall model can dislodge the mental images and assumptions about the system hidden in the minds of individuals and lay them bare before the whole team. This process helps to identify and resolve what may otherwise have been unknown differences of opinion that could have crippled the project months down the road. The ultimate goal is to provide the team with a common and agreed upon understanding of the overall system before it starts [Palmer03].

PLANNING FOR THE END

Most traditional projects (or at least traditional project plans) end with a formal project close task and perhaps a lessons learned activity or document. Before the close there is perhaps a deployment support period and before that most definitely a release. Earlier still, in the plan, all the work to be performed is laid bare and scheduled. From the point of the plan, it is easy to see how the project will carry on and eventually expire. As should have already been made apparent in this book, agile projects are not nearly so deterministic. Some agile methodologies do not plan for an end at all, while others may only call for some form of reflective or lessons learned activity.

A sentiment that seems to have been attributed to painting, writing, and many other creative media is that a work is never completed but merely abandoned. This can be the case for software development projects as well. Planning for the close of a project may be a noble goal, but just as many other things cannot be predicted about any given project, such as technological issues and shifts in functionality, so too it seems implausible in the majority of cases to accurately predict exactly how and when a project will end. Most likely, the project will not close at the time ordained in the plan but rather at the point at which the stakeholders decide that putting more money into the project cannot be justified by what the project will produce. At some point, most any project (whether in an orderly or a get-out-of-Dodge fashion) is abandoned.

While agile methodologies recognize this fact about the end of project, this does not mean they do not prepare. As will be discussed in detail in Chapter 14, agile iterations and releases are structured so that the system and any functionality currently under development are never far from a deployable state. Unlike a traditional project, where pulling the money plug could result in the complete depreciation of any work performed since the last actual deployment, agile projects can lose funding at the end of any iteration, and all newly developed functionality will be in a near-deployable state.

AGILE PRACTICE: BLITZ PLANNING[1]

Crystal Clear employs a technique that is a variation on the planning game (discussed in Chapter 13) called *blitz planning* or a *project planning jam session*. The practice provides more focus on project initiation activity, speaks to technical as well as functional aspects of the project, and provides a more substantial plan for both the project's first release and follow-up releases.

Blitz planning may be useful to any small project that has completed little to no initiation activity but needs to get started (or needs a decision on whether it should be started) quickly. It is intended to cover only about three months of activity, though this is often a sufficient period during which to kick off and expect results from a small project.

Purpose and Benefits

The blitz planning practice can enable a potential project team to complete multiple project initiation activities within a single meeting, including the development of a features or task list, the creation of a release-based plan, and even a somewhat informal value assessment. Upon completing the practice, the project team has at its disposal a plan that has been agreed to by every individual or group that has an important association with the project. Issues that often are overlooked prior to project initiation, such as the distribution of work across programmers and what the true pain points are for the business regarding the first few releases, will be addressed within this single meeting. Finally, the collaborative, all-at-once nature of the gathering ensures that issues are discussed while simultaneously producing a quality plan quickly.

Detail

There are 10 steps to a blitz planning session, as illustrated in Figure 12.4.

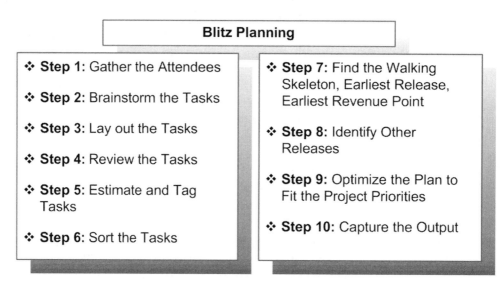

Blitz Planning

❖ **Step 1**: Gather the Attendees

❖ **Step 2**: Brainstorm the Tasks

❖ **Step 3**: Lay out the Tasks

❖ **Step 4**: Review the Tasks

❖ **Step 5**: Estimate and Tag Tasks

❖ **Step 6**: Sort the Tasks

❖ **Step 7**: Find the Walking Skeleton, Earliest Release, Earliest Revenue Point

❖ **Step 8**: Identify Other Releases

❖ **Step 9**: Optimize the Plan to Fit the Project Priorities

❖ **Step 10**: Capture the Output

FIGURE 12.4 The 10 steps to blitz planning [Cockburn04a].

The meeting is attended by the entire team, any relevant domain analysts, and the key users and key stakeholders of the project (or potential project). Attendance of all these groups is highly recommended for an optimal outcome because suboptimal outcomes typically arise when the project manager and the programmers plan without the users and stakeholders or—as bad as it is common—the project manager authors the plan entirely on his own. Additionally, wide participation in the planning process means a more comprehensive understanding of what will need to be done, better estimates, and a sense of collective ownership and responsibility for the plan.

Like the planning game, blitz planning requires a stack of index cards—potentially a large stack of index cards. Each member should grab a handful of cards, begin brainstorming, and start writing tasks. This includes all non-programming activities, including tasks related to analysis, documentation, and infrastructure, anything that may take more than half a day. (Note that blitz planning operates at the task level instead of the story, feature, or use case level.) Once the tasks have been written, they should be laid out on a table in dependency order. Tasks that may be implemented immediately (or in parallel) should be laid out side-by-side on the table. Any tasks that are dependent upon another task should be placed below that task. Duplicate tasks should be discarded. The result of this step may resemble an elongated or extended game of solitaire. The whole set of tasks should then be reviewed by the entire group. Tasks written by someone else may remind a participant of one or more forgotten tasks. These tasks should be written and added to the table.

Now, the tasks are estimated and tentatively assigned to a team member. Programmers write an estimate and an owner for each task on the card. When opinions differ on an estimate, the group should work toward a common estimate. If any individual's name ends up on a disproportionate number of tasks, the team should consider ways of offloading work from that individual and thereby heading off a bottleneck waiting to happen. Finally, tasks that are dependent on an external event or action should be flagged accordingly.

Next, the tasks should be sorted in the order that they may be completed. The sort will consist of multiple, parallel activity streams, possibly by area of development or by owner. This is the first time the lines of tasks may begin to resemble a plan. Task dependencies should receive a greater level of scrutiny, both to flush out where they were falsely placed and where they were missed. Hard dependencies between tasks (such as *define the batch report fields* and *code the batch report*) should be noted on the tasks so that they do not get lost as cards are shifted about.

Once the tasks are sorted, the participants should work together to identify the following releases:

A walking skeleton: This is the completion of code intended for production that demonstrates a simple function being performed from one end of the system to the other.

Earliest release: This is the first opportunity the users will have to see a working version of the system.

Earliest revenue point: This is when the system first begins either making or saving money.

Each of these points may be critical to the project and those who depend on it. The walking skeleton is both a proof of concept for the entire system and a framework on which the features of the system may be built. The earliest release provides both a recognizable achievement for the team and the first opportunity for the team to begin receiving the user feedback that will guide its actions for the rest of the project. The earliest point at which the system can begin to show revenue is the big prize. The earlier the team can get there the better. Any tasks that are not required to meet these three points should be moved to a lower position in the sort. Next the group can identify releases beyond the initial three. In the beginning this may involve identifying clusters of related or high-demand functionality within the sort. Eventually, release points may become time based and set (based on their estimates) to occur at regular time intervals.

Now the sorted task cards may be called a plan, but the plan will need to be optimized to fit the priorities of the project. This process is begun by adding up the estimated duration of all the cards in each release. Cockburn cautions that at this point the group may be in for a significant surprise as the numbers total up far beyond what anyone had expected. If this occurs, it will force the senior individuals to make some tough decisions. The options here run the gamut of possibilities.

- The stakeholder may choose to kill the project wholesale or by turning to an off-the-shelf product.
- Features and the tasks they depend upon may be removed from the plan.
- Someone in the group might spot a way to get to a release that generates revenue earlier by shifting an essential task up the sort and others down.
- A bottleneck might be identified that when addressed speeds up or reduces the risk of a critical release.

Whatever happens, the stakeholder or project manager must not turn on the programmers to reduce their estimates.

Once the group completes the previous step, it has a useable and useful plan. This output must be trapped in whatever mechanism (spreadsheet or tool-based) the team uses for planning.

13 Small Releases

Releases on an agile project begin with the customer identifying a set of features or user stories for the team to complete and end with the delivery of that functionality (or something near it) either into production or for review by the customer. The functionality planned for the release may change either because the customer has exercised his right as the person paying for the software to see the plan change or the team has exercised its right as the guys who have always been honest about their best-guess estimates and never padded them to say that something turned out to be tougher than they had first thought.

THE AGILE APPROACH TO THE PROJECT RELEASE

In agile development the release is generally the largest timebox (the project is not considered a timebox) and is used for planning from a functional point of view. Different methodologies use different names for the release; the Crystal methodologies, for example, call it a delivery cycle. Releases can vary significantly in length, depending upon the makeup of the project and needs of the customer, and are composed of a varying number of other timebox structures, iterations most typically. Generally speaking, a release may be:

- A grouping of two or more iterations that share specific startup and close activities.
- One iteration at the end of a sequence of two or more iterations, the output of which is intended to be production worthy, though it still may not go into production.
- The same as an iteration. In this case, every completed iteration must be production worthy. This is a unique mechanism that, in addition to following the norms discussed in this section, is discussed in Chapter 14, "Executing Iterative Development," in the section "Sprints and Other Releasable Iterations."

The term *production worthy* refers to an ideal state and will differ by project and methodology. At its simplest, production worthy is the closest the development team can bring the system to a deployable state at the end of each release. Often, before being deployed to real users, the production candidate will go through some form of system integration and user acceptance testing (UAT).

Something that must be kept in mind is that, while the project team may deliver a production-worthy release on a regular schedule, the customer does not need to actually put every one of those releases into production. This decision must be left to the discretion of the customer. However, if the customer decides at the last minute that he wants a release to go into production, the team should have provided him with a solid enough build that this request can be met.

RELEASE PLANNING

As discussed in Chapter 10, "Agile Management," agile projects have a spike in planning activity prior to the beginning of each release. In agile development, the release timebox provides a significant and sufficient period of time for forward-looking planning. On the average agile project, this period is somewhere between two and four months. However, on some projects releases may occur more frequently than once a month, and on others a single release can last more than a year, although, in that case, projects are using either iterations or some other sub-release mechanism to deliver production-worthy code to users and testers more frequently for review.

Typical Release Planning Activities

The activities that an agile team completes during a release can vary according to its project environment. These factors include, among others, how much of the project has been planned up front, the presence or absence of a team customer, the nature of its contract, the amount of functionality it completed in the previous release, and the degree to which the functional scope of the project shifted over the previous release.

In general, prior to initiating a release, a project team will work with its customer (or, if it has no customer, then on its own) to complete the steps listed in Figure 13.1 and discussed in the following sections.

Release Planning Activities

❖ **Step 1**: Update the List of Work

❖ **Step 2**: Prioritize the List of Work

❖ **Step 3**: Determine the Release Date and the Amount of Work the Team Can Complete

❖ **Step 4**: Select the Work to Be Completed During the Release

❖ **Step 5**: Plan the Development Activity for the Release's First Iteration

FIGURE 13.1   Typical release planning activities.

Step 1: Update the List of Work

The list of work is whatever features, user stories, or other gadgets the project team is using to capture whole bits of functionality. The project team and its customer need to update the items on this list based on any information each party has learned during the previous release. This should include the addition of any new work that has been identified for the project, the removal of any work that is no longer intended for the project, and a reaffirmation of current estimates.

If the team does not yet have a list of work (or if it has burned through its entire backlog of work and has an empty list of work), then it will need to compile a new set of features or user stories before planning the release. This topic is discussed in Chapter 12, "Project Initiation," in the section "Gather a List of Features."

Step 2: Prioritize the List of Work

If the project team has a customer, he should complete this step based an any input the team has to offer. Important information the team has to offer may include known risks, known unknowns, and dependencies between items on the list. Techniques that may be used for prioritizing stories are discussed in Chapter 11, "Features and User Stories."

Step 3: Determine the Release Date and the Amount of Work the Team Can Complete

These are interdependent variables. Typically, an agile team will know how much work it can complete in a given week or iteration (see the discussion on velocity in Chapter 10). Typically, this step will begin from one of two starting points. Sometimes the release date will already be fixed, and determining the amount of work the team can complete during the iteration is a simple calculation. Other times the customer will need to determine an appropriate date for the release, taking into account the speed at which the team has said it can complete work and the needs of the users and business.

Step 4: Select the Work to Be Completed During the Release

Again, if the project has a customer, he must complete this step. The customer's decision should be based on the amount of work the team has said it will be able to complete, his opinion of what functionality is most important to be delivered first, and whatever additional advice the team has to offer.

Step 5: Plan the Development Activity for the Release's First Iteration

This step is more of a placeholder. It is meant to remind the reader who may be new to agile development that while the release-planning process has been completed, the project team does not simply get to run off and start programming (or even designing). Before these activities can occur, the team needs to plan an iteration, which will be discussed in the following section.

Sometimes (and in some methodologies) the features that will be completed in each iteration in the upcoming release are determined at this time. For more information on how features may be elected for development during an iteration, see Chapter 14 in the section "Typical Iteration Planning Activities."

Depending upon the project environment, steps two and three may be switched. Some customers need to have a certain amount of functionality completed by the project before they can justify a release. Other customers are told what dates they will release on, irrespective of what functionality that may need to be complete. Such dates are just as likely to be driven by the date of a major conference (when the system may be demonstrated) or the IT department's internal processes (such as a release schedule defined at the beginning of the year through the entire year for every project).

Additionally, this set of steps might seem somewhat simplistic, but bear in mind that, unless the project team has combined the release and iteration into a single timebox, additional planning activity will take place at the beginning of every iteration within the release.

Methodology-Specific Approaches to Release Planning

In addition to the generic approach to planning a release discussed previously, this book also details three methodology-specific approaches to release planning:

The Planning Game: This technique was pioneered by XP and is discussed later in this chapter as an agile practice. One specific intent of the planning game is to bring together parties who may have a strained relationship (for example, your average business and IT managers) to plan in a less formal atmosphere. The planning game provides a set of rules for planning that are clear and concise and strive to respect the needs and feelings of both the project and its customer.

Blitz Planning: This technique is introduced in Crystal Clear and discussed as an agile practice in Chapter 12. While blitz planning is introduced as a full project planning technique, it may also be used to plan successive releases within a longer project. Blitz planning aims to get all the individuals required in the planning process into one room so that each may have an opportunity to add his two cents to the planning process.

The Sprint Planning Meeting: This is a major part of the Scrum methodology and may be used to plan both standard releases and releasable iterations. This technique is discussed in Chapter 14 in the section "Sprints and Other Releasable Iterations."

Each of these practices goes into greater specifics about and inserts a few unique twists into the release planning process.

CHANGING THE FUNCTIONALITY AND DELIVERY DATE OF A RELEASE

A functionality or delivery date change for a release may be caused by either the customer or the project team. Typically this change will be the result of the customer wanting additional functionality included within the release or the project team acknowledging slower progress than planned.

Changes Initiated by the Customer

On an agile project, scope does and is expected to change during the course of the release. While scope occasionally shrinks during a release, it is much more common to see it increase. The majority of agile projects are happy to see functionality shift in the midst of a release, with one caveat. Either the amount of functionality that is added to the project—measured in ideal time or some other effort-based metric—must be balanced by the removal of a similar amount of functionality or the release date must be moved to accommodate the time required to complete the additional functionality. DSDM actually plans for such contingencies by stipulating that a release and its constituent iterations should not be filled more than 60 percent with must-have features. The rest need to be of a lower priority. That way, when new features are identified in the middle of the release, it is clear what pieces of functionality may be shoved out.

Arguably, it is better to implement a feature (or user story) swap than to move a release date. Moving the release date extends the timebox planned for the release, somewhat blunting the benefits derived from the use of a timebox, such as forcing the customer to make tough decisions and ensuring that the team delivers some amount of usable functionality in a timely manner. At the same time, the project team needs to work with its customer, and if the customer determines that another release is useless if it does not contain all the functionality (both planned and added), then the project team needs to work with the customer and move the release date.

Finally, FDD takes a bit of a different approach. It has quantified the amount of shifting scope it will accept during a single cycle of its five phases (which, in many cases, is tantamount to a release). After the scope within a project has shifted by more than 10 percent, the project manager will inform the customer and request that he either remove features from the plan or extend the team's delivery date.

Changes Initiated by the Project Team

Sometimes the development team completes an iteration and realizes that it is irrecoverably behind schedule. The tracking mechanisms that will help the team recognize such a situation are discussed later in this chapter. If it finds itself in this situation, a project team should notify its customer as quickly as is reasonable possible. That way, the customer has the most time to either adjust the functionality or the delivery date of the project so that, regardless of the setback, he will still get the functionality that matters most at the end of the release.

TAKING TIME BETWEEN RELEASES

Some teams run on a release schedule in which a release is completed on one day and the planning meeting for the following release is held on the next. Others may take time between each release to perform system integration, user acceptance testing (UAT), deployment, or other activities as required by the customer or the organization within which they are operating. End-of-release system integration and UAT, for example, are activities that an agile team should breeze through because the team should have performed similar programming-level activities, such as continuous integration and automated acceptance tests, as part of its development process.

Project teams may also consider taking additional time between releases that, instead of being dedicated to wrapping up the previous release, may contribute to the planning and execution of the upcoming release. This time may vary from three days to as much as two weeks and may allow the team to proof new technologies, perform spikes, and investigate and discuss other options for the future of the system. The outcome of these activities should feed directly into the planning process and result in a better-defined list of development tasks with more certain estimates.

Additionally, such down time may be well spent simply as an opportunity to allow the team to take a breather from the fast-paced iterative cycle, where it is not operating under the pressure of a constant (if changing) near-term goal.

TOOLS FOR PLANNING AND TRACKING RELEASES

Agile project teams use a variety of means to store and manage features within and across releases. Spreadsheets seem to be the most common solution, though simple database and task-tracking tools are also popular. As discussed in Chapter 6, "Agile Practices," in relation to agile practices and tools, it is typically best to start with a simple solution and then add process as necessary. In fact, on almost all the projects under my management, we began with a spreadsheet solution before identifying and graduating to another approach, and in some cases we simply never found a need to use anything more.

The typical spreadsheet approach may use one or two sheets, depending on the project and the size of its features. The essential pieces of information to be tracked are these:

Name: This should be short enough to be easily said and understood during planning meetings and hallway conversations.

Description: This should contain any pertinent information that could not fit into the name but should not be more than a couple of paragraphs.

Estimate: As provided by the programmers.

Iteration: This is either when the work has been tentatively planned by the customer (a placeholder) or when the work was actually completed by the team.

Other important pieces of information can include priority, risk rating, the name of the programmer who has agreed to complete the work, and the actual status of the work, such as pending, in progress, completed, or dropped.

Packaged Tools

There are two sorts of packaged tools that may be used for tracking and managing agile features and releases: hierarchical-minded tools (proceed with caution) and agile-minded tools (adopt after ensuring a good fit). Each sort of tool is discussed in turn.

Tools with a strict hierarchical mindset, such as Microsoft Project®, are not recommended for an agile project because they are not built with the notion of a pool of unscheduled and unassigned features. For example, a common activity on agile projects that can be difficult to perform in many hierarchical management tools is to schedule a feature for a given iteration, remove the feature from that iteration when it is clear that all work cannot be completed within the timebox (but to not assign it to any other iteration), and then schedule the feature again two iterations later. These tools simply were not built with the mindset that such activities would be fair play on a software development project.

There are a number of open source and proprietary applications being developed both for managing agile projects in general and targeting specific agile methodologies. Project teams may consider adopting such products to store features and manage iterations and releases. When adopting one of these tools, a team needs to remember that the tool will only be as good as the team using it and the environment in which it is being used. Specifically:

- Will the product be usable by everyone who needs to use it? How much training will be needed to get team members up to speed with the product?
- Is the product truly able to map the way the team works and will it be able to adapt if the team alters its current processes?
- Is the product easy to access and easy to use? Web-based systems, for example, are often heralded as great project management tools because team members can check their assigned work and report status from anywhere, while stakeholders and upper management can often get real-time access to project status reports. For the project manager and tracker, however, such systems can be agonizingly painful when it comes to entering a feature list or updating the status of an iteration. Numerous screens and mouse clicks may be required for such simple activities as entering the tasks associated with a feature or even updating the status of features in progress.

Index Cards Only

Most agile teams use some means of electronic storage for features, though not always. XP purists, for example, advocate that user stories be written and maintained entirely on physical index cards.

The point of this requirement is to keep project planning as simple as possible and to remind the entire team (including the customer) that the goal of the project is useful software and not a detailed, intricate, or perfect plan. While this approach is based on a noble goal and can lead to more collaborative and successful projects, it can also make customers and managers very nervous and inspire questions such as: "What do we do if someone steals the cards?" or "What if there is a fire?" When such questions arise, a project team may want to heed them as a warning that it may be leading its customer into waters where he does not want to swim.

Just to be clear, this discussion pertains only to the use of physical index cards as the sole storage device for system features. The use of index cards (whether handwritten or generated by the laser printer) can be very beneficial at different times during the project and is recommended in other sections of this book.

REQUIREMENTS TRACING

Projects operating within heavier process environments (or even just heavy documentation) may find themselves saddled with the task of tracing requirements. There are techniques agile projects may employ to demonstrate a level of traceability that will appease the majority of customers (though these, of course, will not truly replicate a more formal requirement tracing approach). The difficulty of completing such an activity (and the direction of the solution) is largely dependent upon whether the project has to contend with a non-agile set of requirement documentation, such as use cases).

On projects where functionality is classed solely as features or user stories, this activity could be relatively straightforward. Since the features are in essence the project's requirements, the team has an easy mechanism to use for tracing the progression of requirements. Solution sheets (discussed in Chapter 11) may be written for each feature and focus specifically on the requirements of that feature. Acceptance tests (see Chapter 8, "Testing") can then be written to cover each feature. Approved solution sheets and passing acceptance tests can then be used to trace requirements from identification through delivery. Actual implementations will vary, of course.

Things can grow hairier when the project team has to trace requirements back to a stack of documentation that was written before the project transitioned to agile development. The team will need to tie the features it needs to complete to the requirements nestled within documentation that is essentially external to its activity. Of course, the documentation will need to be vetted to weed out requirements that do not apply. If you think you can throw a fuss and kick and scream your project team's way out of this activity, then do it. If the documentation does not contain explicitly tagged requirements (such as those found on most any RUP project), then you may even have a valid reason for throwing a fit. If the existing documentation is just page after page of text and diagrams with no indication as to what is truly a requirement, then you have a very valid basis for arguing that the documentation simply provides the basis upon which requirement tracing can be performed.

If the existing documentation contains formally called-out requirements, then tracing is possible and maybe even straightforward. The project team will need to collect all the requirements from the documentation into a list, possibly in a spreadsheet, and then tie each requirement to one or more features. Many requirements should be easy to handle and can be tied explicitly to the completion of a single feature. Some requirements may relate to multiple features. Other requirements may be technical in nature and not relate to any features, in which case an acceptance test may be written specifically to address the feature. Solution sheets can, again, be used as necessary to show traceability through the design process. In most cases, a project team will want to ensure that ultimately an acceptance test is written for every requirement once its associated feature has been completed. This should both ensure and demonstrate a sufficient level of traceability.

AGILE PRACTICE: PLANNING GAME

The planning game can turn planning into something that feels less serious and contentious while still adding real value and purpose. It was developed as part of XP in an attempt to reduce some of the emotion and acrimony that often arise when programmers, managers, users, and stakeholders meet in the same room to discuss features, scheduling, and release dates. Specifically, it can help to change a distressed relationship between a project team and the business to one that is more openly participatory and productive. Typically, a single planning game runs the duration of a release, which contains multiple iterations. However, if a project team is running on long iterations (at least four to six weeks), the planning game may be modified to fit a long iteration.

It should be noted that this description of the planning game is based on the original description of the practice (in *Extreme Programming Explained*), which has evolved in multiple directions in the last few years. The original, nonetheless, still stands as a valuable practice in its own right, based on its simplicity of approach and focus on the interaction between the project team and the business.

Purpose and Benefits

The planning game is a good and simple way to do planning on a relatively small project that is following an iterative process. Its straightforward rules provide a common language and process for the project and its customer to use both in planning a release and executing iterations. The moves in the game clearly spell out the rights of each party, such as the business's right to alter the plan in the middle of a release and development's right to not be pushed beyond a speed that it knows is safe. The moves also plainly state the results and repercussions of their use. When adding functionality in the middle of a release, the business must also remove an equivalent amount. While development can state how fast they will program, they must follow the business's direction on what to program.

When the game is used to recover a strained relationship between the project team and its users and stakeholders, then the initial point of the game is to guide all members of the planning discussion through a collaborative planning process while steering clear of minefields related to previous slipped deliveries, misreported requirements, broken promises, and harsh words. Of course, this will not happen if the business is not willing to play along or if the team is not willing to listen and work toward delivering the value requested by the customer. A project that already has a healthy relationship with its customer may continue to follow the planning game by its written rules, adapt the rules to handle planning more informally, or devise a new process altogether.

Prerequisites

The only true prerequisite for the planning game is a willing set of users and stakeholders. However, to be effective at implementing the planning game, a team should have gotten a handle on its development ability to a level at which it can dependably develop functionality. For example, the planning game alone will not help a team that is suffering from chronic quality issues or does not adequately understand the technology with which it is assigned to work. Ultimately, it is probably not a good idea for a project team to try to cut its teeth on agile development through the planning game.

Implementation[1]

The planning game has two participants: development (those involved in building the system) and business (the people responsible for determining what the system will do). This abstraction is meant to de-emphasize the personal histories and feelings of the individual participants. The game "pieces" are the index cards that represent user stories or features, if agile practices from multiple projects are being mixed together. Having user stories on individual cards is an essential component of the planning game. If a project team maintains its user stories in an electronic form, the easiest thing to do is to mail merge them into an index card format, send this to the printer, and make a stop at the office paper-cutter (as discussed in Chapter 11).

The planning game is broken into three phases, each consisting of a handful of moves. The first two phases can be completed in a single meeting. The third phase continues to the completion of the release. The planning game moves are broken out by participant in Figure 13.2.

The first phase is the exploration phase. This is where the complete scope of functionality that may make it into the release is defined and estimated. This phase

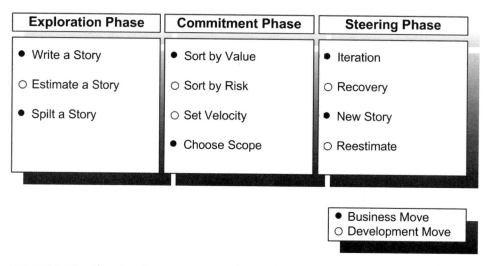

FIGURE 13.2 The planning game moves, by participant [Beck99].

consists of three moves that may be repeated until all the candidate functionality is included in user stories.

> **Write a story:** Business writes a new piece of functionality onto an index card. (Writing user stories is discussed in detail in Chapter 11.)
>
> **Estimate a story:** Development attempts to estimate the story in ideal time. (Estimation and ideal time are discussed in Chapter 11.) If the story cannot be estimated, they must ask business to clarify the story. Business must not force development into reducing its estimates.
>
> **Split a story:** If a story is too large or complex for development or if business decides it wants one part of a story earlier than another, business may rewrite a story on two or more cards.

The second phase of the planning game is the commitment phase. This is where business and development agree on the scope and delivery date associated with the release. The first two moves of this phase help ensure that the business is making knowledgeable decisions about the stories it will queue for the release. The second two moves determine the release's scope and duration. The moves in this phase are made sequentially and include:

> **Sort by value:** Business ranks the stories from most to least essential for inclusion within the release. This move can be performed in a rough manner by stacking the cards into three piles: (1) essential to the system, (2) high value, and (3) nice to have.

Sort by risk: Development ranks the stories based on faith in the estimates they have provided. The rough approach puts the cards into the following three piles: (1) high certainty, (2) moderate certainty, and (3) low certainty.

Set velocity: Development establishes the velocity at which it believes it will develop the release. (Velocity is discussed in Chapter 10.) Velocity will typically be communicated in an amount of ideal time per week or month. The business must not attempt to force development into increasing this number.

Choose scope: Business selects either a release date or a specific number of stories for the release. If the business selects a release date, then it selects an assortment of stories with estimates that add up to the total ideal time available for the release. If the business selects a specific number of stories, then the release date is calculated by totaling the story estimates and dividing that number by the team's velocity.

The third and final phase is the steering phase. This runs from the end of the commitment phase to the end of the release, during which time the team is developing in iterations. Each move during this period typically will be made prior to the beginning of a new iteration. The moves in this phase are these:

Iteration: Prior to the beginning of each iteration, the business selects the stories to be completed by development during that iteration. The number of stories for each iteration is selected based on the total of their estimates and the latest velocity reported by development.

Recovery: During the release, development may conclude that it has overstated its velocity; that is, they are not completing functionality at the pace they had originally thought they could. If this occurs, development may ask business to trim the stories remaining for the release that fit within the time remaining for the release and the new velocity determined by development.

New story: During the release, business may realize that they need a new story to be completed during the release. Business writes the story, and development estimates it. Then business pulls out from the release one or more stories equivalent to the estimate of the story it is adding. Development must honor this request.

Reestimate: Development may grow concerned about the nature of the work remaining in the release. For example, they may learn something during the first iterations of a release that calls into question their estimates for a number of stories. In that case, development may choose to reestimate the stories remaining in the release. If the total ideal time of the reestimated stories is significantly higher than the previous total estimate, business must respond by removing a sufficient number of stories from the release in order to bring the total remaining work in line with the original total estimate.

It is important to keep in mind that the first full cycle of the planning game may shake out some very poor estimates, an inaccurate and fluctuating assessment of velocity, and some less-than-perfect definitions and choices of user stories. This is to be expected. The true benefit from the planning game is not derived from a single cycle but from the improvement associated with incorporating the lessons learned from one cycle into the next. As the project passes through successive releases, business should get better at writing stories, deciding what needs to be included in each release and iteration, and determining when a new user story really does need to make it into the current release. Development, meanwhile, should improve at estimation and assessing its velocity. Finally, the relationship between the two parties should evolve into something that more closely resembles trust and a sense of shared purpose.

If the Project Has Already Begun

The planning game practice can be picked up prior to the onset of any release. In order to do so, the project will need to either have its work already broken out into user stories or features or plan to do so and spend the time required for such an activity during the exploration phase. If the project needs to write user stories mostly from scratch because it has not written requirements or because its written requirements are not amenable to a quick conversion into features, then the exploration phase could take several days to complete.

If the Team Is Beginning a New Project

A blank slate offers both opportunities and challenges for a project team. If most high-level variables have already been set for the team (for example, what they will build and what technology they will use), the business may just begin writing stories in an extended exploration phase. If a lot of things about the project are still up in the air (that is, not much more has been decided than, "We need a project to fix this"), it would be best to consult Chapter 12 in general and the agile practice blitz planning in particular.

Obstacles and Opportunities

The point of the planning game is to get business and development actively working together on a realistic and mutually agreed to plan. The practice should be adjusted accordingly to fit this goal.

Adjust or Add New Moves

This was discussed previously, but it is worth repeating. The point of the rules and the moves within the game is to provide both parties with a framework that allows them to work together and that they both respect and value. If there is something missing or that does not quite fit in the rules, both parties can agree to make a change. Most commonly, a change may entail an alteration of an existing move or the inclusion of a new one. For example, in some environments, both parties may feel it is appropriate to allow development to select a certain percentage of stories during the iterate move because development simply better understands the technical hurdles they face [Beck00].

Adding moves to the game may involve formalizing moves that everyone knows can be made anyway. A change value move, for example, simply allows business to change an existing story during the steering phase. The activities it will set in motion are nearly identical to the new story move. Other new moves may introduce new concepts. A spike move, also played during the steering phase, allows business to request that development perform an immediate activity either to proof an approach or to apply a temporary fix. The code in a spike is disposable (otherwise it would be introduced as a story), and the move, again, spawns the same reestimate and rebalance activities as the new story move [Wiki04].

Do Not Call It the Planning Game

Ever since it was introduced in *Extreme Programming Explained,* the practice has been called the planning game. Nonetheless, the founders of XP and many others have some concerns with the name [Wiki04]. The issue is that calling the planning process a game can be off-putting or trivializing to individuals who value planning highly, causing them to react negatively to the name and miss the actual value of the practice. Calling the planning game something else or merely making it part of release planning may be a prudent action in environments (such as CMM and RUP) where planning and scheduling are highly valued activities.

See Also

- Beck and Fowler's *Planning Extreme Programming* focuses extensively on planning and executing an iterative process. While the planning game itself goes all but unmentioned, chapters 10 through 16 delve deeper into much of what has been discussed here [Beck00].
- The Wiki page on the planning game contains additional moves and has links to other related topics. Browse to *http://www.c2.com/cgi/wiki?PlanningGame.*

STARTING MONDAY: INSTITUTE SMALL RELEASES

As discussed in Chapter 10, releases provide an excellent timeboxing mechanism for project teams because they force tough decisions about priorities and ensure that something useful is developed and delivered in the near term. Projects can get a significant benefit from planning and executing in short releases, even when only the final release gets deployed and every earlier release only goes so far as to demonstrate working functionality.

It is important to note that short releases cannot simply be instituted on any project by inserting half a dozen demos to customer points within an existing, year-long project work schedule. There are two significant reasons that such an approach will not work. First, this approach does not incorporate a release planning mechanism because the schedule for the entire project is still drawn up in advance. Therefore, this approach will do nothing to ensure that the most important functionality within a project is being identified and developed as the business climate changes and the customer's understanding of the system matures. Second, inserting release points is not the same as planning in timeboxes. It is simply too easy to allow a mere date on a schedule to slip. True small releases, which rely on a timebox mechanism, have established end dates. Changing the end date of a release affects the start date and the duration of the next. With timeboxes it becomes easier to argue that functionality needs to shift, not dates, ensuring that something new and useful gets delivered at the end of each release.

Possibly the simplest way to begin using small releases may be to build off the Scrum sprint. In a sprint, the customer presents the project team with the highest priority functionality, and the team selects from that set of items the amount of work it believes it can complete within the upcoming release. If the customer is not satisfied with the work selected by the team, then smaller bits of functionality are scoped into and out of the release until both the customer and the project team are satisfied with the agreed-to functionality.

Two characteristics of the sprint help keep this process simple. First, a single sprint with a recommended duration of 30 days is small enough that it can operate simultaneously as a release and iteration. Second, work does not need to be broken into features or user stories in order to pursue this approach. The Scrum sprint and the sprint planning meeting are discussed in Chapter 14.

There are numerous other ways a project team may institute small releases. The team may choose to first break all its existing near-term work into features and user stories, which is discussed in Chapter 14. The team may want to embed several short iterations within each release. For each project, such decisions should be made based on the current condition of the project.

14 Executing Iterative Development

In This Chapter

- An Agile Approach to Iterative Development
- Iteration Planning Meeting
- Monitoring Progress Within the Iteration
- Changing the End Date of the Current Iteration
- Changing the Functionality of the Current Iteration
- Abnormally Terminating an Iteration
- Adapting the Iteration
- Sprints and Other Releasable Iterations
- Working Without Iterations
- Agile Practice: The Task Cycle
- Starting Monday: Begin Iterating

The traditional approach to project execution in software development entails an upfront and phased plan (such as define, design, build, test, deploy) broken down into individual task packets and rolled up into a hierarchical WBS or Gant chart. Agile development advocates a procession of short iterations (typically one to eight weeks), each with its own define-design-build-test cycle. These iterations lead to regular releases of small functionality, enable progress tracking that is more reliable than phased approaches, and provide an opportunity for regular feedback from users to the project team.

AN AGILE APPROACH TO ITERATIVE DEVELOPMENT

Iterations are the timebox in which agile projects actually queue up and complete whole features or user stories. Scheduling only complete pieces of functionality within the iteration is one way that agile projects ensure that an iterative process regularly delivers new functionality that is useable, of sufficient quality, and what the customer has requested. This is just one benefit provided in the agile approach to iterative development. Others include:

- Iterations allow a customer to change the direction of a project at the beginning of each iteration, thereby queuing up whatever functionality is actually most relevant and valuable.
- Iterations enable the prioritization of risk. At the beginning of each iteration, and based on what the project team has most recently learned, the plan may be altered to attack elements of the project where technologies may be unproven or estimates are widely uncertain.
- Iterations can ensure that a system never strays far from a deployable state, since only whole features are planned within each iteration.
- Iterations provide regular cycles that can be used as feedback loops to measure project progress and team productivity.
- Iterations can provide an easy end to a project. This occurs when the customer no longer values any backlogged functionality sufficiently to pay for an additional iteration.

The average iteration varies in length between one and four weeks. However, some methodologies, such as Crystal and ASD, allow iterations as long as two or even four months.

ITERATION PLANNING MEETING

The iteration planning meeting is probably one of the most recognizable characteristics of the agile approach to iterative development. Prior to the beginning of every iteration, the entire team will gather within its open workspace, a conference room, or (for very large teams) some other space that can accommodate the entire team. The meeting serves both to plan the upcoming iteration (where everyone on the team has the opportunity to know what is going on and provide input where necessary) and to actually kick off the iteration.

Typically the planning meeting occurs in a single day, although some planning activities are often performed prior to the actual meeting. This is the case even for large project teams with long iterations. These variables, of course, influence the overall length of the meeting. A small team executing one-week iterations may be done with the meeting in an hour. A large team running monthly iterations may take an entire day to complete the meeting.

The planning meeting is an integral part of an agile and iterative process. It is the time at which the customer may step in to adjust the direction of the project, based upon either internal or external factors. It is the point at which the entire team comes to a consensus about what they are going to do for the iteration and how they are going to do it. It is when each member of the team agrees to and accepts responsibility for the work he will perform during the upcoming iteration.

Typical Iteration Planning Activities

The actual activities performed by any agile team during its iteration planning meeting can depend on a number of factors, including:

1. The size of the project team and the duration of the iteration (as previously discussed).
2. The agile methodology the project team is most closely aligned with.
3. How tightly the activities for each iteration were scripted during the planning session for the release.
4. Whether the customer actively participates with the project team in the iteration planning process.
5. Whether the team performs some of the iteration planning activities in advance or all at once.

Depending upon the project team and agile methodology, the customer may or may not be engaged in iteration planning. Having the customer take part in planning an iteration is strongly recommended, but many teams simply cannot get the customer to focus regularly on iteration-level activities. In any case, the project team should work with the customer, if at all possible, to complete steps 2 through 4.

Not all steps will be taken by every team. Furthermore, the team may reorder some steps to fit its needs (such as steps 1 and 2). Finally, these steps assume the team already has a defined schedule for iterations. Typically this will be based on either a fixed duration (such as two weeks) or a specific schedule that was set out at the beginning of the project or release (for iterations of five weeks or more).

Steps Taken Before the Iteration Planning Meeting

The steps in this section closely resemble the activities during the planning of a release (discussed in Chapter 13) because this portion of the iteration planning process allows the customer (or the project team) to adjust the plan for the iteration. Possibly the climate of the customer's business has suddenly changed. Perhaps a key client has requested that a new feature be included in the project two months ahead of schedule. Maybe that third-party invoicing package did not include all the features the sales guy said it would. Whatever the case, now is the time for the customer or the project team to adjust the release plan to compensate for unknowable events.

Many teams will perform the first four steps in the days leading up to the planning meeting with discussions held between the customer, the project manager, and any relevant domain or technical experts. In this more common case, the entire

Pre-Meeting Activities	Iteration Planning Meeting
❖ **Step 1:** Determine the Amount of Work the Team Can Complete	❖ **Step 5:** Present the Features
	❖ **Step 6:** Decompose Features into Estimated Tasks
❖ **Step 2:** Update the List of Work for the Release	❖ **Step 7:** Programmers Sign Up to Complete Tasks
❖ **Step 3:** Set a Goal for the Iteration	❖ **Step 8:** Confirm Reasonable Commitment by Both Individual Programmers and Entire Team
❖ **Step 4:** Select the Functionality	

FIGURE 14.1 Typical iteration planning activities.

project team meets only to complete steps 5 through 8. Some teams, instead, will complete all eight steps with a single meeting on a single day. Finally, teams with a less participatory customer or a fixed release plan may skip these steps altogether.

Step 1: Determine the Amount of Work the Team Can Complete

Two inputs will factor into this activity. The first input is the team's estimated velocity for the upcoming iteration—that is, how much work the team believes it can complete per day or per iteration. Calculating velocity is discussed in Chapter 10, "Agile Management."

Second, the team needs to consider the actual amount of time (in days or weeks) it will have to complete work for this iteration. The team must assess whether holidays, vacations, or any other activities that will keep one or more programmers from doing their work (such as company-wide meetings and training seminars) will have a significant impact on the amount of work it may complete during the iteration. On many occasions, lesser holidays and individual days are simply forgotten about. On shorter iterations this can have a real effect on the ability of the team to complete its work. For longer iterations (of four weeks or more), week-long vacations are known to have been overlooked during the planning process to similar effect.

What the team must ultimately decide here is whether it can treat the size of its upcoming iteration as similar to previous iterations. If the iteration size is similar, then the team can simply use its velocity as calculated to indicate how much work it should plan for the iteration. If the team is embarking upon an iteration that is significantly larger or smaller than its previous iterations, then it will need to adjust the amount of work it believes it can do based on its velocity for a typical iteration.

Step 2: Update the List of Work for the Release

This activity is similar to one performed during the release planning period. The customer and the project team need to ensure that the list of features or user stories associated with the release is completely up to date, including individual estimates and overall prioritization.

When planning an iteration, the project team needs to be interested only in ensuring that work intended for the current release is up to date. Of course the project will still want to track work proposed for the following releases so that features may be added, adjusted, or altered, but this work should have no bearing on decisions to be made for the current iteration within the current release.

Step 3: Set a Goal for the Iteration

The customer sets the goal for the iteration. If the customer is not involved in iteration planning, then the goal is set by the project team. The goal may be a specific set of functionality, an attempt to reduce risk (by tackling the features with the least trusted estimates), or whatever else seems most pressing.

Not every project team will need to do this, but sometimes a team may find itself looking at a handful of stories (queued up for a release several iterations away) and not knowing what to do first.

Step 4: Select the Functionality

This step does not occur in every project environment or agile methodology. Sometimes functionality for a each iteration is predetermined when release planning is performed.

Two common and similar techniques are used by projects to determine the functionality a team will complete in each iteration. The most significant difference in these approaches is that the first relies on features that have already been estimated by the team and the second approach does not.

> **When the List of Work Includes Estimates:** In the first approach (which relies upon the team having completed step 1), the customer selects an amount of functionality equivalent to that amount of ideal time the team has said it can complete.
>
> **When the List of Work Does Not Include Estimates:** In the second approach, similar to that used by Scrum to plan its sprints (discussed in detail later in this chapter), the customer prioritizes in sequence the features that most need to be completed. The team then indicates the amount of functionality that it believes it can complete during the iteration, starting at the highest priority feature and working down the list. If the customer is not happy with the amount of functionality chosen by the team, he may enter into negotiation until both parties are satisfied with the decision.

Steps Taken During the Iteration Planning Meeting

This is the part of the planning meeting that requires participation from the entire project. These steps (or a variation of them) should be completed during a single meeting that is attended by the entire project team, its customer, and any other relevant domain experts. The steps may be completed in one of two approaches:

By feature: In this approach, a single feature or user story is introduced, steps 5 through 7 are completed, and the project team moves on to the next story. The process is repeated for every feature that has been included in the iteration. The last step, step 8, is performed only once at the end of the meeting. The advantage of this approach is that it provides continuity for each feature—discussing, dissecting, estimating, and divvying it up—before moving on to the next.

In sequence: In this approach, the team just burns through steps 5 through 8 in sequence, performing each one in order for all the stories scheduled for the iteration. This approach works best when the team has only a limited period of time with the customer and domain experts, presumably at the beginning of the meeting.

Step 5: Present the Features

This step is as straightforward as it is essential. Someone—the best candidate may be the customer—should present the feature to the project team and answer any questions members of the team may have.

Step 6: Decompose Features into Estimated Tasks

Here the team will embark upon one of the essential activities in more agile approaches: features or user stories (ideally, written by the customer and in the customer's language) are broken into technical tasks that are understood and may be implemented by the programmers. Besides mere translation, there are other significant benefits that agile teams derive from breaking user-understood features into programming-oriented tasks, and they are worth mentioning here.

A single programmer typically does not complete all the functionality for a single feature. Sometimes this is because of time constraints (in the case of larger stories) and sometimes because different programmers have knowledge and skills specific to the varying technical activities that need to be completed to implement a single feature.

Breaking larger features into smaller tasks allows a better capability to track progress within the iteration.

The process of breaking a feature into tasks typically entails a handful of decisions to be made about how that feature will be designed into the system. Therefore, by performing this activity during the planning meeting, the entire team has the opportunity to collaborate on the high-level design for that feature [Cohn04].

Once a feature is broken into tasks, those tasks need to be estimated. Typically, the estimated duration for a task should be somewhere between two hours and two days. Anything smaller can be rolled into another task to avoid too much clutter.

However, if a very small task really should be tracked independently, it can be labeled a point-one (see the discussion of point-one tasks later in this chapter). Estimates of more than two days suggest that the team has not sufficiently thought through (or possibly knows enough) about the task. Such estimates should be treated with skepticism and if possible should be split into additional, smaller tasks.

Step 7: Programmers Sign Up to Complete Tasks

Typically, one or more programmers agree to take ownership of each task. It then becomes the responsibility of that programmer or those programmers to see that the task is completed. In some agile methodologies, the owner is not even bound to complete the task. If he has too much work of his own, the owner may instead ask another programmer who finished his tasks ahead of schedule to complete it. It is not important who completes the task, only that it is completed. Making sure that someone has taken ownership of every task, however, ensures that no task simply falls through the cracks, because at the end of the iteration someone is going to have to stand up and say whether the task got done and, if not, at least provide a reasonable explanation why.

Step 8: Confirm Reasonable Commitment by Both the Programmer and the Team

At this point, nearly all the work of the planning meeting is complete except for one thing: the sanity check. Each programmer should confirm that he is comfortable with the amount of work he has accepted in the iteration, and the project manager or team lead should keep an eye out for programmers who have a habit for taking on more than they can actually handle.

The same sort of check should be made for the entire team. When the estimates for the stories and the estimates for the tasks derived from those features are added up, are the numbers reasonably close? Typically, the total of the tasks will be greater because programmers have a tendency to round up when estimating, but the number should not be significantly greater. If it is, the team may have to go back to the customer and discuss the possibility of pulling a feature or two from the iteration. If the total estimate for tasks is significantly less than the total estimate for features, then the team should revalidate the outputs of steps 6 and 7 and, if the discrepancy holds, approach the customer about adding a feature or two.

Not Enough Work to Fill an Iteration

It can (and unfortunately does) happen that the team may be at the onset of a new iteration and the customer does not actually have enough work (either in features or user stories) at hand to fill an entire iteration. Perhaps there is work, but the experts necessary to define it adequately are not available. Perhaps the company is in the process of redefining its strategy for the system, so the customer is simply unsure of what actually needs to be done. Regardless, the dilemma is the same: The iteration contains more time than the customer knows what to do with.

If the customer is not adamant about getting the problem resolved, the project manager may need to step in and try to find a solution. The confrontational approach (advocated in the past by some Agilists) is to have the team go on strike until an iteration's worth of work can be defined. Three other, more pragmatic approaches may also be pursued.

First, the team might run a shorter-than-typical iteration. The only team this approach will certainly not work for is one that is running one-week iterations. A second approach, assuming that the customer is willing, is to have the project team fill the extra time with other tasks that it has wanted to do or that it feels will result in future benefits. For example, the team may complete a spike or begin to implement a test data maintenance practice. Third, the team can complete low-priority work such as documentation that may have little immediate value but will most likely be required at some point in the project.

Working with Shared Resources

On an agile project (and probably most any other project), having a part-time resource on a team can be difficult. First, because the individual has multiple sets of responsibilities, he is less likely to see the success or failure of his own performance as being tied to the success or failure of any given project team. Second, the individual typically gets pulled in a variety of directions by his different masters, thrashes as he attempts to switch tasks, and ends up being less productive. Third, the project manager may spend a not insignificant amount of time trying to retain a sufficient amount of the individual's time. This is especially the case when the shared individual has a clear preference for one of his project responsibilities over another. Finally, just when you need him most, he is likely to be nowhere to be found.

At the same time, management sometimes has little choice but to accept a shared resource on the project. In such a case, the best approach may be a two-pronged approach. First, come to an agreement with the individual's other managers on a simple sharing plan. It will probably involve the division of a commonly understood time period, such as two days a week on Project Foo and three days a week on Project Bar. Beware, however, of assigning calendar-specific periods to shared time (such as Monday and Tuesday on Project Foo and Wednesday through Friday on Project Bar). Although in practice the individual may land on a schedule such as this to reduce the intrusion of one project into the other, the formal agreement between managers should not go into such specifics. What if one project has an emergency on the wrong day? What if there is off-site training two weeks in a row? What about sick days? A complicated and calendar-specific agreement is likely to run aground on too much detail.

Working with a shared resource will cause a couple of small changes to the iteration planning process. First, prior to each iteration, the project manager should confirm with the individual that he will be able to provide the agreed amount of time to the project. This should not be taken as an assumption, nor should the project manager assume that such information will be provided in a timely manner. Second, if the individual is not able to make the agreed effort for two consecutive iterations due to being pulled into activities on another project, the project manager must assess the effect this has on the team's velocity and, if necessary, inform the business of the situation. Staying proactive—as opposed to being reactive—can reduce some of the hassle of working with a shared resource, especially when things start to go wrong.

Variations of the Iteration Planning Meeting

As mentioned earlier in this section, each agile methodology has a slightly different flavor of meeting that it uses to kick off its iterations. These meetings are often adapted by individual teams to fit their particular project environments. Ultimately, there is a large variety of similar (but not the same) planning meeting formats available. In this chapter, two such approaches are discussed.

> **The sprint planning meeting:** Later in this chapter, in the section "Sprints and Other Releasable Iterations," the textbook approach to a Scrum sprint is discussed. Note that the sprint is also cited in Chapter 13 as a release planning approach, which of course it is.

> **The task cycle weekly meeting:** Later still in this chapter, in the section on task cycles, the weekly meeting for this practice is detailed. This approach might apply well for one- or two-week iterations and incorporates triage as well as planning activities. Note that some straightforward modifications will need to be made to adjust the meeting to handle features or user stories instead of tasks.

MONITORING PROGRESS WITHIN THE ITERATION

For anything but one-week iterations, it is a good idea to monitor progress during the iteration instead of waiting to be surprised (or surprise the team's customer) by what is or is not accomplished during the iteration wrap-up. Regular stand up or daily Scrum meetings (both discussed as agile practices in Chapter 17) may provide an unscientific but sufficient measure of progress for iterations of up two weeks in length. For anything longer, a project team should really have a process in place for gauging progress within the iteration.

Assess Progress at the Iteration Halfway Point

Depending on the size of the project, the length of the iteration, and the complexity of what is being done, it may be sufficient for the team to collect its bearings and assess its progress when it is halfway through the iteration. The team can do this by holding a halfway point meeting [Martin02].

At the meeting, the team should total the amount of work it has completed and compare it to the amount of work it planned to complete for the iteration. Depending on the practices a team is following and its interpretation of those practices, a team may measure one of a few metrics. Typically this metric may fall within one of two categories:

- The total ideal time of all the features, user stories, or tasks the team has completed versus the total amount of ideal time it set out to complete.
- The total number of tasks the team has completed versus the total number it has to complete.

Basically, the numbers should show that the team is roughly half done at the halfway point.

If the team is clearly behind schedule, it has two options. First, it can redistribute work across the members of the team in an attempt to make up the shortfall during the remainder of the iteration. Second, and if the first option will likely not succeed, the team needs to notify its customer about the situation and, with his help, shave a sufficient amount of functionality off the release so that it will be able to complete the remainder by the end of the iteration.

If the team finds itself ahead of schedule, it needs to ask itself whether it is sufficiently ahead of schedule to request that the customer identify additional functionality to be completed during the remainder of the iteration. If so, then the team is in the enviable position of having to go to the customer and ask him to identify which feature he would like to have sooner.

Use a Burndown Chart

Teams can monitor progress in a similar fashion to that done during the iteration's halfway point but do it on a regular and even daily basis. While many agile methodologies have embraced this idea, Scrum has come up with the best name for it: the burndown chart [Schwaber04]. There are more advanced methods of charting progress across iterations and releases, such as the burn up chart. These are discussed in Chapter 16.

Burndown charts are built through a very simple process. At the beginning of the iteration, the team adds up all the work that needs to be done in the iteration. This total amount of work left to be done is then calculated on a daily basis, taking into account features that have been completed, reestimated, or otherwise removed from or added to the iteration. These calculations are usually done in a spreadsheet or other tool that will automatically generate a graph similar to those depicted in Figure 14.2.

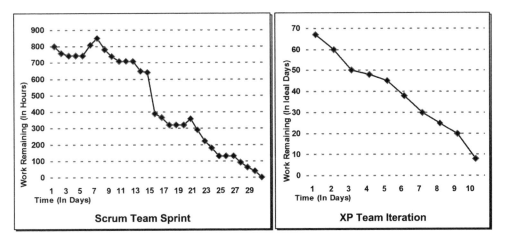

FIGURE 14.2 Sample burndown charts for Scrum and XP projects.

The first illustration in Figure 14.2 is meant to be true to Scrum, and the second is true to XP. Beyond the superficial use of work hours (for Scrum) and ideal days (for XP), the observant reader might notice that in the Scrum chart the total amount of work actually shifts up as well as down. This is the result of programmers in the sprint reestimating their tasks on a frequent basis, which may or may not occur in XP.

These simple graphs can convey an amazing amount of information. In both cases, the teams were not able to complete the amount of functionality they had initially set out to complete, although this is not so obvious in the Scrum team's graph, for reasons that will be explained momentarily. In both cases, either the teams' estimates were off or some other external factor made each team less productive than it usually would be. It is worth noting that agile projects often meet their iteration goals; iterations with such conclusions, however, make for uninteresting examples.

In the sprint team's example, there is a sudden drop in the amount of work that the team still needs to complete. This was not the result of the team working consecutive all-nighters or over the weekend. Rather, this is when the team realized it had more features to complete by the end of the iteration than time available to do it. In this case, the team would have had to go to its customer and have the remaining features for the iteration reduced. The Scrum team then completed that reduced number of features in the second half of the sprint.

In the XP team's example, it most likely became apparent to the team that it would not complete all its user stories sometime in the middle of the iteration. If the team did not already know which user stories were less important to its customer, it would have had a conversation with the customer at that point to find out. Instead of reducing the scope of the iteration, the XP team simply made sure it completed the most important user stories until iteration's end.

Burndown charts must be reviewed on a regular basis to be useful; automatically generating but never reviewing them will not do a project team any good. Some teams like to share the burndown chart with the customer on a regular basis, and others prefer to use it internally and involve the customer only when the need to talk about functionality arises. Such decisions rely both on the methodology the team is following and its relationship with the customer.

CHANGING THE END DATE OF THE CURRENT ITERATION

The smaller the iteration, the less willing Agilists are to let the end date slip. This is because moving the end date negates most of the benefit that an iteration derives from serving as a timebox. Once this psychological barrier has been broken, some rightly fear, the customer and the project may decide it is OK to let dates slip in following iterations. Tough decisions may thus be side-stepped, and urgently needed functionality may be slower in coming.

On larger iterations, those that take more than four weeks to complete, it can actually be difficult to dissuade a customer from wanting to make that first small shift in the end date. When the iteration is already four weeks long, what does a couple of days matter? Or worse, when the iteration is eight weeks long, what does an extra week matter? Rules stated clearly upfront instead of being brought up when the team is under fire may help mitigate some of those pressures. For example, Scrum (recommended sprint length: 30 days) strictly outlaws movements in the date [Schwaber01]. If the customer believes he needs to change the direction of the project team that badly (and this goes for any functionality changes the customer may have as well), his only option is to cancel the sprint outright.

On smaller iterations, the approach can be similar to the one taken by Scrum. Especially when the iteration is only a week or two in length, the project team can muster up some formidable arguments, such as that it will break the rhythm in the team and that one more week really will not make a difference.

One final point. The members of the project should never be the ones lobbying to change the end date of the iteration. In so doing, they would be breaking a rule that is in their own interest, short-circuiting a feedback loop, and sending the wrong message to their customer.

CHANGING THE FUNCTIONALITY OF THE CURRENT ITERATION

Altering the functionality within an iteration is a bit more of a nuanced topic than altering the date. Again, there is the question of the size of the iteration. In addition, there is the question of who instigates the discussion. Three possibilities are discussed. The first two are straightforward: Either the customer requests a change in the work for the iteration or the project team recognizes that they are working faster or slower than expected, which is not an uncommon occurrence on agile projects. The third is more difficult to detect and is based on a rule developed on one of my past projects; the no snow days rule reminds people that when they are blocked from work on all the tasks they have been assigned, they do not simply get to go home. These three situations are discussed in the following sections.

Customer Requests a Change During the Iteration

The agile methodologies are split on how to address customer-initiated changes in the middle of an iteration. For example, they are planned for in DSDM (as discussed in Chapter 13) and strictly forbidden in Scrum. In the project trenches, customer changes and how they are addressed may depend largely on the length of the iteration and the relationship between the team and its customer.

On teams with longer and even medium-size iterations, many Agilists are more willing to contemplate or will even openly accept customer-instigated changes to the functionality within an iteration as long as an equal amount of functionality is removed from the iteration and work on that functionality has not already begun. This is essentially the same response as the customer will get when he wants to change functionality during a release, though many teams will not be as enthusiastic to see functionality shift within an iteration (see Chapter 13).

Project teams running shorter iterations will be more reluctant to entertain functionality swaps and will likely get fewer requests for it because their customer should not have to wait more than a week or two at most to get his new functionality into the next iterations. Teams running one-week iterations may even argue that there is no reason to bring up the topic because once it is debated and decided the team may have already started the next iteration.

To be clear, this does not mean that teams running on smaller iterations should not allow the customer to swap functionality within the iteration, simply that the project team is within its rights to seek significant justification for such an action. Shifting functionality in the middle of a short iteration, even when that functionality has not yet been touched by a programmer, can put a small strain on a team. People have to be pulled into conference rooms. Programmers are told don't do this, do that. Regular interruptions such as this can make a project team feel like it is losing control.

Project Team Reports That Actual Progress Is Not in Line with Estimates

Sometimes in the midst of an iteration a project team determines conclusively that it is ahead of or behind schedule. In some cases this realization will require an immediate meeting with the customer, and in other cases the team will already know what to do. Typically, if the team has an active customer, it will need to go to the customer and ask for a quick decision. Either the team cannot do everything, and something needs to be removed from the iteration, or (and we all love it when this happens) the team is about to run out of work and needs to know what it should attack next.

On other occasions, the customer may have done a thorough job of prioritizing functionality for the entire release. In that case, the team will already know what it should not do or what it should do next. All that is left is to break the news to the customer. In the final scenario, the team may have a customer who does not get involved in iteration planning. When this is the case, the team will have to make the decision on its own. Additionally, the team will need to assess whether the discrepancy between estimated and actual effort will have an impact upon the overall outcome of the release. If so, then it will need to contact its customer.

No Snow Days

Sometimes development tasks get blocked by events external to the project, and programmers may find themselves with all their other tasks complete well before the end of the iteration. In such a situation, when there is work left to complete, people can fall into a snow day mentality. That is, instead of going to the team lead, project manager, or customer in search of additional work, people may just take the time and spend it on whatever task most appeals to them, which even when related to the project, may not be of particularly high priority.

Programmers and project managers must be on guard against snow days. It may seem like a rather innocent thing to do: "Mike did not get the data specifications for the XML task from the folks in accounting, so he decided to fix that annoying font issue in the order screen instead." Nonetheless, a handful of snow days can set the project back from completing priority functionality by the same amount of time.

ABNORMALLY TERMINATING AN ITERATION

When necessary, iterations can be ended prior to their planned completion dates. Reasons for such an action include:

- The customer decides he no longer wants the functionality that is being developed.
- The customer decides there is other functionality that the team must put its attention toward and drop everything else in the process.
- The technology that the team is using to complete the functionality for the iteration has proven to be unusable [Schwaber04]. This situation may occur if the customer, for example, directs the team to spend the majority of the iteration on setting up and interfacing with a third-party product.

In the first two cases, the cost of making such a decision lies with the customer. He of course should be informed of the true cost of his decision, but the decision is his to make. In the last case, the decision will typically be initiated by the team and agreed to by the customer.

ADAPTING THE ITERATION

The iteration, as defined by the agile methodologies, is a very flexible construct that can be adapted in all manner of ways to fit the peculiarities of individual team environments and even individual team members. This section contains a few things teams may do to tailor the iterative mechanism. For an example of full-fledged adaptation of the iteration, see the "Agile Practice: The Task Cycle" section near the end of this chapter.

One-Week Iterations

One-week iterations may be frightening to some individuals because they suggest that the team needs to be constantly producing in order to meet a steady stream of one-week goals. This fear is understandable, though misguided. Shorter iterations actually help to maintain a more sustainable pace of development activity.

The average agile iteration runs between two and four weeks. The extended period of time, even at two weeks, will likely cause a rhythm of less and then more work, as illustrated in Figure 14.3. This is because teams too often get into the habit of taking it easy for the first half of an iteration and then working overtime in the office to catch up during the last half of the iteration. This cycle is self-reinforcing because it is only natural to want to follow a period of overwork at the end of one cycle with a period of underwork at the beginning of the next. Of course, also as illustrated in Figure 14.3, two- and four-week iterations still do a much better job of leveling out the pace of work than a traditional development process, which merely becomes sustained overtime near the end of the project.

One-week task cycles engender a stable 40-hour workweek because a constant near-term goal keeps the team from taking a resting period or having to make up for a resting period with an overtime period. The fear from weekly iterations comes from the thought of having to work an overtime period every week. Since the overtime period never occurs, one-week iterations actually feel less harried than longer iterations.

Alistair Cockburn provides a few cautions (and tips to address them) about weekly iterations [Cockburn04a]:

The rhythm becomes too monotonous: This is when the drip, drip, drip of near-term goals begins to resemble Chinese water torture and people begin to go batty from essentially doing the same thing week after week. Occasionally

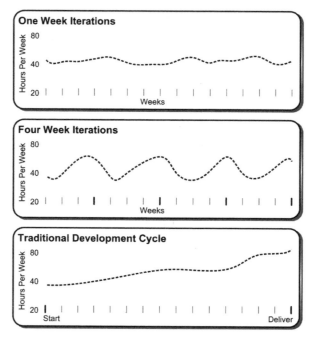

FIGURE 14.3   The work curve flattened across one-week iterations.

varying the length of the iteration can help to address this. So can providing some free time between releases (see the "Taking Time Between Releases" section in Chapter 13 for more information on this approach).

Users stop viewing completed functionality: Because functionality is completed so frequently, the team will fall away from regularly showing completed functionality to the users. To overcome this, projects may embed weekly iterations within a month- or two-month-long super-cycle mechanism to ensure a regular schedule with the customer or users to review all recently completed functionality. Also, projects with an onsite customer (see the agile practice in Chapter 15) should not experience this problem even with weekly iterations.

Nothing new to reflect on: Because a week goes by so quickly, teams that get together at the end of an iteration to reflect and identify lessons learned are likely not going to have much to talk about. Instituting a super-cycle of iterations should provide a solution to this problem.

The planning session for a one-week iteration should last only about an hour and may include the wrap-up activity for the previous iteration. Teams executing one-week iterations should also seriously consider holding the planning meeting in the middle of the week as discussed in the next section. Finally, for more tips on executing weekly iterations, see the section on task cycles near the end of this chapter.

Begin the Iteration in the Middle of the Week

The workweek starts on Monday and ends on Friday, so typically teams start iterations on Mondays and end them on Fridays. However, ending the previous iteration and starting a new one in the middle of the week has several advantages.

First, the majority of holidays land on a Monday or a Friday. This is not too bad because a holiday means no one will be around, and the day can simply be shifted over. However, people tend to use spare vacation days for the occasional three- or four-day weekend. Scheduling around this activity, especially for iterations only one or two weeks in length, becomes a bit more dicey. Does the team move the beginning of the iteration just because one person will not be there, or do they simply assign him the tasks no one else wants? Trickier still is when a project begins to acquire traveling team members. People who fly in at the beginning of the week and fly out at the end are necessarily going to wreak havoc on a Monday-to-Friday iteration schedule.

Tuesdays, Wednesdays, and Thursdays are much less likely to be affected by these activities. The project team may meet first thing in the morning or at the end of the day, so for example, a team may have an iteration wrap-up meeting late Wednesday afternoon and an iteration planning meeting first thing Thursday morning.

A final benefit to this approach is that people who enjoy doing a bit of work on weekends will always know what they should be working on over the weekend. (One assumes these individuals are working on the weekend because they prefer flexible work schedules, not because they are given too much work to do.)

Stretch Goals

Some teams may prefer to set stretch goals for each iteration, to queue up more work than they can actually complete. Depending on the temperament of the team, this may be a very effective practice, encouraging programmers not to relax when they are low on work (either because their tasks were overestimated or are being blocked) and enabling them to complete more work in a single iteration than they initially thought they could.

When setting stretch goals, the team should watch for two pitfalls. First, lessened morale can result from the team frequently not hitting its stated goal; this can happen even when everyone knows the goal was not meant to be met. Second, managers and programmers alike will need to remember to heed and not violate the sustainable pace of the team; otherwise the stretch goals will ultimately result in the sort of unreasonable goals that burn out project teams.

The key to stretch goals is that the team needs to buy into them. Otherwise, those two pitfalls are all but certain to happen.

Use Point-One Tasks to Track Issues

The name *point-one* is derived from the smallest reasonable amount of time (.1 ideal days) one might consider providing as an estimate for a task that needs to be done. Point-one tasks may be associated with features, user stories, or iteration task lists to ensure that an activity or issue is performed or resolved instead of merely forgotten. These are meant to be little things, the kind of stuff that someone says, almost in passing "yeah, I'll do that while I'm working on this other thing" or "I'll e-mail Bob and get his opinion." Examples of point-one tasks include:

- Getting the correct name for a field on the order cancellation screen from Joe, the user who knows everything about order cancellations. This may be a reminder intended for the project manager, who needs to get the information for a programmer.
- Correcting the misspelling of the word "colour" in the item lookup screen. This may be a reminder for the programmer working on a task on that screen.

Whatever it is, it may not take much effort to be done, but it needs to be done. The point-one weighting given to such tasks is meant to convey that they may be very lightweight, but they are not free. Enough point-one tasks will add up to real work for the team.

SPRINTS AND OTHER RELEASABLE ITERATIONS

In Scrum, the release and the iteration are combined into a single construct: the sprint. This 30-day activity serves as a timebox for both planning functionality and development activity.

In other agile methodologies that follow the short iteration and small release approach, occasionally a team will treat the activity as a single timebox, typically with a period of four to six weeks. In such a situation, the team delivers a release in a deployable state to the customer at the end of every iteration. This approach may be well suited for a Web-based, thin-client, or back-end application where deployment does not entail touching a multitude of workstations and the users are comfortable with a gradually changing system, as opposed to one that changes only every year or so.

An obvious advantage of the sprint and the releasable iteration is that new functionality may be released at the earliest possible opportunity. The business should, of course, always have the option of not deploying at the end of one iteration and simply waiting until the next. An obvious challenge, which a competent project team should be able to rise to, is that the quality of the system must always be maintained at a high level. Doing so should entail many of the programming practices discussed in Chapters 7 and 8, including build automation, automated testing, acceptance testing, and continuous integration, among others.

Sprint Planning Meeting

Because it folds all functional and technical planning activity into a single timebox and the meeting for that timebox into a single day, the sprint planning meeting provides a good example for the type of meeting required to plan a releasable iteration within an agile-minded project, one that has a customer, plans by feature or user story, and follows an iterative process.

The sprint planning meeting is actually two meetings that are timeboxed to four hours each and meant to be completed within the same day. In the first meeting the team assists the customer (called the *product owner* in Scrum) in selecting the functionality for the upcoming sprint. In the second meeting, the team converts the features requested by the customer into a list called the *sprint backlog* of specific and estimated tasks [Schwaber01] [Schwaber04].

Define the Sprint Objective

The first meeting is attended by the entire project team and the customer. As necessary, domain experts and other individuals may be called in to provide information or for consultation, but these individuals should not remain in the room beyond the time during which they are needed. The entire list of features currently assigned to the project should be updated prior to the meeting. In Scrum, this list is called the *product backlog*, and it is typically owned by the customer.

The customer begins the first meeting by presenting and describing the highest priority features to the team; typically this will entail only a handful of items from the top of the product backlog. Members of the team may provide input and suggestions to the customer related to the items discussed or other features included in the product backlog. The team and the customer then work to define the sprint objective: those features that will be completed during the upcoming sprint. The customer indicates to the team what features should be completed. The team asks the customer and any individuals it invites into the room questions about the functionality in order to understand and estimate. The team may inform the customer that it can complete a greater or lesser amount of work, and the customer adjusts his feature request accordingly. The entire meeting is timeboxed to four hours. Even if the team is not certain it can handle a specific number of features for the sprint, it will have to agree to a specific set that it can take into its next meeting.

Define the Sprint Backlog of Tasks

The second meeting is attended solely by the team, although the customer must be available in case the team needs to call upon him. The team may again call in experts as necessary to answer questions and provide additional information. The team begins the meeting with the sprint objective defined in the previous meeting, the features the customer has requested the team complete during the sprint.

The team spends the meeting breaking the features into estimated tasks that will typically take four to sixteen hours each to complete (this process is discussed in greater detail earlier in this chapter). The team may perform whatever architecture or design activity is required to reach a set of specific tasks. In Scrum, unless a technical requirement is called out as part of the description of a feature, it is assumed to be at the team's discretion as to how it will implement it. The task list will represent the team's best current understanding of everything that must be done to build and deploy the features. It will be the team's plan for the upcoming sprint, and it will of course be altered and updated as the team progresses and learns through the course of the sprint.

Sometimes during its discussions a team may conclude that it has agreed to more work than it can complete within the sprint. When this occurs, the team calls the customer into the meeting and asks the customer to remove one or more features from the sprint objective. If removing features will not solve the problem (because they are not of the right size, there is only one feature, or the customer still wants to have everything), the team and the customer can work together to whittle at the functionality within the features until the team is comfortable that it can complete all the work within the duration of the sprint.

Finally, this second meeting is again contained within a rigid timebox of four hours. If the team has not completed all its task definition and estimation activity by this time, it will need to punt and complete these activities as part of its execution of the sprint.

Maintaining a Strategic Vision

The releasable iteration always has a near-term goal, which is to prepare all queued functionality in a production-worthy manner by the end of the iteration. What it is susceptible to, however, is the loss of strategic vision on the part of the customer [Beck00]. Essentially, the business can easily become too involved in adding a handful of new features and changes each iteration but forget to think six or even three months out, resulting in a system that may be overdeveloped in some less-important aspects but underdeveloped in key areas. Such drifting may be mitigated with a mission statement or metaphor (see Chapter 12) to remind the business of its overall objectives. It may also be corrected by instituting a larger, lightweight timebox, such as a quarterly milestone. This approach enables the business to plan in the large and review progress every few iterations in relation to its longer term goals.

WORKING WITHOUT ITERATIONS

Occasionally, for any of a handful or reasons, a project team may be unable to define a timeboxing mechanism to execute an iterative process. This could occur in periods of extraordinary change, at times when the technology being employed is essentially unknown and therefore the feasibility and time-to-completion for the majority of tasks is unknowable, and in the unfortunate circumstance where a project team is disallowed from establishing any sort of formal iterative mechanism. In such situations, the use of a wall work queue may enable a team to continue to use some agile techniques such as user stories, binary status reporting, continuous planning, and burndown charts.

It Does Happen

Teams really can be told that they cannot operate with even the simplest of iterative mechanisms. Sometimes a manager overseeing a project (especially when he is also the customer of that project) can fail to see the value in an iterative approach. Such an individual may see an iterative mechanism of even a week as too long to address the changes and new features he thinks up in the middle of the day. Unfortunately, and as unhealthy as it may be, he may see his ability to step in at any point of time and redirect the team as more important and valuable than the inefficiencies that arise when people thrash from one task to the next, when they do not have enough control over their work environments, and when they never have the chance to truly grasp even a near-term goal. Finally, while the incorrectness and insufferability of such a situation may be debated, the reality is that it is a situation within which some teams must work.

The recommendations in this section are based on the experience of a project that was in place where iterations simply could not be effectively employed. The project was building an internal system for a consulting organization, so as any experienced consultant should know, this meant staffing was always an issue because people were regularly pulled to do billable work. This particular team had only two permanent members, both of whom were only part time on the project. The remainder of the team consisted of individuals who would be briefly assigned to the team, typically immediately after joining the company and before being pulled onto a client project.

Simple but Sufficient Estimates

The team defined all new work as features, attempting as best as possible to stick to the agile definition. In addition to features, the team needs to identify, complete, and resolve both defects and issues.

Because of the fluid environment of the project and the difficulty in estimating non-feature bits of work, it was decided that specific estimates would be unrealistic. Too often, we concluded, the estimates would not be made by the same person who would complete the task. Since the different individuals flowing into and out of the project had varying levels of skill and experience with the technology, specific estimates (such as half a day) could not be counted upon. Instead, the team chose to use a very simple system of estimation based on five values:

Tiny: Work that would take less than an hour.

Small: Work that would take less than a day.

Medium: Work that would take less that a week.

Large: Work that would take less than a month.

Huge: Work that would take more than a month.

These labels allowed everyone on the team to quickly grasp the level of effort behind each task without conveying the sense of unrealism that might be associated with a specific number of hours or days.

The Wall Work Queue

The team had one significant thing going for it: No matter who constituted its membership during any given week, the members sat within the same large workspace. Iterations, a collaborative customer, and dedicated team members are all things that we did not have, but we did have an open workspace. The team also had an issue management database that it was required to use to track new features, defects, and issues. We used this in tandem with a big, empty, white wall that framed one side of the open workspace.

Because we never knew how much time the team would be able to put toward the project during any given timebox, we devised a wall work queue to manage the team's activity. The framework of the wall work queue consisted of Post-It® notes used to identify four different zones on the wall. These were:

Immediate work: Work estimated as tiny or small and considered urgent.

Short-term: Work estimated as tiny or small and not considered urgent.

Long-term: Work estimated as medium, large, or huge that should be completed.

Hold: Work of any estimated size that had been identified but that should not be worked on currently.

Features, issues, and defects were typically mail merged from the tracking tool onto index cards that were stuck on the wall with tape loops. If a new item came up during the middle of the day, it was written on a Post-It, stuck in the appropriate grouping on the wall, and tracked in the tool later in the day. Figure 14.4 illustrates an example of how the Post-Its and cards are placed on the wall. (See Chapter 11 for more detail on what information is typically kept on these cards.)

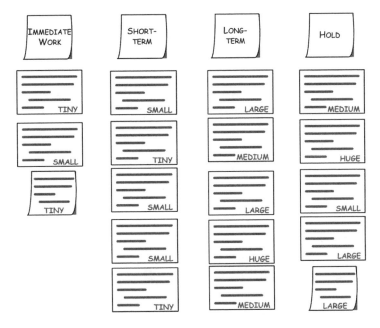

FIGURE 14.4   An example wall work queue.

Whoever was on the team during a given day knew the rules of the wall work queue. Any item under immediate work had first priority and should be completed prior to working on anything else. Any item under short-term could be picked up any time there was no work under immediate work. Items under long-term either had an owner or were waiting to be assigned, and work on these items stopped whenever an item showed up under immediate work. No programmer owned more than one item under long-term at any given time, so there was no question of what long-term item he should return to when all immediate work and short-term items were done.

If a programmer did not know whether to continue on his long-term item or complete an item in the short-term column, he consulted one of the two permanent members of the team, who best understood the team's priorities and current objectives.

As soon as a programmer completed a task, he moved the card out of the work queue and stuck it on a completed zone on another wall. These completed items were recorded in the tracking tool at the end of the day.

The wall work queue has several benefits. First, it provides a very visible, simple, and easy-to-alter plan. Second, it reduces the time it takes programmers to switch between tasks. If someone completes a task and looks up to think about the next thing he needs to do, he is likely to see the cards on the wall, which will serve as an immediate reminder of the plan. There is no need for this individual to have to recall a conversation earlier in the day or have to hunt down one of the permanent members of the team. Third, someone new to the team can quickly acquaint himself with the plan. He does not need to wait for an iteration planning meeting to select a set of tasks or learn to use (and remember to consult) an online tracking system. Fourth, discussions about work items and prioritization can be completed faster because the plan is there for everyone to see, gather around and discuss, and even alter simply by moving a card. Finally, the team has a clear indication of progress on a daily basis. The cards in the first two columns fluctuate regularly as new work flows in and as the team quickly disposes of strings of tiny and small items. This way, the team can see when it needs to get serious about clearing out the immediate work and short-term items and has an immediately visible report of its progress toward such goals.

AGILE PRACTICE: THE TASK CYCLE

The task cycle is a lightweight, one-week-long, iteration-like activity that allows a more agile management process to be inserted into a wide variety of project environments. It is a practice that has been in my toolbox for a couple of years and that other agile teams have landed upon in one fashion or another. It can be embedded within existing project timebox mechanisms such as releases, phases, and iterations of two weeks or more, is meant for smaller teams, although it can be scaled as discussed in Chapter 20, and is driven by one weekly, team-wide meeting.

Purpose and Benefits

Task cycles deliver much of the same benefits as well-executed one-week iterations, while being more versatile. First, they can fit in almost anywhere, such as with a long iteration, a short release, or even a phase- or waterfall-driven plan. Second, the task cycle is very well suited for environments of high change and many unknowns, such as prototyping and working with new technologies. This is because the short duration of each task cycle provides the team with a steady cadence of small, valuable, and near-term goals; frequent assessments of progress; and the opportunity to redirect the priorities of the project on a weekly basis. Finally, the task cycle foments greater communication between the project and the highest levels of management. Since planning is tuned and status is assessed by the entire team on a weekly basis, the task cycle facilitates greater collaboration between the project team and its management. Additionally, it enables better communication with project stakeholders because the result of each completed task cycle—an up-to-date task list—can be quickly converted into a burndown chart or other highly visible progress report.

Detail

The task cycle is similar to many agile notions of an iteration. It may, in fact, be referred to as an iteration and may take the place of an iteration. The element that most distinguishes the task cycle from other agile iterative structures is that it is concerned with completing tasks instead of features. At first this seems to contradict the agile value of always delivering usable features. In fact, the task cycle does not contradict this value; it merely leaves the responsibility of delivering features to the next mechanism of aggregation: an iteration, release, or project phase, which from here on will be referred to as a "release" for the sake of brevity. Figure 14.5 illustrates how the task cycle fits into a variety of release mechanisms.

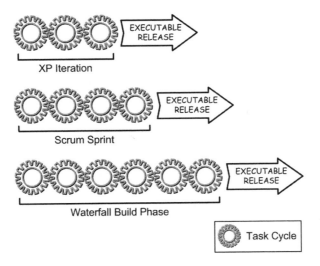

FIGURE 14.5   Fitting the task cycle into a release mechanism.

Task cycles focus on planning and tracking the work that the team has agreed to complete in conjunction with a variety of release-level timeboxing mechanisms. The task cycle is driven by a single meeting that represents the end of one release and the beginning of the next and is typically held in the middle of the week. Figure 14.6 illustrates task cycle activity within an iteration or release.

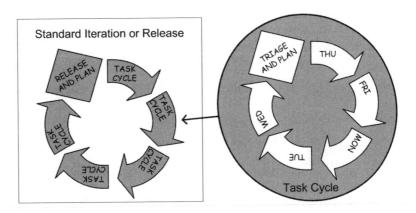

FIGURE 14.6   Task cycle activity within a release mechanism.

The task cycle's weekly meeting is a structured activity based on two distinct activities: task triage and task planning. The entire team attends the meeting, preferably in person but via speaker-phone if necessary. The meeting is coordinated and run by the project manager or team lead. An up-to-date list of all the tasks that need to be completed during the release must be available at the meeting.

Task Triage

This is the portion of the meeting where the previous task cycle is closed out and when the team reports completed work and traps new knowledge. Depending on the size of the team and the peculiarities of a given week, this part of the meeting may take between 5 and 20 minutes. The following activities are performed in order during the meeting:

Step 1: Close Out the Tasks in the Current Task Cycle

The team goes through the list of queued tasks for the task cycle being closed and records the status of the task as either completed or not completed. Like many other agile timeboxing approaches, credit is not given in terms of percent-complete. However, when a task has been started but not completed, the task owner is given the opportunity to provide a new estimate for the task based on how much work is left to be done. Sometimes this new estimate may be higher that the original estimate, indicating that the task owner has progressed far enough to learn that the task was initially underestimated.

The team should not assume that a task that was not completed in the present task cycle must be queued for completion in the next, because the priorities, based on both business demands and technical risk, can change from one week to the next. An incomplete task should be queued into the next task cycle only if the team is certain that there is nothing more urgent that could bump that task out of the plan for the coming week.

Step 2: Identify Any Tasks That Were Not Planned but Were Completed

Sometimes, for a variety of reasons, a task that had not been queued for a task cycle gets done anyway. This may be due to a previously unknown dependency, a programmer who was more efficient than planned, or someone taking the opportunity to knock out an easy task while completing a related activity. Regardless of how it occurred, the task needs to be marked as complete.

Step 3: Remove Tasks That No Longer Need to Be Completed

Because of business or technical reasons, some tasks simply turn out to not need to be done. Often a requirement is refined out or a programmer realizes that the design of a given feature can be simplified so that the technical activity related to one or more tasks is no longer necessary.

Step 4: Add New Tasks to the List

And then there are the requirements that get refined in and the technical tasks that no one thought about at the beginning of the release.

Step 5: Refine Estimates

This is the last step in capturing the knowledge. If the team learned something during the current task cycle that affected his estimate of a task that has not already been discussed, it should be brought up, and the task should be given a new estimate.

Task Planning

This is the portion of the task cycle weekly meeting when the team queues up work for the new task cycle. Like the triage activity, this portion of the meeting should take between 5 and 20 minutes.

Step 6: Determine the Amount of Time Available in the New Task Cycle

As noted earlier in this chapter, when the steps to be taken during the iteration planning meeting were discussed, any number of variables can affect the total amount of time the entire team has available to work on tasks, including holidays, individual vacations, training activities, and responsibilities to other projects. Therefore, the amount of time available for work should not be taken as a given and should be reaffirmed at the beginning of each cycle.

Step 7: Determine the Goal of the New Task Cycle

Identifying a task cycle goal is similar to identifying an iteration goal, with the potential for less customer involvement and minus the requirement to complete an entire feature. Potential goals may include tackling the riskiest and least well-known tasks, queuing up and removing dependency tasks, and completing all the tasks for one or more user stories.

In practice, teams should first identify and attack the tasks that are the riskiest and have the least certain estimates. In doing this, the team will reap one of the major benefits of task cycles, the ability to prioritize and address risks early (and uncertain estimates are definite risks). This way, the activities that are most likely to affect the outcome of the release will be performed early in the release, the extent of their impact will be known early, and the project will be able to react sooner instead of later.

When the team feels confident about its ability to complete the remaining tasks at something near their estimates, it should turn to completing features. This should be done for the same reasons that features are completed during iterations, as discussed earlier. Nonetheless, it is worth remembering that completing all the tasks related to a feature may not mean that the feature is complete. Any acceptance criteria for the feature must also be taken into account, such as the passing of acceptance tests or user review and sign-off, and these activities may be included under the feature as specific tasks.

Step 8: Select the Tasks for Development

After a goal for the task cycle has been identified, this should be a relatively straightforward activity.

Step 9: Determine the Owner of Each Active Task

Not every project team will need to complete this step. Teams that employ class ownership will likely already know who will complete each task, and this would have been factored into the selection of tasks. Nonetheless, as is the case with features and iterations, specific owners should agree to take ownership of each task in the task cycle.

Implementation

For agile project teams or non-agile teams that have already adopted certain agile practices, transitioning to task cycles should be rather painless.

If the project is already using short iterations or small releases and already has a list of features broken into tasks for the current release, then it can easily transition to task cycles. The only question for this project team is whether to embed task cycles into its existing iterative approach or replace its longer iterations with more frequent task cycles. Two-week iterations, for example, may be easily replaced with weekly task cycles. Four-week iterations that result in production deployments, meanwhile, should have task cycles embedded into them.

A project team that is feature and iteration driven will simply need to break its features for each release into tasks to begin using task cycles.

If Project Work Is Not Organized into Features

If the project team is not using features (or a feature equivalent, such as user stories or use cases) to trap requirements, perhaps it should adopt this practice first. Features provide thumbnail sketches of the system in development that help the entire project visualize its different aspects and goals, and an efficiently run string of task cycles will guarantee only the steady completion of tasks, not useable features or a system that delivers value to its user.

If for whatever reason the project team cannot use features but has a list of tasks identified, it may still employ task cycles, notwithstanding the reservations just expressed. In this case, the project will need to define and estimate all of its work for the current release into tasks. These tasks can then be fed into task cycles.

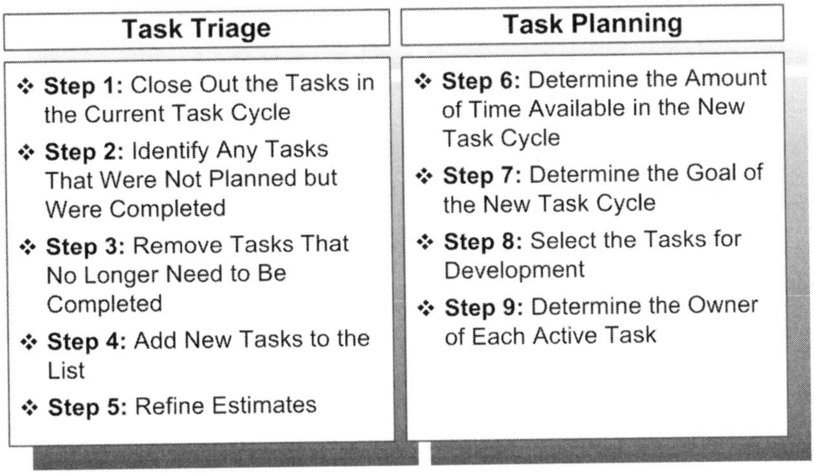

Task Triage	Task Planning
❖ **Step 1:** Close Out the Tasks in the Current Task Cycle ❖ **Step 2:** Identify Any Tasks That Were Not Planned but Were Completed ❖ **Step 3:** Remove Tasks That No Longer Need to Be Completed ❖ **Step 4:** Add New Tasks to the List ❖ **Step 5:** Refine Estimates	❖ **Step 6:** Determine the Amount of Time Available in the New Task Cycle ❖ **Step 7:** Determine the Goal of the New Task Cycle ❖ **Step 8:** Select the Tasks for Development ❖ **Step 9:** Determine the Owner of Each Active Task

FIGURE 14.7   Activities during the task cycle planning meeting.

Opportunities and Obstacles

The task cycle is meant to be very versatile, so there are several ways it might be adapted and altered on-the-fly to address a changing project environment.

Vary the Duration of the Cycle to Fit External Factors

Holidays, vacations, and other duties can reduce the time of a task cycle to the point at which it would be difficult to guarantee the completion of many tasks. For example, the American Thanksgiving holiday typically entails a four-day weekend for the entire team, even before people begin using their vacation days to turn it into either a five-day weekend or a one-week vacation. Additionally, on small projects, the extended absence of two or more individuals due to vacation time, extended training sessions, or the completion of other duties can have a similar effect. Finally, members of the business such as the customer, users, and domain experts may have duties to perform or other obligations that influence the timing of iterations. For example, many accounting groups need to spend several days at the end of each month or quarter performing reconciliation activities and may not be available to provide detail on features or even answer questions. Under any of these circumstances, it makes sense to schedule a cycle of two weeks duration. Typically, there will be no change in the nature of the meeting or the way the project operates over the extended cycle.

There Is Not a Sufficient Amount of Work to Plan a New Task Cycle

Because task cycles assume that functionality has already been selected for development via a larger iteration or release, the problem of not having enough work to plan a new task cycle will typically result when the majority of remaining tasks are blocked by external dependencies. Assuming the team has been using task cycles throughout the release, they should have seen this coming for a couple of weeks. Of course, in some project environments, issues like these are not dealt with until they rise to the level of an emergency.

One mitigation technique that may do some good is for the team to sketch out a simple task dependency chart in order to identify the tasks that are being blocked by external factors and the other tasks that may be backed up behind those blocked tasks. For example, a blocked task to finish capturing the low-level requirements on a given feature will block the majority of other tasks related to that feature. Simply by performing the activity, the team may realize that some tasks it assumed were dependent upon other blocked tasks may in fact be worked on.

Next, the team can identify the highest-value blocked tasks. These are the tasks that block the largest amount of estimated work and that may be most easily un-blocked. The team can then focus its attention on unblocking those specific tasks. Sometimes there are specific things the team can do to remove or overcome the ex-ternal dependency. For example, if the team is waiting on a component from an-other team, it might mock up that component instead. This might not be an ideal solution, but after reviewing its options the team may determine that the possibil-ity of some rework is preferable to the certainty of no work.

Finally, the project manager or team lead may take the results of the dependency analysis to a stakeholder or other individual with some authority. Instead of simply announcing "We're stuck," the project manager can explain: "The team is blocked here, here, and here. We've done some thinking, and if you can help us here by talk-ing to this person, we will be able to move forward with another two weeks of work. By then, these other blocked issues should have resolved themselves." It should be obvious which presentation is going to elicit more help for the team.

Switch to Daily Cycles for Short Periods of High Change

During certain periods, a week of planning can actually be too long. Such periods may include extensive testing sessions, such as system integration and acceptance testing, or periods when there is a high level of change. At such times, it is understandable that a project team might not be able to predict the nature of work even one week out; however, to be clear, this should not be the norm. In such cases the team may revert to brief meetings on cycles on a daily basis. These meetings should not last more than 10 to 15 minutes and may resemble a stand up or daily Scrum meeting.

Merge the Task List with the Project's Issue List

Maintaining one document is typically easier than two. Additionally, issues often arise out of weekly meetings when the task list is actively being worked. All issues on a project that is executing task cycles may fit nicely into the task list as point-one tasks (discussed earlier in this chapter). They may be tracked just like any other task and queued for an iteration, tracked as part of a release, or put off for attention in a later release.

STARTING MONDAY: BEGIN ITERATING[1]

Iterations and task cycles are very flexible. They do not need to be implemented within any particular release mechanism or even on a particularly agile project, keeping in mind, of course, that the true benefit of agile practices comes when they begin to feed on one another. Frequent, short, iterations correctly implemented will almost certainly benefit a project team that is working with no real schedule or a team that has a full-scale WBS but no understanding of how to stick to it.

In order to implement an iterative approach a project team must, at the very least, have:

- Selected and agreed upon an iterative mechanism such as two-week iterations, a 30-day sprint, task cycles, or a wall work queue.
- All the work for the near future (for example, through to an upcoming release) defined as features, user stories, or tasks.
- Estimates for all the near-term work.

Adopting iterations then depends on the state of the project team's current work schedule or lack thereof. If a project team has a fixed scope or duration but no formal project plan, it should readily be able to switch to an iterative approach. In that case, a project will need only to agree upon or identify the items just listed. It can then begin experimenting with an iterative approach.

If a project must follow traditional development phases and there is little likelihood of getting that restriction repealed, the project has several options. First, the project might be able to run iterations within the phases. Task cycles might best be adapted to fit this approach. Second, the project might reduce the size of the define, design, and test phases so that the low-level activities from those phases can be performed in an extended, iteration-laden build phase. This means the project still has to perform some amount of upfront work, but it should also be able to transition to iterative development after a short period of time. Third, the project may consider adopting FDD or some variation of it. The methodology stipulates some upfront define and design activities and may be a good fit in this situation (see Chapter 3 for more information on FDD).

Lastly, if a project team has a strict WBS and a customer or manager making them stick to it, the one option the project may have available is to keep two sets of books. First, based on my own firsthand experience, this really can happen in very heavy process environments. Second—and just to be clear—there is nothing disingenuous in the practice of keeping two sets of books. No one is trying to cheat the IRS or even his customer. However, if the upper management or the business requires a regularly updated WBS, especially if it needs to be maintained in a specific tool, and cannot be talked out of it, the project team has little choice but to use this option if it still wants to use an iterative approach.

The approach is simple and typically arduous for no one but the project manager. Essentially, the project manager completes a detailed WBS at the outset of the project that represents his best guess at how the project will be performed and is completed to a level of detail sufficient to what is needed (and not a single line more). At the same time, the project manager completes a list of features for the team to actually use during the project. The team follows an agile management and programming approach with the features in as much as is possible, and the project manager makes all the changes necessary to the WBS to keep it in sync with what is actually occurring in the project.

So the project team has two sets of books. The first set of books is for the team so that it can operate with a more agile planning tool. The second set of books is for upper management or the business or whoever absolutely needs to see a regularly updated WBS. Both books say the same thing, just in different ways. Think of it as double-entry accounting with a twist.

15 The Customer

In This Chapter

- Who Is the Customer?
- An Agile Approach to the Customer
- Getting a Customer
- Challenging Customers
- Agile Practice: Onsite Customer
- Starting Monday: Build a Closer Relationship with Your Customer

Traditionally, the analysis and requirements definition for a project is completed by or with the help of the users and stakeholders, and the development team is left alone to get the system built on time. Then the users and stakeholders reengage at some point during the testing phase, only after the system has been completed, to ensure that the system has been built to do what was needed and that it does so in a quality manner. This process could sum up the lifetime of a one-month or even two-year project following a traditional software approach.

Agile development calls for the customer to be available throughout the project lifecycle. This does not mean that the customer needs to sit with the project every minute of every workday, although there are benefits to this approach, as are discussed in this chapter, but the customer must be sufficiently present or available to perform the following duties:

- Represent the interests of the business, users, and stakeholders
- Help drive an iterative planning process
- Assist with requirements refinement issues as they arise

The customer is the most important person in agile development. He has different names, depending on what agile methodology is being used and from which side you are viewing him. XP uses the term *customer*. Scrum calls this individual the product owner, and DSDM calls him the *ambassador user*. Crystal Clear has two roles that together act as the customer: the *ambassador user* and the *executive sponsor*. Although they have different names and can take somewhat different roles in each methodology, these are all the same person or group of people. In this chapter we will discuss who the customer really is, how to engage him, and how to work with him to produce a better system.

WHO IS THE CUSTOMER?

In this book and across agile development, the customer has two very common manifestations. It is important to understand the difference.

The Traditional Customer

This customer is the one that we will not be discussing in this chapter.

This is the client, the company, the CEO, the stakeholders, the users, the business, and everyone else the project is trying to please by doing a good job. When someone shrugs and says, "He's the customer," this is typically the person being referred to. This customer is important, and we want him or them or it to like us because he/they/it pay the bills and decide whether or not to retain our services.

Someone who is not working as a consultant, contractor, or vendor may not refer to this entity as the customer. Rather, someone else might say "the business" or perhaps even "my boss."

The Agile Customer

This is the customer we will discuss in this chapter.

As noted previously, the agile methodologies have varying names and specific duties for this customer, but the role can be generalized (and idealized) as an individual who:

- Understands the purpose of the system both as a user and from a more strategic, organizational level
- Is regularly available to the team
- Is empowered and willing to make decisions

A customer could be more than one person and does not need to be able to make all decisions without consulting colleagues or supervisors. The customer could be a group of individuals who work with one another to speak with one voice. The customer could also be a person who has little decision-making authority himself but is highly effective at getting various parties within the traditional customer to come together and make the tough decisions for the team. (This may be a good way to describe the average Scrum product owner.)

Ultimately, whether one or more persons, whether empowered or simply a very effective facilitator, the customer needs to be able to deliver coherent, actionable, and usually correct answers in a timely manner.

AN AGILE APPROACH TO THE CUSTOMER

A good customer collaborating with a good development team can significantly increase the success of a project [Cockburn04]. The benefits can span across many of the team's activities. First, the continuous involvement of the customer in the team's activity results in a superior and more accurate trapping of user requirements within code. This saves time for everyone over the long run because users will need to file very few do-over requests during the testing phase and after deployment.

Second, customer-driven agile planning all but ensures that only the relevant functionality goes into the system instead of a plan or contract dictating a laundry list of functionality, any item of which may or may not really be relevant. This means that the most important functionality gets to the users first, and the functionality that has grown irrelevant gets buried. Once again, less time is expended by the team, and more value is delivered to the users.

Finally, superfluous analysis activity is reduced if feature and requirement definition is performed only when it is most relevant, days or even moments before the code is written. When a programmer sits down with a customer days before coding a feature, activity is reduced on two fronts. On front one, time is not lost trapping information in a document for the sole purpose of storing it for three months until a programmer who was not on the team when the document was created can pull it from a shared drive and code it. On front two, no time is lost on features that are not coded because the features were never queued for development, so no one ever took the time to refine the requirements.

Let's revisit that last sentence just to clarify a point. In agile development, a team performs the analysis and requirement definition on a feature only after it is certain that the feature will be needed and only immediately before it is actually programmed. This means that even if an agile project is required to create the same level of documentation as a traditionally minded project, the agile team will still take less time because it will never spend the effort documenting features that do not make it into the code. Of course, to operate in this fashion, the project needs to have a good customer assigned to it.

Finally, in agile development, the team's ability to communicate with the customer regularly and the customer's physical proximity to the team really do matter.

For a customer to be most useful, a member of the team should be able to locate him, pose a question, and receive an answer in a timely manner. Furthermore, Agilists value face-to-face conversations. There is a lot of communication that just does not transmit over a phone line, much less e-mail.

GETTING A CUSTOMER

An agile-minded project may gain a customer either by strengthening the lines of communication with the business representative a team already has or by helping the business identify and provide a customer for the team.

A project typically will not get a customer without asking for one and then explaining why it wants one and how he would provide a benefit and then explaining the same thing again to two or three more people. Anyone requesting to have an agile customer assigned to a project should be clear about what he is requesting. Nearly any project can benefit from having an individual available who can provide quick explanations and decisions on the inevitable gaps between requirements. For a customer to be truly useful, it should take less effort for a programmer to locate him and ask a question than it would take for that programmer to dream up a solution. Projects following a traditional software development approach may not be ready for a customer willing to queue up functionality by iteration or even release. A customer who has come to know the nature and capabilities of a good team may help convey the benefits of agile planning to the powers that be.

What to Look For in a Customer

The qualities to look for in a customer are these:

- Knows the business domain
- Understands and appreciates the objectives of the project
- Has sufficient time to work with the project
- Has a history with and is respected by the business, users, and stakeholders
- Can assist the business, users, and stakeholders in making decisions
- Is authorized to and capable of making informed decisions
- Is not afraid to take responsibility for his decisions
- Is willing to compromise and is not a perfectionist
- Has some political savvy

A project may not get everything on this list. In an agile project environment, it will be possible to get most or all of these attributes in a customer. In a traditional project environment where a customer is being assigned to a project team, that team may consider itself fortunate if the assigner earnestly considers all these attributes, no matter the end result.

Boehm and Turner provide a useful and amusing acronym for an effective customer, calling him a CRACK performer. Such an individual is Collaborative, Representative, Authorized, Committed, and Knowledgeable [Boehm04].

Distance Matters

All agile methodologies call for a customer who is engaged in the project and easily accessible to the team, but some methodologies take this desire for an accessible customer to the extreme. Specifically, XP calls for the team's customer to be located in the same physical space as the team itself. In *Extreme Programming Installed*, Jeffries, Anderson, and Hendrickson provide an excellent illustration of the benefit of this practice:

> One day on Ron's last visit, the customers had to get to another work site for machine access. They told the programmers where they were (two floors down and a few offices over), and left their phone number and beeper number. Sure enough, in the afternoon, someone had one of those questions. But the programmer knew Pam wasn't there. He didn't call her—instead, he guessed about the code and wrote a note to ask her later. [Jeffries00]

Just to reiterate, the programmer knew where the customer was. He has the customer's phone number and beeper that the customer left for him to use in just such a scenario. He guessed anyway. How many of those guesses do programmers forget to follow up on? How many of those guesses, do you suppose, make it into the average project release?

Obviously, many projects will simply never be able to get a customer located with the team. This is not a requirement of any agile methodology. Even XP understands that it must be foregone at times.

The actual implementation of this XP-inspired agile practice, an onsite customer, is discussed later in this chapter.

Does the Team Have the Right Customer?

Once the project team has a customer, the team should make sure it has the right customer. This is not akin to looking a gift horse in the mouth. The right customer is one who truly speaks for the users, the business, and the stakeholders and provides the project the information it needs to build the correct system and satisfy the business, users, and stakeholders. Disastrous consequences can occur if the team's customer is not who he seems to be.

An acquaintance of mine was a programmer on a team that was doing the requirements analysis on a project for a nationally respected newspaper's online division. The project manager was a well-spoken advocate of agile development and spoke at length to a couple of business managers about the benefits of agile development. The business managers agreed that for the design and development phases of the project the team should head off in a more agile direction. The output of the analysis phases was to be a high-level requirements document and a proposal (including cost estimate) for completing the design and development of the system. Based on his conversations with the business managers and their recommendations, the project manager directed the team to produce and then delivered a requirements document composed of user stories and an agile-minded proposal with a cost estimate for only the first three months and with a price tag for the following 15 months. The project manager delivered the documents through the business managers to the company's upper management, who flatly rejected the proposal. The vendor lost the client, and some months later learned that one of the big consulting firms was at the paper redoing the analysis on the same system.

In this case, the project manager failed to confirm that the business managers he had connected with so well sufficiently represented his customer. As it turned out, there were other business managers who were concerned about the prospect of an agile process, whose voices the project manager had not heard. When upper management consulted with all the business managers, they heard these concerns clearly. Furthermore, upper management wanted a fixed price proposal and was entirely unprepared to receive any open-ended cost structure. Whether the two agile-minded business managers failed to communicate this to the project manager or whether he simply failed to hear it is not known. Nonetheless, the project manager either never considered or did not sufficiently investigate the acceptability of the cost structure in his proposal. Ultimately, he incorrectly identified his customer, and the consequences were severe.

This experience may describe an extreme situation, but it goes to show how things can go wrong when a project manager or team mistakenly assumes the validity of a customer or the information being received from him. This should not be misinterpreted as an admonishment to a project team to second-guess its customer. Rather, agile development is founded on trust. However, if a team's customer is newly assigned or newly found or information has been presented to the team that just does not sync, then that team should perform some due diligence. It should speak with some of the users and stakeholders and someone in the business. Ultimately, the team needs to make sure the lines of communication between its customer and those individuals are intact and operating correctly.

If a project team discovers that it does not have the right customer, this is actually good news. This means that the team has recognized a significant pitfall in its path before falling into it (at least before falling fully into it).

CHALLENGING CUSTOMERS

There are tough customers that you can't work with, and then there are challenging customers who may be challenging through no fault of their own that you can work with.

Customers a Team Cannot Work With

Some customers are tough because it is in their nature. Regardless of whether they are intentionally obnoxious or just oblivious, some tough customers are just pushy, bossy, manipulative, non-collaborative, duplicitous, and just not good people. This is an abusive customer. A project team may do what they can to try to work with him. The project manager may try to appeal to his better side. Then the manager may try to get him replaced. In the end, something must be done to change or replace this individual. At the very least, he is a team morale problem waiting to happen. At the worst, he will be the single greatest reason for project failure.

Some tough customers are not abusive but are still all but impossible to work with. At a very large client, one of my project teams was assigned an information manager (IM) whose sole responsibility was to stand on the fence between IT and the business and act as the conduit for communication between the two groups, who were allowed to communicate only in the presence of the IM. This IM seemed to have some understanding of the true meaninglessness of his job, since he took an even more conservative cut at the rules and disallowed any communication between the project team and the business. At the same time, it became clear that the IM was ineffectively communicating the needs of the business, and it took days to get even simple questions answered. Finally, the project team chose to take action. The IM was wined and dined to no effect, and then the IT manager was consulted, getting sympathy, but no action. Finally, after nearly six months, the team connected with the business manager, who expressed surprisingly similar frustrations with the IM. An alliance was formed. The business manager met with the team and made her direct reports available to the programmers as necessary. Both groups conspired (an ugly word but necessary) to prioritize features, refine requirements, and keep one another apprised of status. Because the IM's office was located in a different building two miles away, he was never the wiser.

Customers a Team Can Work With

Other customers are tough because, maybe through no fault of their own, they are unable to provide an agile team with some of the basic things it would expect from a customer. Perhaps this customer has too much on his plate, perhaps he is located in a different state, or perhaps he knows nothing about the application. This individual may simply have been handed the responsibility, and there is no way of getting out of it. Hopefully he is interested in doing the job and making the best of an imperfect situation. At the very least, he may know his responsibilities and work with the team as much as he can. This is a tough customer the team can work with.

The Know-Nothing Customer

An amicable and competent customer who knows little to nothing about the application that is being built but was assigned to the team anyway is a bit like a blank slate. He can be as good as the project team makes him. This means an investment of effort from the project manager and analysts and maybe the programmers. If this individual has a desire to learn and is not too burdened with other responsibilities, he may become a true asset to the team.

There is one caveat. To be a true value to the team, the know-nothing customer need to have or be capable of quickly building a good relationship with the system's users and stakeholders and be able to work with those individuals to provide direction and answer questions for the project team.

If the know-nothing customer can bring the users and stakeholders to the table and is willing to give the team perhaps a day of his time every week, then the rest is up to the project team. The team will need to mentor this customer in the important aspects of the system and include him in discussions regarding the system's features, requirements and, potentially, high-level design. As with so many other things in agile development, this process may initially slow down the project, but its result—a well-connected, knowledgeable customer with an excellent rapport with the team—may become invaluable.

The Limited-Time Customer

This customer probably has a vested interest in the work the project is doing and wants to collaborate with the team and make the right decisions, but he is overburdened with work and has only a very limited amount of time every week to work with the team. If this individual recognizes the value of working with the team on an ongoing basis, as opposed to providing all of his input upfront and seeing only status reports until the system is complete, then you should be able to work with him.

Working with a limited-time customer on a simple project might not be too tough. A good, straightforward strategy is to appoint a member of the team (project manager, analyst, or possibly a programmer) to represent the customer to the team. This person should have a solid understanding of the domain and will filter requests and questions to the limited-time customer, addressing what he can on the spot and sorting out the rest with the customer offline. Finally, make sure the customer attends planning meeting and is prepared and willing to select the features to be developed for each iteration (if this is required of him) and release new code to him as often as he will let you [Jeffries00].

Another possibility on a relatively simple project that may be used in tandem with a team member who represents the customer is to send one or more team members to train on the system. Using this approach, team members may shadow users or become apprentice users for a period. While there is not a lot of data on this approach, anecdotal evidence suggests it provides a better understanding of the users and the way the project will affect them [Cockburn04].

To work with a limited-time customer on a complex project, the team will need to do all of the low-level (and possibly even high-level) analysis and research for him. This may mean pulling in domain experts to assist the team. If the team has the time to spare, it may mean having one or more people book up on the domain. It may mean dropping into a more traditional requirements-gathering mode at the onset of the project or prior to each iteration. In addition, team members may have to hold meetings with multiple users to get the information they need to complete one feature.

The project team requires the following of the limited-time customer:

- The selection of features to be completed before each iteration
- The ability to identify individuals within the organization who know the requirements for each feature
- The authority to make those individuals available to the team
- Quick answers for the most urgent questions

If the customer has requested a feature, appointed the user or users who know how to define it, and makes himself available to handle true roadblocks, then an agile team can develop features in nearly the same fashion as it would with most any other customer. That is, it will be able to refine the requirements of the feature and implement it in the code in a single iteration.

One of my projects worked successfully with a team of customers like this. The project was rebuilding the enterprise reporting system for a medium-size corporation. Our customers were the directors or assistant directors of the different divisions that would use the reports. They were all smart and competent people with lots of drive and responsibility and willing to work together and make tradeoffs and tough decisions, but they had little time for us. While the team was following XP practices, its overall approach better resembled the five-phase approach of FDD. The team brought on two additional analysts and interviewed the users in each division to define a list of requirements based on their input. This process took a couple of weeks, and its result was a list containing system features and groups of reports for the system. Each item on this list of work carried a rough estimate and enough of a description to make it clear what it was, why it was important, and who it was important to. We then began iterative development, meeting with the customers two days before the beginning of each iteration so that they could reprioritize the list of work, queue items for development, and advise the appropriate users to make themselves available to the team for that iteration. Occasionally a feature slipped because the user was not able to find time for the team soon enough, but this was not the norm, and the customers were happy to trade this occasional slippage for the direction they were able to provide to the team.

The Remote Customer

Working with a customer that the project team rarely (or never) meets face-to-face can be similar to working with a limited-time customer. Though the team may get more of a remote customer's time (several hours a week instead of one or two), it will still need to prepare and package a lot of things for him. In addition, one thing the team will get less of (and this will matter) is face-to-face communication.

Because communication is always handled over e-mail, telephone, or video conference, it may take longer to build a rapport with this customer. In addition, here are a few recommendations regarding regular interaction with a remote customer:

- Be proactive with communication. Think ahead about what will be discussed with the customer before calling.
- Realize that direct questions and honest answers may be necessary to compensate for an inability to express nonverbal cues [Wallace02].
- Plan on misunderstandings due to the media used for communication. To compensate for this, maintain a regular communication schedule and be wary of a lack of communication [Jeffries00].

Whatever a project team does, it should make sure to keep the communication flowing.

The Non-Committal Customer

Sometimes a customer seems to refuse to commit to enough work in a timely enough manner to keep the team moving or has a pattern of changing his mind after having made a decision. Such a customer can be one of the trickiest to deal with. The first thing to do with a customer like this, however, is to make sure the team simply is not dealing with a limited-time customer in disguise. If the team spent more time performing analysis and digesting issues prior to engaging the customer, would he be more willing and able to make the required decisions? It is worth keeping in mind that, unfortunately, not every limited-time customer is going to announce that he is not making decisions simply because he lacks the time to educate himself on every subject and issue. Sometimes the team will need to figure this out on its own.

The next thing to consider is whether this indecisiveness is a short-term or long-term problem. If it is short term and related more to the situation and less to the particular customer, there are strategies discussed in Chapter 14, "Executing Iterative Development," in the section "Not Enough Work to Fill an Iteration," that may help the project through this rough patch.

Finally, if the customer really does seem to have a problem with commitment, there is no right answer for this predicament other than having him replaced. If the customer has no problem identifying the things he wants done but simply refuses to work within an iterative structure, the team might implement a wall work queue, as explained in Chapter 14. The team will be less effective working without an iterative timebox, but it may remove the regular struggle associated with hunting and gathering for work. Another option may be for the project manager to identify the stakeholders of the project and bring them into the planning process and meetings. This will be a less than perfect scenario because the project team may then end up with a collective customer who speaks with more than one voice, but again, it may be better than operating a project with constant indecision.

AGILE PRACTICE: ONSITE CUSTOMER

So much documentation stems from having to store requirements that are teased out of the user's head until the programmer can get around to writing them as code months later. More time is lost correcting the guesses programmers make about what needs to be filled into the gaps between requirements when there is no domain expert to ask. More time still is lost because programmers could not conceive of tests that resembled the realities of the production environment. And even more time may be lost when the project deploys a release to the users and, based on that release, the users realize that the project needs to deviate from the plan in the very next iteration, but no one tells the project team. What if you could stuff all these impediments into a box, slap a stick of dynamite on it, and send it to oblivion?

An onsite customer will not do this for a project team, but it could get the team as much as halfway there.

Purpose and Benefits

Besides the general and significant time savings that result from having an onsite customer, there are three main benefits. First is expert steering of the project based on customer feedback and the latest changes in business climate. Second, questions about requirements are either settled on the spot or given to a person (the customer) who has a vested interest in seeing them answered promptly. Third, lower defect rates can be achieved, based on the existence of tests that replicate the real use of the system in production.

Prerequisites

The onsite customer practice has three requirements:

- An agile-minded team with big plans and the discipline and determination to get it where it wants to go.
- A project team that is located within the same physical space. Better yet is a team that has implemented an open workspace environment (see the agile practice in Chapter 17, "Communication and Collaboration").
- A willing customer.

Implementation

To prepare for the onsite customer practice, a project team will require the following ingredients:

> **One customer:** Consult the section "What to Look for in a Customer" earlier in this chapter. And this needs to the real McCoy—he needs to really represent the interests and interested parties of the traditional customer.
>
> **A slice of the customer's workweek:** Being an onsite customer is real work. The project can negotiate the size of the slice based on its needs and the graciousness of the traditional customer.
>
> **A desk for the customer in your workspace:** Yes, he is moving in with the project team, although he is allowed to bring his work with him.

The customer simply interacts with the team exactly as he would if he were not sitting right alongside them, but he does a lot more of it. The customer is immediately available to field any question about requirements, he knows exactly the progress of the team so he can better direct it at the onset of every iteration, and he has been allocated additional time to mull over and write the acceptance tests (see this practice in Chapter 8, "Testing") that will keep most defects from escaping the programmer's pen.

Opportunities and Obstacles

This whole chapter could have been titled "Taking Baby Steps to Get to an Onsite Customer." Consult the earlier sections in this chapter for the tips, tricks, and words of caution on this practice.

STARTING MONDAY: BUILD A CLOSER RELATIONSHIP WITH YOUR CUSTOMER

Does your project team have a real customer? If so, are you taking advantage of his time and knowledge in the best way possible? If your team does not have a customer, is there one or more individuals (a user, stakeholder, or business manager) with whom your team has a good rapport and works with on a regular basis? Is the absence of anyone resembling a customer the single biggest factor impeding your team from being more agile? Regardless of what sort of customer your project team has (or does not have), is there a way you could establish a closer relationship that would benefit everyone?

The project team will likely need to make the first step in building a closer relationship with its customer.

16   Reviewing and Reporting Progress

As discussed in the section on continuous evaluation in Chapter 10, "Agile Management," agile projects rely on two essential forms of feedback: those derived from metrics and those that come from people. This chapter describes several varied techniques recommended by agile methodologies and used by agile projects both to track progress through the collection of metrics and to monitor the state of the team by conducting reviews.

TRACKING PROGRESS

The charts and reports discussed in this section may help the team lead or project manager assess the progress of the project with minimal time and hassle. They may, for example, indicate whether the project is on time or roughly measure the overall quality of the code. Good metrics have a nasty habit of making bad news almost impossible to miss. But is it not better to know about bad news early, when something can be done about it?

These techniques have other benefits as well. They may be used, for example, to explain to the customer and management how an event or new process affects the progress of the project. If something helps to boost productivity, it should be seen as a sudden shift in the level of progress. If an event or new process adversely affects the team's productivity, it will be clearly illustrated in a progress chart as a drop in productivity.

Work Remaining

In Chapter 14, "Executing Iterative Development," we discussed tracking progress within an iteration using burndown charts. The work remaining chart is a similar style of chart that may be used to track progress over an entire release (or even a small project). The work remaining chart displays the amount of work a team has to complete at the beginning of each release and should look something like the examples in Figure 16.1.

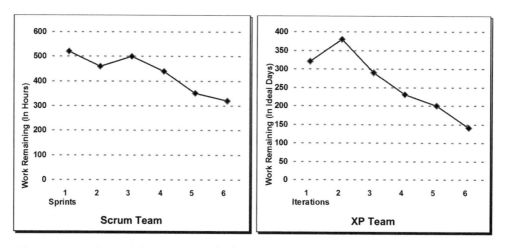

FIGURE 16.1   Example work remaining charts for a Scrum project and an XP release.

Like the burndown chart, the charts in Figure 16.1 depict project teams making steady progress toward an ultimate goal that is only a few iteration or sprints away. Each project had a period when its estimates were revised upward. This likely was the result of one of two situations: Either each project team learned that the work to be performed was more difficult than originally thought or each team agreed to take on additional scope this period.

The work remaining chart is useful for visualizing overall progress toward the completion of a specific goal. For releases and projects where either time or scope is relatively fixed, this chart can also provide an overall indication of the velocity of the team: how much work the team is completing in each iteration and whether that number is consistent over successive iterations. Such information can be useful in determining whether a team will reach its goal for the release or project, deciding how much work the team can take on in an upcoming iteration or sprint, and analyzing whether specific internal or external factors have affected the progress of the team.

The work remaining chart has a significant shortcoming: There is no way to tell why the work line has shifted up or why it is not falling as fast as one might suspect. Were the team's original estimates too low? Did the team agree to additional functionality? Did other external factors reduce the amount of time the team had to spend on the project? These shortcomings will be addressed in the next charts we discuss.

Burn Up Chart

The burn up chart adds a second series of data to the work remaining chart. As illustrated in Figure 16.2, the amount of work actually completed by the team in each iteration or sprint is easily determined by reading the work completed bars at the bottom of the graph.

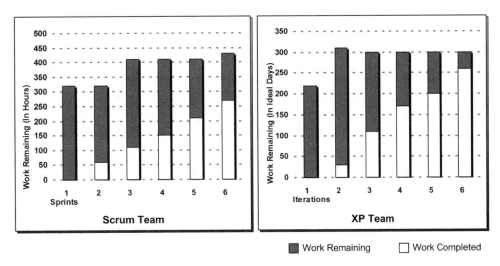

FIGURE 16.2 Example burn up charts for Scrum and XP teams.

The burn up chart more accurately depicts the velocity of a team by separating the amount of work completed and the amount of work remaining in the project. It also illustrates how actual and perceived amounts of work can vary during a project or release by tracking how the total amount of work changes over time. The Scrum project's burn up chart may depict a well-disciplined team churning out functionality while the customer continues to add functionality to the project. Meanwhile, the XP chart shows a project team, probably rather new to agile development, that is still finding its project legs.

Finally, it should be noted that the amount of work remaining does not distinguish between functionality added or removed by the customer and re-estimation by the team. While the chart may be adjusted to include this information by splitting work remaining into two data series, it should be rather apparent to anyone with knowledge of the project whether re-estimation or new functionality caused a shift in work remaining. Furthermore, for project teams that have a policy of not re-estimating features once a release has begun, this is not an issue at all.

Advanced Charts

The burn up chart can be modified to provide additional information for the project team. Also it can be altered to communicate the team's progress more effectively to members of upper management, who do not care about things like velocity or ideal days. An example set of charts that I regularly use on my projects is shown in Figure 16.3.

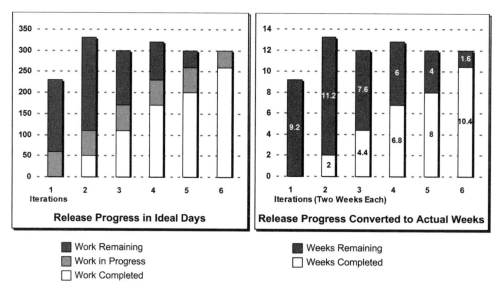

FIGURE 16.3 Advanced burn up chart with a version for upper management.

These two charts are meant for two different sets of people. The one on the left includes a third data series: the actual work in progress at the beginning of the iteration. This allows managers to quickly compare on an iteration-by-iteration basis how much of the work was actually completed in comparison to the amount that was planned. It also allows for a retrospective of the team's velocity. The team in this example has been planning at a steady rate of 50 ideal days per iteration and doing a good job of completing the work as planned, although they hit a snag in iteration five.

When applied to other teams, this chart may show velocity increasing, or velocity decreasing, or a team that consistently plans more than it can do in an iteration.

The chart on the right is meant to be shown to upper management and other individuals who have no specific knowledge of the project or agile processes. This chart is based on the simple progress chart, but the ideal days for each segment have been divided by the team's weekly velocity for the release. (Note that the team in this example is running two-week iterations.) This chart display to managers the same information an agile project may use to determine whether it is on target for a release. Specifically, it shows how many weeks of work the team has remaining, based on the work it has completed thus far. In the example, the project team should be aiming to complete two weeks of work per iteration to be on target. These charts may not matter much to managers when they first see them because anyone can play with numbers to make up a plan that looks good. The charts will begin to mean much more after managers have seen them several iterations in a row, when the team has stated every time how much work it intends to complete and then has to come back with an honest answer. Also, both charts can be shown—and the conversion process can be briefly explained—so that upper management can appreciate the substance behind the summary that they are being provided at the beginning of each iteration.

Charts like the ones in Figure 16.3 can force the team to have some very frank conversations with upper management. This is a good thing, generally speaking. Even when progress does not look good, if the project manager has a good explanation, a good director will give him credit for seeming to have a handle on the situation and give the team time to sort things out.

Tracking Progress Without Hard Estimates[1]

FDD does not estimate work in the same way most other agile projects do. Instead of providing specific estimates, FDD simply groups work into feature sets that can take anywhere from one to two weeks to complete. The upshot is that FDD projects, as well as any other projects that do not use specific estimates for work, do not have specific estimates on features or tasks that they can feed into the charts. FDD solves this issue by setting very specific milestones for each feature, as illustrated in Figure 16.4.

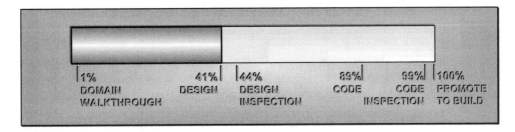

FIGURE 16.4 Measuring milestone-based progress for an FDD feature set.

FDD selects these milestones because they are hard to fib about. For example, either a team has completed its design activities or it has not. FDD determines how complete a feature is, based on the specific percentage associated with the most recent milestone the feature has reached. FDD recommends a specific set of percentages (see Figure 16.4) but advises that these numbers should be altered if a project is aware that an activity consistently takes a different amount of time. The numbers derived from these milestones may then be rolled up to track a project's overall progress within a release or iteration (if this approach has been adopted by a non-FDD team that is following a standard, iterative approach) and to generate charts and reports.

FDD also has a specific approach for producing reports that will be shown to management, often called parking lot diagrams, as illustrated in Figure 16.5.

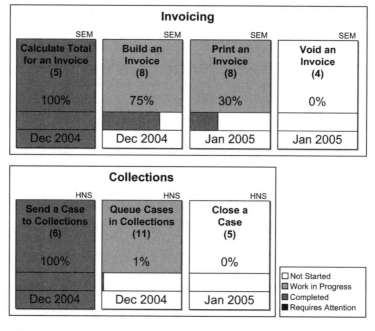

FIGURE 16.5 A management-level report for an FDD project.

FDD employs color to help illustrate progress and highlight areas of concern. For each feature set, yellow indicates that it is in progress, green indicates that it is complete, white means it is not started, and red indicates an issue that requires attention. The initials of the chief programmer who owns each feature set are printed in the top-right corner. This management report can help the project manager and even upper management get a sense of the overall progress of the project, quickly identify what is ahead or behind schedule, and target tasks that are blocked or are otherwise in need of assistance.

Treat Perfect Progress with Suspicion

Estimates are almost never completely on target, technical unknowns pop up out of nowhere, and meetings happen. One thing agile development wholeheartedly accepts is that nothing goes according to plan for long, which is another reason agile projects just keep on planning for short periods.

Perfect progress across multiple iterations or even through the completion of a single long iteration is positively rare (see Figure 16.6 for an example). It has been my fortune to see it happen only once, and that team was cooking the books. It turned out, several iterations farther down the road—after missing its release date by two weeks—that the team in question had not actually completed everything as indicated in their progress report.

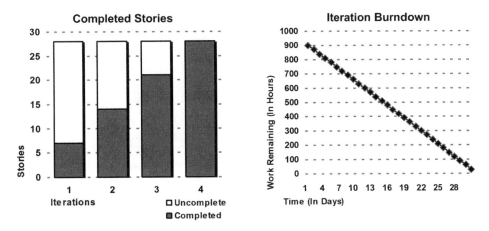

FIGURE 16.6   Examples of perfect progress; don't believe it.

TRACKING OTHER FACTORS

Agile teams often use other metrics to track progress in areas not related to the completion of tasks, features, and user stories. These metrics are typically most beneficial for temporary use to assess and monitor an issue that has already been identified through individual observation. When using a metric to identify and resolve a specific issue, it is important that teams stop generating the metric once the issue has been addressed. As discussed in Chapter 5, "Going Agile," continuing processes beyond the point at which they have already served their purpose can both unnecessarily slow down a team and encourage individuals to focus on goals that do not bring additional value to the team.

Three examples are provided in this section. The first is a metric that some teams will track constantly. The second and third are examples of metrics that should be used only when needed and then discarded.

Total and Passing Acceptance Tests

A very common metric used by agile and non-agile teams alike is the total number of acceptance tests that are run and that pass at the end of each iteration. Traditional project teams may use a similar metric with system tests. The graph produced by this metric may look something like Figure 16.7.

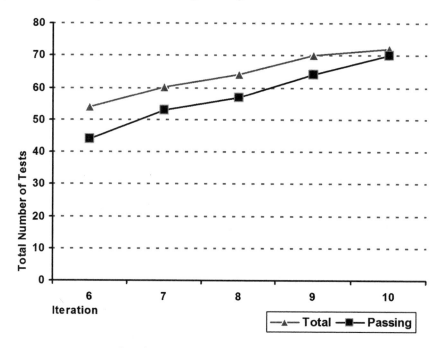

FIGURE 16.7   Total and passing acceptance tests at the end of each iteration.

Depending upon the team, this metric may be temporary or permanent. Teams that do not stipulate that all acceptance tests must pass at the end of every iteration will probably revisit this metric every iteration to ensure that an acceptably small number of acceptance tests are failing. Project teams that require that no feature can be considered complete until it is integrated into the code with all the acceptance tests passing will want to use this metric when the rule has been broken for an iteration or more.

Total Number of Unit Tests

This is a metric that may be useful when a team is just beginning to adopt automated unit testing or when the project manager or team lead recognizes that the team has fallen off the testing bandwagon and needs to climb back on. The metric tracks only one thing: the number of automated unit tests actually run during the last build of the day, as illustrated in Figure 16.8.

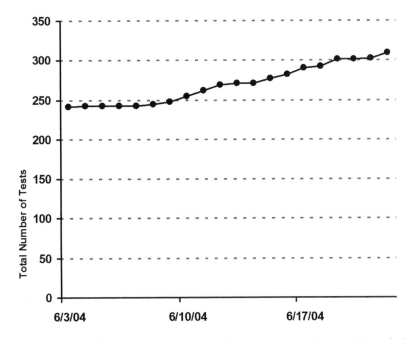

FIGURE 16.8 The total number of running unit tests at the end of each day.

It may not be best to monitor this metric continuously because increasing the number of unit tests in the system is almost never the project team's primary objective. Focus may be put on the issue if the team lead or project manager suspects that programmers are writing a sufficient number of new tests. This is likely to happen on teams that have recently changed over to agile development or teams that have adopted only a handful of practices. If the team is working on new functionality, the project manager can pretty much expect the total number of unit tests to increase. In my experience, once the programmers know that management is watching this number, it will start to trend upward. Of course, the team lead or a senior programmer should confirm that the new tests are testing meaningful functionality.

Estimated Versus Actual Work

A metric that can be of real assistance to programmers is one that shows objectively how their estimates compare to actual work performed. This metric is not one to be used on every project. First, for all the data used in this technique, the programmer who completes a task must be the programmer who estimated that task. Second, actual time for work must be tracked. Third, the technique can be too easily misunderstood in stressful environments as micromanagement. Nonetheless, when used responsibly, the metric can be a powerful technique for helping developers improve their estimates.

The only data required for the technique is the most recent tasks completed by one or more programmers and the actual and estimated hours for each task. The data should be plotted onto a scatter graph, with the estimate of each task following the x-axis and the actual time worked following the y-axis (the axes can be swapped, of course). Then add three lines to the scatter graph: one right up the middle where $x = y$, one where $2x = y$, and one where $x = 2y$. (Apologies to everyone, including me, who has forgotten their basic geometry.) This graph is illustrated in Figure 16.9.

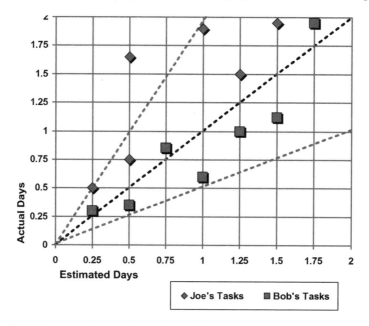

FIGURE 16.9 Comparing estimated versus actual work.

In Figure 16.9, the squares represent tasks completed by Bob, and the diamonds represent tasks completed by Joe; both are programmers on project Toh Ria. The darker dotted line in this graph (where $x = y$) represents the exact point for any given task where estimated and actual work meet. In our example, Bob got very close to meeting this goal twice, with a task estimated at .25 days and another estimated at .75. The lighter dotted lines represent the boundaries beyond which a task takes twice as long (where $x = 2y$) and half as long (where $2x = y$) as estimated. Joe exceeded this boundary condition once, where his actual work was more than three times his estimate. Joe came very close to the same boundary condition, where the actual work required to complete a task was twice the estimate, two more times: once with a task estimated at .25 days and once with a task estimated at 1 day.

Figure 16.9 provides a different message for each programmer. Bob, for one, provided estimates for his tasks that were about as good as anyone could reasonably expect. Perhaps he is actually overestimating his tasks a little, but more tasks than this would need to plotted to be sure. Joe, on the other hand, is clearly underestimating his tasks, and Figure 16.9 makes this readily apparent. The feedback here for Joe is not merely that he needs to become more conservative in his estimates but that he should look back at and evaluate the specific tasks that were so far off. Perhaps all these tasks were related to working with the application's servlets, or perhaps they were all related to areas of the system Joe had not worked in before. Perhaps there was nothing special to these tasks, and he really does simply need to be more conservative in his estimates. This is something that Joe should decide now that he can see how and where his estimates are dramatically off.

Again, project managers and team leads should be very careful using this metric. It must be made completely, utterly, and unmistakably clear that this graph is being shown only to help programmers better perform their estimates and in no way is meant to suggest that programmers need to do a better job of meeting their estimates. Finally, this is most definitely a temporary metric. It should be used sparingly when the manager or lead recognizes that estimates for one or more programmers (or the whole team) are wandering far from reality.

CONDUCTING REVIEWS

As discussed in Chapter 10, agile projects look for regular feedback from their members in order to adjust the heading of the project in light of all manner of internal or external factors. Most of the agile methodologies encourage feedback through the creation of open workspaces and the implementation of daily (or at least frequent) short meetings. If a project is already doing these things, it may need to do little or nothing more to solicit feedback, especially if the project is relatively small and executing short iterations. In place of or in addition to these very informal approaches, some methodologies recommend review meetings at the end of a long iteration or short release. Typically, there are four categories of topics that may be discussed during these meetings [Highsmith02]:

- The customer's point of view regarding the current state of the system
- The programmers' point of view regarding the current state of the system
- The overall state of the project team and the practices and processes being followed
- The status of the project

Review sessions can give project teams the opportunity to come together and assess what they have been doing both correct and wrong. They can then set out simple objectives to encourage more of the correct and less of the wrong. Two different review sessions are discussed in this section. Both focus on acting on what is discussed in the meeting. Not doing so would of course negate nearly the entire point of holding the session in the first place.

Sprint Retrospective[2]

Scrum employs a meeting with a very simple structure to be held for up to three hours. This meeting can be used to gather feedback from the team and convert it into activities that may be implemented as early as the following sprint. The entire project team attends the session, and the team's customer may attend as well. The steps in the sprint retrospective are summarized in Figure 16.10.

The Scrum Retrospective

❖ **Step 1:** Every participant tells what he thought went well about the previous iteration and what can be improved upon in the next iteration

❖ **Step 2:** The entire group reviews and prioritizes the list of issues

❖ **Step 3:** Issues are discussed (and an actionable solution sought) on a priority basis until all issues have been discussed or the meeting has run out of time

❖ **Step 4:** Actionable solutions should be written as features and added as a priority to the project's list of work

---

FIGURE 16.10   Steps in the sprint retrospective [Schwaber04].

The facilitator of the meeting—on a Scrum project this is the Scrum master—opens the meeting by asking every member of the team to answer two questions.

- What things went well in the last iteration or sprint?
- What are areas of improvement for the next iteration or sprint?

Each participant answers both questions, while the facilitator compiles a summary of the answers. After everyone has answered both questions, the group reviews the answer summary and prioritizes them for discussion. This prioritization of issues and the meeting's timebox of three hours should focus discussion on the most import problems facing the team. The team should discuss each item in turn until it has run out of time. Any actionable solution the team agrees upon should be written as a feature or story and be included as a priority item in the team's list of work.

It is essential for the facilitator of the meeting (Scrum master, project manager, or team lead) to remember that his role in this meeting is to facilitate. A project-wide review will be most effective only when, in addition to identifying issues, the project team collectively identifies and solidifies around a solution to each issue.

Reflection Workshop[3]

Attendance at the reflection workshop is similar to that of the sprint retrospective: the project team, the customer, and anyone else the project team believes may have valuable input to give. The workshop is driven with a visual diagram. The diagram may be written on a flipchart or a whiteboard. What is key is that the results are captured somewhere and then displayed in a prominent place. The diagram should include three boxes labeled Keep These, Problems, and Try These. A sample blank diagram is shown in Figure 16.11.

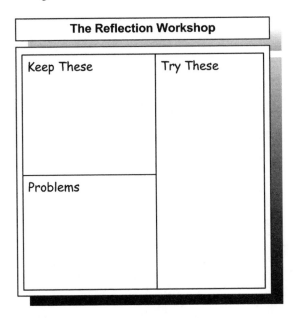

FIGURE 16.11   Opening diagram from a reflection workshop [Cockburn02].

The input for each box should be rather self-evident. Keep These and Problems address what the team has done well and what the team would like to fix moving forward, mirroring the two questions asked at the beginning of the sprint retrospective. Try These is for potential solutions and improvements. The name of each section in this diagram can change. What is important is their meaning. For example, The Good, The Bad, and The Ugly may be used to set a more laid-back tone for the session.

The facilitator should start the discussion on a positive note with what the team is doing right and then transition over to any problems the project is experiencing. The facilitator should try to sum up related good points and problems as much as possible. Problems specifically should be trapped in the diagram and not brooded upon in long-worded descriptions or lengthy going-nowhere-fast discussions.

The point of the meeting is to move on to solutions, and the facilitator should get there once the major pluses and problems seem to have rattled out from the project team. If the list of solutions grows too large, then the facilitator should try to focus the team on which ones are most important and which ones the entire group can unite behind. Here it is important to recognize that silence is not always synonymous with agreement.

Once the team has come to a consensus on a few actionable items to focus on in the immediate future, the meeting has served its purpose. The result of the meeting must then be placed in a highly visible place to remind the project team of its stated goals. Finally, the diagram from the previous reflection workshop may be brought in at the beginning of the next to give the team a chance to review its earlier comments and assess progress.

BE MINDFUL TO NOT OVERREACT

Just because a metric is flying south (or north, depending on what the metric is meant to measure) does not mean there is an issue that must be addressed with a process change. Nor is this the case if a programmer comes to a stand up meeting with his hair on fire because of a problem he encountered the day before. Teams that are constantly adjusting the way they do things should be wary of overreacting and responding too much to any single event. We have to think carefully about implementing a process to address an issue that has arisen only once. It may be a real event that could happen again, and perhaps there is a simple process that may guard effectively against a reoccurrence, but perhaps we will only be busying ourselves with securing the barn door after the thief has made off with the horses and while he is making his way into the pigeon coup.

Anyone who has sat through more than a handful of real estate closings and has had to sign sheet after sheet of a thick stack of paper has likely heard that there is a lawsuit behind every document. The implication is that bank attorneys have responded to each lost lawsuit by producing a new document that, when signed, will immunize the bank from that same form of loss in the future. The result is that even a simple refinance can take two hours or more of just signing documents. Perhaps this solution works for a process that the average individual may enter into only a few times in his lifetime. However, one should be able to easily imagine that, if a project team were to follow this approach and augment its process every time something goes wrong, there would at some point no longer be time left in the day for programming.

17 Communication and Collaboration

In This Chapter

■ An Agile Approach to Communication and Collaboration
■ Engendering a Communicative and Collaborative Culture
■ Comparing the Daily Scrum and Stand Up Meetings
■ Agile Practice: Stand Up Meeting
■ Agile Practice: Daily Scrum Meeting
■ Agile Practice: Collocated Team
■ Starting Monday: Increase Communication

One cornerstone of an agile project is a culture of good communication and collaboration, both internally and with the parties that it interacts with.

AN AGILE APPROACH TO COMMUNICATION AND COLLABORATION

A truly agile project requires a culture of open communication and collaboration in order to thrive. This is because agile processes and practices are tuned to work with and complement human nature and the way healthy groups interact. These processes help programmers adopt better habits (such as infusing testing throughout the development process). They help managers understand and trust the things they hear from programmers (through agile planning, estimation, and execution practices). They keep everyone honest about progress (based on the timeboxing mechanisms built into iterations and releases). Finally, many agile practices assist teams in fostering and maintaining a communicative and collaborative environment.

Some difficult work may at times be entailed in establishing and maintaining such an environment. The first half of this chapter will discuss some actions to take and not to take to foster communication and collaboration within a project. The second half of the chapter will discuss three agile practices that also contribute toward this goal. These are stand up meetings, the daily Scrum meeting, and the collocated team. Many other agile practices also directly contribute to a more communicative and collaborative project by fostering communication within the project team or between the team and its customer. These include but are not limited to collective ownership, feature teams, an onsite customer, pair programming, blitz planning, and the planning game. Each of these practices is discussed elsewhere in this book.

ENGENDERING A COMMUNICATIVE AND COLLABORATIVE CULTURE

As a project begins its transition toward agile, the culture of the team, the dynamic between its members, and its relationship with the business can all undergo marked change. There will be lots of opportunities to encourage or discourage proper interactions between individuals. Here are some big ticket things that should be done.

Strive to Make Decisions Based on Consensus

This can be a new experience for a manager or team lead who is used to telling people what to do and not having to provide much justification for his decisions. It can also be challenging for programmers who are accustomed to being told what to do and not having to bother with providing input and sharing with others what they really think. But this is a significant issue because open communication and self-motivated individuals are perpetuates for many agile practices. Additionally and generally, agile practices cannot be correctly implemented without the feedback that comes from team members who believe their opinions matter.

It is in the project's benefit that any changes related to agile practices and affecting the programmers, management, or business be discussed with the affected parties before any definite plans are laid. Then strive for consensus. For development practices, obtaining team-wide buy-in will increase both the likelihood of success and the speed with which each practice is adopted. Some management practices such as ideal day estimation and short iterations may be adopted without the involvement of the business, but others such as small releases and user stories can be profoundly difficult to implement without the support and participation of the business. For both development and management, decisions that have the buy-in of all parties will foster a better environment for communication, collaboration, and feedback.

Alternatively, there are real perils in not heeding this advice. Even a single agile practice introduced without the consensus and buy-in of the team can hurt morale. This is no exaggeration.

At one time, the author was observing a team during its transition to agile. The team leadership had decided to transition to user stories. Without sharing anything with the rest of the team's programmers, the team leads got together with the business and wrote up a small stack of story cards. They then invited the programmers to a conference room where they presented the completed and pre-estimated story cards and announced that since the team was going XP, now would be a great time for each programmer to start selecting what work he wanted to do. No one elected to take on a story. During a later discussion, the team lead admitted that he was surprised at the programmers' lack of enthusiasm. He honestly believed that the programmers would grow more assertive and collaborative simply by being allowed to select which stories they would work on. The opposite appeared to occur. The programmers communicated even less during that meeting than usual and left the conference room with story cards they had not chosen but had been assigned. For some reason, it never occurred to the team lead that the means by which he was introducing change (without consulting or even giving a heads-up to the programmers) only made them react as if they were victims of this change. By merely dropping a prefabricated agile practice on the programmers, the team leadership succeeded only in encouraging each programmer to hide farther back in his cube, hoping the next rogue agile practice might mistake him for a tech writer and overlook him. Ultimately, there was a huge misapplication of XP here, but people make mistakes when learning, and the team leadership should not be treated too harshly for this. Nonetheless, had the team leaders communicated their plan to the programmers prior to meeting with the business (or even after), the concerns of the programmers about accepting work with estimates they had no say in, about wanting to have some time to consider the work entailed in each story, and about their desire to have a voice in the technical design behind the story may have been heard. Had this happened, that demoralizing meeting might not have happened.

Establish a Common Area

Important collaborative discussions can be stifled in an environment of low-walled or closely packed cubes. Programmers need to have a common area where they can have impromptu design discussions or work out other issues and where they can talk without worrying about disturbing other individuals not associated with the project. Some teams will already have addressed this issue by collocating the team or establishing a war room. If not, then some sort of area (a conference room, a corner of the office, anywhere easily accessible) needs to be requisitioned. The area needs only to have a few everyday items such as chairs, a table, and a markerboard.

This area does not need be out of earshot from the team itself. In fact, other team members overhearing conversations is often not a bad thing.

Post Important Information in a Highly Visible Place

Information important to the daily functioning of the team such as the work schedule and progress should not be squirreled away in project plans and status reports seven levels down in some folder on a shared drive. Too few people, unfortunately, even review such documents when they are received in e-mails. Instead, information important to the daily operation of the team should be posted on a wall near to the team, in plain view, and kept up to date. This will set a subtle but constant reminder that openness is encouraged in the project's culture.

Examples of information to post include:

■ Work queued for the current iteration
■ Work completed and remaining for the current release
■ Acceptance test results
■ Coding standard (as long as it has been agreed to by the entire team)

Alistair Cockburn refers to such postings as *information radiators* because similar to heat registers they radiate information upon passersby. He recommends placing such posting in hallways or other high traffic areas [Cockburn01a]. Keep in mind that these postings must be constantly kept up to date. If they do not regularly take on new shapes depicting the progression of work, they will become as inconspicuous to team members and passersby as the ubiquitous, ultra-bland, framed office art.

Institute Openness from the Top Down

A project manager or team lead, simply by the way he interacts with the team, can do an awful lot to either encourage or stifle communication. A leader sets the culture of communication and collaboration on the team by how he engages and responds to individual team members and how he encourages individuals to engage and respond to one another. This includes the basic rules of common courtesy and professional behavior, which studies have found to be lacking in the IT profession [BCS04]. This section discusses some behaviors a leader may choose to follow and encourage in others.

Talk Less and Listen More

This is the obvious item on the list. But it is something we all too often forget. When we interact with others, they build an impression of how we react when we are given information. Do we appear attentive and interested, bored and fidgety, or do we merely cut others off and talk over them? Not only do the latter two habits impede our ability to gain sometimes vital information, but by exhibiting these behaviors repeatedly we can actively discourage others from wanting to communicate and collaborate with us.

Ask Questions Instead of Guessing at Answers

Guessing at answers is a habit we may all be guilty of at times. It is also a habit that may have a devastating effect on the project if it is the reason why an important bit of functionality is delivered in an unusable condition. Every member on the team needs to understand the importance of and the need to take the time required (both of himself and others) to get things right.

Talk More and E-Mail Less

Anyone who has ever worked on a team where programmers who sat yards away from one another still felt compelled to launch long e-mail missiles about code-related issues will know this is one very obvious sign of a bad communication culture. Face-to-face communication takes less time, guarantees that the other parties at least receive the message, and provides for all manner of feedback that cannot be delivered in ASCII text.

This suggestion is based on a personal experience with a team that, even though its entire membership was located in a space of 100 square feet, suffered from serious communication problems that were, in turn, the result of a team lead who was asleep at the wheel. Programmers composed finely crafted e-mails about their positions regarding the coding styles of other programmers. Everyone was congenial enough to not mention by name the other programmers they were not happy with. In all likelihood, most of the e-mails went unread anyway.

Bad News Is Better than No News

This one really is on the shoulders of the project manager or team lead. Most any reasonable person will immediately recognize that shooting the messenger is a lousy practice even for despots. But many of us forget that in small groups where communication is vital, we must even be wary of shooting the occasional culprit. Managers obviously want team members to act responsibly, professionally, and in a disciplined manner, thus minimizing events that might result in the communication of bad news. When bad news does arrive, teams benefit much more when those culpable present the news in a timely manner instead of sitting on it until it is too late.

Give Them Time

Sometimes you need to slow down in order to go faster.

Most project teams are accustomed to running almost constantly (a topic addressed in the discussion on sustainable pace in Chapter 10, "Agile Management"), and it may feel very unnatural to give everybody some time to catch their breath so they can really delve into a new practice, evaluate their progress correctly, and get the thing working right. To make sure there is time for this process to happen, management needs to set expectations both within and outside the team at a reasonable level. Additionally, for project managers and team leads, giving programmers time may mean being patient during periods of high pressure and stress and trusting that everyone is doing the best he can. For that matter, even if someone truly is not performing up to par, this can be investigated and addressed when the high-tension period has passed.

COMPARING THE DAILY SCRUM AND STAND UP MEETINGS

Before we proceed, it is worth taking a few sentences to discuss the similarities and differences between the stand up and daily Scrum meetings. At first, these two practices may seem to be essentially the same except that the daily Scrum is an integral part of the Scrum methodology, and the stand up meeting has been adopted by XP and DSDM. However, in their detail these practices have significant differences.

The daily Scrum is led by the Scrum master (who is a member of management), and stand up meetings are typically organized by the programmers and either facilitated by the group as a whole or the programming team lead. While some Scrum teams do stand for a meeting, standing is a requirement of the daily stand up. The act of standing is one significant way participants keep a stand up meeting brief. In the daily Scrum, the Scrum master is explicitly charged with the responsibility of keeping the meeting short, and the meeting terminates after 15 minutes regardless of whether everyone has had a chance to report status. Stand up meetings may be skipped or stopped and started again, while daily Scrums provide a level of visibility for the project that disallows the team from canceling them on a whim. Finally, the stand up meeting is attended only by programmers and possibly the project manager, while daily Scrums may be attended by a variety of individuals from outside the team, although only the team participates.

The lines between these two practices can blur, and this is quite appropriate. Some daily Scrums have a rule that everyone must stand [Schwaber01]. In some cases, stakeholders may attend a stand up meeting. The two practices are presented here because they represent two different (but not incompatible) approaches to meet similar goals. They may be blended as necessary.

Which practice should a team choose to start with? The most significant difference between the two practices is whether the meeting is merely a design and programming-level activity (stand up) or intended for programmers, management, stakeholders, and the like (daily Scrum). Determining which groups will attend the meeting should tell a team which practice to start with.

AGILE PRACTICE: STAND UP MEETING

Regular conversations about progress and direction are an essential but often neglected component of teamwork. Every experienced software development practitioner should be able to easily recollect at least half a dozen scenarios where the sinking thought "if only I'd known they were working on that" flashed through his mind. For the project's programmers, stand up meetings may be the simplest and best way to reduce the occurrence of that sinking feeling.

Stand ups are short meetings (typically 5 to 15 minutes) where the team touches base on the work each member is doing. During these meetings, programmers may report status, coordinate activities, ask for or offer assistance, and provide early warnings about significant technical and people issues.

Purpose and Benefits

Stand up meetings are called stand ups for a reason. All attendees must stand during the entirety of the meeting, thereby encouraging a speedy meeting so that everyone can get back to the more important things he has to do. Good stand ups have a rhythm where one individual speaks, a question or two is exchanged, a topic may be flagged for a follow-up discussion, and the next individual speaks. No lengthy conversations are allowed. One purpose of stand ups is to identify topics that need to be discussed, but then those topics should be sidelined for discussion only by the necessary individuals after the stand up is completed. This allows everyone else to get back to work.

Stand up meetings may not benefit every agile team. Small teams that are collocated may not have much use for them. Stand ups become more of a requirement the larger and more dispersed a team becomes (see Figure 17.1 for an illustration).

Finally, stand up meetings really are pretty much for programmers. This allows them to have an open and honest discussion about progress on tasks and the nature of the code without having to worry about a customer or manager misinterpreting or reading too deeply into their words. If the team requires a mechanism that incorporates management or stakeholders, try the daily Scrum meeting, discussed in the next section.

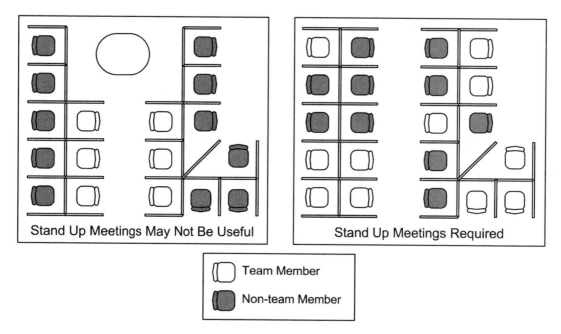

FIGURE 17.1 The need for stand up meetings may be determined by team size and location.

Implementation

Typically, a stand up is held at the same place and the same time every day. The team usually gathers in a circle. The meeting can be a free-for-all or structured. A small team with members who already have a good working relationship may not need to have any structure beyond identifying the order in which people will speak (typically clockwise or counterclockwise). Other teams may need a specific question or set of questions that each member will run through and a moderator who keeps things moving and cuts off side conversations. Questions answered during the stand up may include:

- What did you complete yesterday?
- What will you work on today?
- Have you encountered any roadblocks?

Stand up meetings are a good place for identifying problems, but they are not the place to solve those problems. Issues and problems that filter out of the stand up meeting need to be addressed as follow-up discussions. This is rather essential because it is rare that an issue arising out of a stand up actually affects the entire team. Long discussions on topics that do not involve the whole team will cause disinterested members to mentally wander off and even conduct side conversations. Repeated long discussions will discourage the timely appearance of those disinterested team members.

Stand up meetings are typically easy to initiate (few people will push back on a practice that is only supposed to take 5 to 10 minutes a day). The challenge comes in keeping them running smoothly, ensuring that everyone makes the meeting on time, grabbing and focusing everyone's interest for 5 to 10 minutes, and not wasting anyone's time. Some teams will actually institute a simple list of rules in an effort to keep the meeting running smoothly and on track.

Opportunities and Obstacles

Stand up meetings may take a surprising amount of tweaking and fussing. Their usefulness, the way they flow, and attitudes toward them may shift quickly based upon changes in workload and team composition.

People Are Arriving Late or Missing the Stand Up Altogether

This is feedback being expressed either intentionally or unintentionally by one or more members of the team. It may mean one of several things and entail a number of solutions. When discussing the issue with the team, there are a number of causes to consider:

- Is the meeting simply scheduled at a poor time (for example, too early or too close to lunch)? Can everyone agree on a better time?
- Are people just forgetful? If so, can some sort of alarm (either within Lotus Notes® or the big thing with bells on the wall) be used to remind people?
- Are one or more people upset or bored by the increasing duration of the meeting? If so, skip to the next section, "The Stand Up Is Routinely Taking More than Ten Minutes."
- Do people want fewer meetings? Stand up meetings are meant to help the team coordinate their activity on a daily basis. Some teams really may not need this level of formalized coordination, either because members communicate freely or because code is not shared collectively. If this is the case, try scaling back to three meetings a week or even two.

The Stand Up Is Routinely Taking More than Ten Minutes

First, is someone actively managing the stand up? If not, should someone such as the team lead pick up that responsibility? Some groups self-manage themselves very effectively. Other groups under the responsibility of self-management just start sucking mud. This is in no way a statement on the group's individual members, just the particular group's dynamics. Sometimes very smart, very enthusiastic people need someone to keep them on track.

Next, are people entering into side conversations at the meeting or discussions that should be scheduled as follow-ups after the meeting? The group can make an explicit rule prohibiting side conversations. Additionally, hold the meeting by a marker board and institute a rule that once a follow-up conversation has been written on the board it can no longer be discussed during that meeting.

Finally, try bringing a stick to the meeting. Don't beat anyone with it. But call it something corny like the talking too much stick. Keep it in a place where anyone can get it quickly (perhaps on the floor in the center of the group). If a conversation that does not pertain to the meeting has gone on too long, any team member may make a big to-do of taking up the stick.

The Late Afternoon Stand Up

Stand up meetings traditionally occur in the morning, but this may not be appropriate for every team. Some companies allow a very open start time. Although it once was my privilege to see an architect throw a snit about being told he had to be in the office by 11 a.m., this is not the place to debate how lenient company policies should or should not be. If your company allows flexible and individualized work times and it is difficult setting a time before 1 p.m. for the stand up meeting (when you take into account that some people might want to eat lunch as early as 11 a.m.), consider an afternoon stand up. The afternoon stand up may be a bit more historical (for example, "I did this and that today"), but it still serves as a means of sharing information and might even allow programmers to coordinate on times they will arrive in the morning to work together.

AGILE PRACTICE: DAILY SCRUM MEETING

The daily Scrum meeting, which obviously originated in the Scrum methodology, shares similarities with stand up meetings. Like the stand up, the daily Scrum focuses on a quick daily discussion of progress, attempts to ferret out issues and obstacles, and pushes off nonessential discussions to other venues. The daily Scrum differs most markedly from the stand up by inviting stakeholders, upper level managers, and other interested parties to observe. The daily Scrum has a bit more structure than stand up meetings. The final, meaningful deviation from stand ups is that at daily Scrum meetings, attendees are permitted to sit.

Purpose and Benefits

The Scrum has several goals [Rising02] [Schwaber01]. First, it serves as an opportunity to constantly tune the priorities of the team. Note the use of the word "tune" and not something stronger like "change." The daily Scrum is not the place where work is ripped out of the schedule or shoved in; it is where the team can refocus its effort from one area of planned work to another. Such decisions may be based on the team being ahead of or behind schedule, the availability or absence of specific team members or domain experts, the unexpected ease or difficulty of a given feature, or any other number of other factors.

Second, the daily Scrum keeps everyone informed on progress as it is made and obstacles as they are encountered and overcome. This can encourage a sense of common cause from programmers all the way up to stakeholders. It also expedites the process of clearing the trickier obstacles because stakeholders become aware of them sooner.

Third, the meeting enables the project manager to learn about and target any obstacles that the team has found in its way. It is then the project manager's responsibility to see that these obstacles are removed or that a safe path around is found as quickly as possible.

Finally, the meeting is a mechanism for tracking the completion of work. For projects using Scrum, this information will later be fed into an updated burndown chart (as discussed in Chapter 14, "Executing Iterative Development"). Projects not following the Scrum methodology can still use this input to track progress on tasks, features, or user stories toward their own iterations or other timeboxing mechanism.

Implementation

The daily Scrum meeting distinguishes between team members, who are called pigs, and everyone else, called chickens [Schwaber01]. The labels are based on an old anecdote where the pig turns down a chicken's proposal to open a ham and eggs restaurant. The pig's rationale is that he is committed to the endeavor while the chicken is only involved. Several of the Scrum meeting's rules arise from this analogy. Specifically, pigs (the team members) sit at the meeting table and participate actively, while chickens (business people and stakeholders) may sit or stand at the periphery of the team and are not allowed to speak during the meeting. These rules serve to expedite the meeting, allowing the team members to plan and communicate, permitting everyone else the ability to know the exact progress of the team, and getting it all done in an allotment of 15 minutes.

The meeting should be held in the same room at the same time every day. This room (dubbed the Scrum room) should have table, chairs, marker board, speakerphone, and door. If there is no room that can be reserved at the same time on a daily basis, the team should make due with whatever it has. In any case, the focus should be on keeping the meeting location and time as constant as possible.

All team members must attend the meeting. If a team member cannot attend physically, he may attend via speakerphone. If he is unable to make the meeting at all, the team member must communicate his status in advance to someone who will represent him at the meeting. If too many chickens attend the meeting (too many meaning there's not enough space for everyone or so many people causes too much commotion), the team is empowered to limit the number.

Finally, every daily Scrum involves the same three questions [Schwaber01]:

- What work have you completed since the last Scrum?
- What work do you plan to complete before the next Scrum?
- What, if anything, has gotten in your way?

The discussion should stick to these three topics. As with stand up meetings, any discoveries (issues, problems, opportunities, and so forth) should be queued for follow-up discussions.

Opportunities and Obstacles

The daily Scrum is a vital component of the Scrum methodology. If it does not flow smoothly day after day, the whole process is disrupted. It is also a mechanism that can expose team members to the highest levels of an organization. This may be why, in *Agile Project Management with Scrum,* Ken Schwaber comes down pretty hard on tardiness, talking chickens, and most other rule breaking activities [Schwaber04]. The remedies he proposes include:

Tardy team members: Fine them a buck on the spot.

Team members who do not follow the rules: Remove them from the team.

Members of the business and stakeholders who do not follow the rules: Exclude them from future meetings.

If you are disinclined or disallowed from using such tactics, consult some of the tips in the stand up meeting's "Opportunities and Obstacles" section.

See Also

- Schwaber and Beedle's *Agile Software Development with Scrum* provides a very thorough description of the daily Scrum [Schwaber01].
- Linda Rising's useful article "Agile Meetings" is based on the daily Scrum and can be found at *http://members.cox.net/risingl1/articles/STQE.pdf.*

AGILE PRACTICE: COLLOCATED TEAM

This practice should not be underestimated. Collocating a team is more than simply arranging to have the entire project situated in the same building, on the same floor, or even within a shot put of one another. Collocation means having the whole team in a single space that facilitates communication and collaboration. That way people can easily interact with one another, ideally so they don't even need to get out of their seats, and people have enough space to break off into ad hoc groups that can work apart from one another.

Purpose and Benefits

Collocated team spaces have several advantages. First, people can be more easily and quickly found. If the individual you want to speak with is in the team area, the most you will have to do is turn around. Even if he is not there, you have just saved time as a consequence of the team being collocated because you did not need to call, e-mail, or walk over to his space to find out if he is available.

Second, people can easily find space to work together. A collocated team should have the space for people to pair up and group together to work on and solve all manner of issues. When was the last time you spent five minutes looking for an available conference room to do some group work? If your team does not work in a common space and you do not have your own office, this was probably not very long ago.

Third, an openness with information and of ideas is fostered. When you work in an environment where questions and ideas are regularly exchanged in open air, it becomes more difficult to not share and collaborate. Suddenly, conversations may be overheard not accidentally but intentionally because every discussion in the team space becomes the property of the entire project. A topic discussed between two people may pull in two more and grow into a full-fledged design discussion. A question about a user request may suddenly grow into a team-wide examination of the priority of a particular user story. Crystal refers to this phenomenon as *osmotic communication,* and it is one of the required properties of Crystal Clear (see Chapter 3, "The Agile Methodologies") [Cockburn04].

Fourth, messing with the furniture in an office (moving desks and reconfiguring cubes) sends a strong message to the team. In essence, the result of our endeavors is more important that the sanctity of the environment within which we all work.

Finally, given all the above benefits, one might expect a boost in productivity. There is some research to support this assertion. One University of Michigan study performed in 2000 with teams working in war room environments found that "radically collocated teams" are at least twice as productive as their non-collocated counterparts [ScienceDaily00]. It should be noted that the researchers believed it was not merely the open workspace setting that provided this boost in productivity but also the techniques that the teams were able to use as a result of being collocated.

Implementation

Creating a shared workspace has everything to do with the organization within which you work. Is it a small, carefree shop where such innovations are encouraged? Is it a 10,000-person company with a team of fire-belching managers who get bent out of shape when workstations are moved without proper notice? At your workplace, does the unionized facilities staff file a complaint if people switch cubes without their assistance (been there)? If so, can you gauge the distance between bending and breaking a rule?

Are You Working in a Preconfigured Space?

In *Extreme Programming Explained,* Kent Beck quips that he often starts projects "with a screwdriver and an Allen wrench" [Beck99]. It really is worth remembering that cubes are meant to be reconfigured. Figure 17.2 demonstrates how the same space and partitions used to create a typical cube farm can be reconfigured to form a collaborative space.

The collocated team layout in Figure 17.2 is based on a "caves and commons" approach. The goal behind the approach is to provide people with access both to "commons" where they can interact together and "caves" where they can work alone (for e-mail, document review, and other independent activities) [Cockburn02].

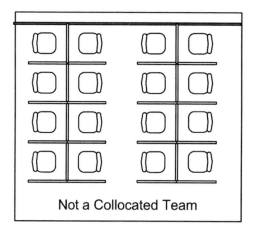
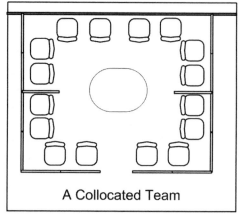

Not a Collocated Team   A Collocated Team

FIGURE 17.2 Cubes can be reconfigured

Do You Have the Ability to Fashion a New Space?

In *Agile Software Development with Scrum*, Schwaber and Beedle propose a large room with no fixed partitions or heavy furniture where team members can shift their spaces about to form workgroups, break those groups apart and form different groups, and then break off and do individual work. Imagine the buzz and energy that may come from this regular shifting of space and the easy ability to communicate verbally and visually across the open space of the room [Schwaber01].

This approach takes into account the latest innovations: wireless networks with improved security, phones that work over IP, electrical outlets set flush into hardwood or tiled floors. Desks, marker boards, and even wall partitions can be purchased on a set of wheels.

Opportunities and Obstacles

There are many variables to consider when instituting an open workspace. A few are discussed here.

Adjusting to the New Environment and Getting Along

In order for an open workspace to succeed, the project team needs to be a group of people who, at the very least, play well with one another. Loss of private space or even worse an office can cause real trauma to some individuals. Before transforming the team workspace, it might be a good idea to identify these individuals in advance, engage them in the process, and counsel them through the transition. The University of Michigan study mentioned earlier observed that while teammates do not often look forward to moving into shared quarters, they realize over time the ultimate benefits of easier coordination, improved problem solving, and faster learning [ScienceDaily00].

Collocating in Time

If the team is all working together in one space, but half the team starts work at 7 a.m. and the other half does not get in until 10:30, it may not achieve the desired benefit of an open space. Project teams typically operate best when they can control their working hours separately from the rest of the organization, but they also work best when they synchronize their hours and maximize the potential for collaboration. A stand up meeting scheduled not too early may be a good way to get everybody on the team coming to work nearer to the same time, while also tapping into the other benefits of the practice.

The Lead Programmer Has No Time to Complete His Own Work

One recognized pitfall of an open space environment is that the team's lead programmer (or some other important team member) may be so interrupted with questions and helping others that he does not have time to complete his own work. One solution that project teams attempt is to move this individual out of the open workspace and into a nearby office with a door. But this solution either robs the team of a valued resource or simply does not solve the problem, because the team is still in the habit of going to that individual whenever there is a question [Cockburn01a]. Alistair Cockburn has proposed a solution to this dilemma, dubbed the *cone of silence*. At its most simplest, the lead programmer or whichever individual is too often interrupted to complete his work finds a place and a time where he works apart from the team without interruption. This could mean leaving the office at 5 p.m. and then working at home. An even better solution is an office on the other side of the building to which he can retreat for a few hours each day [Cockburn04b].

Cube Retooling Is Not Allowed in Your Organization

In larger organizations this can be a real issue. If you cannot move the team to a better space, can you move individuals around to create pockets of open workspace? For example, is there a manager sitting by a programmer who could swap spots with another programmer, so that at least some of the development staff are collocated? Can the team or a significant portion of it commandeer a conference room? Basically, get creative.

STARTING MONDAY: INCREASE COMMUNICATION

A team does not simply learn one day to interact on a higher level. Increasing team communication and collaboration is a process that takes time and regular attention to progress. There are several small actions that could be taken today that might nudge the team's communication in the right direction. Some of these actions may be taken by any member of the team. Some may require the authority held by a project manager or team lead.

Actions Anyone May Take

These are ideas that have a low likelihood of backfiring.

Work on Your Own Communication Style

Encourage communication by example. For most of us, that likely means trying to listen more and assume less. For others, however, it may actually mean trying to speak up more. Either way, it is something nearly all of us can work on, and regardless of its effect on the team, it is something that could benefit each of us.

Float the Idea of Stand Up Meetings

Would the team benefit from a daily infusion of communication? Grab a couple of programmers and try out some pros and cons. Have your own list of pros and cons ready before approaching other members of the team.

Investigate Another Practice

Do not forget the other agile practices listed at the beginning of this chapter that encourage a more communicative and collaborative team culture. Perhaps one of those practices would fit the team better.

Actions the Project Manager or Team Lead May Take

These are the people who are positioned to encourage a better dynamic among team members and between the team and the business and users.

Take People to Lunch

This suggestion entails more than playing the role of the relationship guy. If you take the project team out, ask them what you could do to help them work better as a team. If you lunch with a member of the business or a stakeholder, ask whether and how he would like to become more involved with the team. Sometimes a positive effect can be gained just by mentioning such topics.

Post a Team Metric

Identify a public place that is well suited for posting team information. Then identify a metric that might benefit the team by being posted. Are unit tests or acceptance tests failing too often? Throw up a chart. Is the team making good progress on the user stories for this release? Apply positive reinforcement and post a graph.

You will likely want to vet this idea with one or two people before doing it.

Institute a Daily Scrum

Consider the idea of a daily Scrum, both to encourage communication between the team and to keep the business better informed. Do not take any immediate action, but weigh the pros and cons for a few days.

Take Down a Cube Wall

And finally, it is time for a crazy idea.

Is there another member of the team sitting on the other side of your cube partition? If you have the authority, consider taking down that wall. The action certainly will not go unnoticed, could make a real statement, and may help you gauge how receptive the team might be to a more open workspace.

18 Documentation

Documentation is a serious hazard to productivity for two reasons. First, when programmers are writing documentation there are design, coding, and testing activities that are not being done. Second, unnecessary documentation, just like any other form of mundane and uninteresting labor, hurts morale, which in turn hurts productivity.

Nonetheless, there is a necessary place for at least some documentation in nearly every project, just as long as it is not the driver's seat.

THE PERILS OF DOCUMENTATION

When and why can documentation be a road hazard? Let's consider the illustration in Figure 18.1, which is a simplification of an actual CMMI implementation.

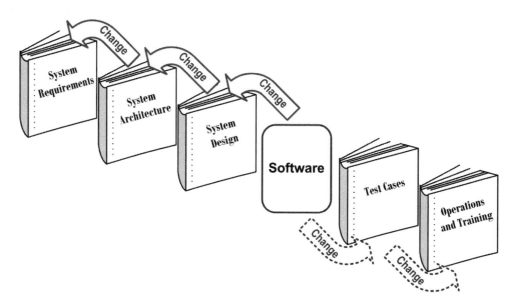

FIGURE 18.1   Changes propagating through heavy documentation.

The figure illustrates the levels of documentation that may exist in a traditional, waterfall-inspired development process. The arrows demonstrate how a change to code (driven, for example, by an altered, missed, or new requirement) may need to propagate all the way back up the documentation chain. Then, once the application goes live, changes will need to propagate down the documentation chain as well. One can easily image how a process like this can choke an agile project, where regular requirement changes are accepted and even encouraged. One can even imagine how a process like this might choke a project based on traditional development processes where change requests and missed requirements are getting out of hand.

Nonetheless, it must be acknowledged that this is perhaps the best documentation solution for a traditional development process. Maybe the requirements analysis is bang on, maybe the architects all have 10 years with the technology, maybe they all know their stuff, maybe the programmers know enough to span the gaps that inevitably litter the requirements and design documentation, and maybe the system is being delivered into a relatively unchanging business climate. That's five instances of maybe. Do we sum, multiply, or square to determine probability?

It is rare that projects fully shed all their unnecessary documentation requirements. To be entirely fair, a heavier approach to documentation can be valuable and potentially necessary to some projects (especially large and complex ones), just as long as the desire to document does not override the need to build a working and useful system.

AN AGILE APPROACH TO DOCUMENTATION

Different agile methodologies require different amounts of documentation. A good rule of thumb, though, is that agile requires "just enough" documentation.

Agilists recognize that documentation is an important part of nearly any software-related endeavor, but it is typically a poor excuse for communication. People communicating with one another is what gets requirements designed and implemented. Written documentation, on the other hand, is much more useful for telling others after the fact what decisions were made and what goes where.

Agilists will always choose working software over documentation. A working system can make do without documentation. Documentation, meanwhile, merely pines for a working system.

Finally, documentation should be easy to maintain and update. Good documentation may follow the same principles as the agile practice of simple design:

> **Consider the Simplest Thing That Could Possibly Work:** How often may comments in code replace separate design documents?

> **You Aren't Gonna Need It:** Will anyone really use the document? If you are certain they will, then generate the document.

> **Once and Only Once:** As illustrated in Figure 18.1, the same information captured in multiple documents can take quite some time to update. If the information must be kept in a document, try to keep it in only one document.

Consult the simple design practice in Chapter 7, "Design and Programming," for more explanation of these items.

At its worst, agile sees excessive documentation as an impediment to a healthy and productive relationship between a company and the firms it enlists to build software for it. This is because documents and detailed specifications can actually give less-than-competent and disingenuous firms a readily available source of cover [Highsmith02]. Lots of documents and formalized review procedures provide the vendor with excuses such as:

- But it says right here . . .
- You approved this.
- That was never in the specification!

Granted, such groups will likely not be given the opportunity to repeat their missteps, but that does little for the here and now.

POOR EXCUSES FOR DOCUMENTATION

In his essay "Agile Documentation," Scott Ambler lists seven felonious reasons why documentation may exist [Ambler03]:

- The requester wants to be seen as in control.
- The requester is justifying his existence.
- The requester does not know any better.
- Because the process says so.
- The stakeholders want to know everything is okay.
- The documentation is required for another group to understand the system.
- It is stipulated in the contract.

All of these are bad reasons to create documentation. In some cases, there may not even be a real audience for the documentation that is being produced. In other cases, the intended audience may never read the documentation, especially if they had no hand in its creation. Still other cases are the result of ignorance and other intentions that are not worth dwelling upon.

MINIMIZING DOCUMENTATION REQUIREMENTS

What can teams do to clear some of the more onerous documentation responsibilities off the deck of the ship? Here are a few strategies.

Seek an Alternative Solution

Potentially the first and best approach is to apply a bit of reality therapy to seemingly onerous documentation requests. One might politely inquire as to why the documentation is required and, again politely, explain why significant documentation can be detrimental to an agile process. On rare occasions, a customer may not have a good rationale for the documentation except that "we've just always done it this way" and will forego the requirement when presented with a valid case against it. A bit of wishful thinking, yes, but this has happened.

On other occasions, a bit more investigation might reveal that while there is a valid need to be satisfied, the documentation route may not be the best approach. For example, on some projects, it may be all but essential to keep management and business informed of development progress. Daily reports can take a significant amount of time to compile and often go unread. A more appropriate and less time consuming solution may be a daily 15-minute status meeting between the team and the business (modeled on the daily Scrum, discussed in Chapter 17, "Communication and Collaboration").

If there is a valid purpose for the documentation, one may still assess whether an alternative process could be employed to achieve the same goal. For example, if the documentation is intended for the maintenance team that will support the system after it is deployed, perhaps members of the support team could instead each spend a week working with the development team to get some hands-on knowledge of the system.

Finally, if the documentation requirement cannot be waived, can it be pared down to lessen the amount of effort entailed while still addressing the underlying goal? For example, maybe the maintenance team can be brought in to at least tell the programmers what information they want in the system documentation and what does not need to be there. This strategy would serve a dual purpose of allowing programmers to write only what has been explicitly requested (instead of guessing at everything) while simultaneously increasing the possibility that the management team will actually read and refer to the documentation because they had a hand in fashioning it.

Break Out Documentation as Separate Work

This is probably the most common approach. Agile teams that are requested by their customers to perform significant amounts of documentation will break the work out into features, make estimates, and present the documentation tasks to the customer alongside all the other features that may be queued up for the next iteration. This approach both helps the customer to appreciate what is typically the overhead cost of documentation and lets him prioritize the work with everything else that needs to be done.

Vendors are warned to deploy this option with care. The occasional client has been known to react very negatively to the suggestion that he pay separately for documentation, especially after a contract has been signed. Some reconnaissance may be required to determine whether this is a viable front.

Incorporate Documentation into Tools the Team Is Already Using

The point of documentation is to trap information. Living code is the ultimate documentation mechanism because it both tells the system how to operate and can be read as a set of instructions. The closer the team can move a documentation requirement toward the code itself, the simpler it will be to meet that requirement. For example, a process where design documentation is recorded in the comment blocks above methods and objects and then extracted into a separate document by a process such as JavaDoc is less costly than a process where design documentation is completed in a word processor. Maintaining design documentation within code is cheaper, first because a programmer does not need to open a separate document with a separate application to make documentation changes that reflect his activity in the code. Second, there is no separate system that must be devised for sharing and merging a word processor document that requires occasional updates by each programmer on the team.

Another good example involves the documentation of test cases. A former team of mine working in a heavy process environment once received permission to forego a client's company-wide requirement that test cases be written from a specific template and stored in separate documents. The team instead satisfied the requirement by using a tool like JavaDoc to generate a single document from information embedded in the comments preceding automated unit test methods.

Use a Wiki

One of the real problems with documentation is that there has, to date, been no good method of managing updates to word processor documentation in the way that source control tools manage updates to code. Time is lost regularly as people queue to update a 30-page document. Potentially worse, two people update the document at the same time, and one of them is left sorting out the mess. (Word processors are now coming bundled with merge tools, but they are still less than perfect.) Finally, and we have all probably witnessed this situation at least once, one person may inadvertently save over another person's changes. How long does it take to pull the backup tapes? Do you even have backup tapes?

Consider using a Wiki for many forms of project documentation. A document that is well divided across multiple Wiki pages will allow for simultaneous updates as different people work on different portions of the text. Additionally, a Wiki incorporates many of the rigors of source control into a simple interface, including versioning, rollback, and very rudimentary file locking, so that at least you will know that someone has gotten there before you.

To get a feel for how a Wiki may work for shared documents, try the Wiki Wiki Sandbox at *http://c2.com/cgi/wiki?WikiWikiSandbox*.

Of course Wiki documents do not have the same polish as documents created in a word processor. At some point, the text may be extracted from the Wiki. Then polish may be applied in any measure.

Get the Requestor to Take Responsibility for It

If a specific group either within or outside of the project is requesting the generation of a document solely for its own use, it may be possible to push the responsibility for the creation of that document back upon the group. In this case, the project manager or team lead may offer to make members of the team available for input or review sessions but leave the actual task of writing the document (and the bulk of the work) on the shoulders of the requestor. It may be important to pursue this strategy not from the perspective that the project team is refusing to do the writing itself but rather that the team is willing to stretch itself and lend a helping hand.

Get Someone Else to Do It

Experiences with this approach may be mixed, but when a project is under a pile of documentation requirements, a valid though potentially last option is to bring in a technical writer or other such individual to spearhead it. The technical writer will certainly not be able to take over all the work, but he may be able to write training manuals; distill documentation out of design discussions; render paper and pencil diagramming into a line drawing; and collect, edit, and merge paragraphs of technical information speedily authored by otherwise occupied programmers. This is certainly not a perfect solution, but if no other strategy prevails, this one may have to do.

However, pay heed to a quick warning based on personal experience. While a good technical writer may bring real productivity gains to a project, a poor—or poorly selected—technical writer may bring only grief. Specifically, an individual brought in to assist with documentation because he was cheap without being vetted by the programmers he may work with and without real knowledge of the domain or technology associated with the work will most likely make a bad situation worse.

DOCUMENTATION AT THE START OF A PROJECT

On most projects, there's a burst of documentation right at the beginning. One wonders if there is a better way to channel enthusiasm.

Agile methodologies agree that documentation in software development should be kept to a minimum but differ significantly on their approach to documentation at the start of the project. XP is set at one end of this spectrum, permitting (but not stipulating) the generation of nothing more than a box of index cards. FDD is probably at the other end of the spectrum. Its first phase is to form a modeling team and generate an overall model of the system to be developed. This may seem heavy weight, but FDD was, after all, developed for large projects in large organizations.

Startup documentation has its merits. The process can help the team define where it is going and how, generally, it intends to go there. The product that the process produces can communicate this same information to others, and the artifact that was once the original product may be used for measuring progress and deriving lessons learned. Ultimately, most Agilists agree that some form of startup documentation is important as long as it does not stifle the team's enthusiasm.

Define a Mission or Metaphor

The project mission statement and the XP practice, metaphor, are both described in Chapter 12, "Project Initiation," along with some methods to go about writing them. Ultimately, this is really the bare minimum of what should be documented at the start of the project.

For a small project with a straightforward purpose and few documentation requirements, a well-crafted mission or metaphor that lucidly states the nature of the system and objective of the project may be all that is needed to satisfy management and get started.

A Simple but Rigorous Set of Mission Artifacts

ASD recommends creating three artifacts at the beginning of each project. These artifacts are meant to define what the project is about, why it is being done, and how it will be done. Their purpose is to focus the initial energy of the project and ensure that the team has a clear understanding of its mission and direction before it casts off into open waters. It is meant to guard against the uncritical full speed ahead mindset that can grip a project at its onset, especially when the project is urgently needed or has been held up by bureaucratic or financial red tape [Highsmith00].

The three artifacts ASD recommends are:

The Project Vision (Charter): A 2- to 10-page document that defines the commissioned system by its business objectives, overall specification, and intended position within the organization or within a competitive commercial market.

The Project Data Sheet: This is a one-sheet overview of the project. It should include the key benefits of the project, overall specifications, and project management information. This can be thought of as an executive summary of the project. It gives outsiders a quick overview of the project. In addition, it can help those working on and involved with the project to stay attuned with the big picture of the project.

The Product Specification Outline: This document is a high-level inventory of the features, functions, objects, performance needs, and other specifications of the system.

These three documents can give a project of significant size or a smaller project with significant documentation demands the business-level clearance and internal guidance necessary to transition to a planning and execution footing.

Model Everything at a High Level

While XP and other small teams may start with a mission statement or metaphor of the system, larger projects may eschew the prose, follow FDD, and go right for a model. For an agile team operating in an environment where architectural models are essential and other early forms of documentation may be forgone, this may be a very effective approach. It is discussed in greater detail in Chapter 12.

Complete a Set of Solution Sheets

Solution sheets are meant to nail down the most important functional and technical aspects of a feature, may be written to resemble lightweight analysis documents, and can be compiled to provide one or more simple but comprehensive system documents at the end of the project. Solution sheets are introduced and discussed in Chapter 11, "Features and User Stories."

DESIGN DOCUMENTATION

Just like documenting your way out of the starting gate, the agile methodologies and the projects that use them differ on the level of documentation produced by the development team. Some of these differences have more to do with team size and the nature of the work, but other differences are founded in the methodologies themselves. Typically, XP pushes for a bare minimum of documentation, DSDM recommends specific documents, and FDD calls for sequence diagrams to supplement its overall model. The rest of the methodologies are either between these points or allow documentation requirements to vary substantially according to the demands of the business and the nature of the technology.

Most every agile programmer endorses some form of design documentation, though opinions may differ over exactly which method is appropriate to meet bare minimum design documentation requirements. The following sections discuss a few ways an agile team can go about providing a bare minimum level of documentation.

Executable Documentation

Many agile programmers argue that executable documentation (that is, the code and its tests) is the best method of documenting the design of the system. Executable documentation entails code that is written in a simple-to-understand fashion and that uses self-describing variable and method names [Fraunhofer02b]. This approach is, of course, premised on a team that not only writes tests but writes them well and thoroughly covers the system.

The argument for treating the code and its tests as a means of documentation is a very credible one. First, the approach results in cleaner code because programmers are constantly aware that their code must not only work but clearly communicate what it is doing. Second, both unit and acceptance tests document the code by means of demonstration. That is, cleanly written tests that thoroughly examine a portion of code reveal both what the code is meant to do and how it goes about doing it. Third, the code and tests on an agile project never fall out of date, ensuring that the team's documentation will always stay up to date. As the system's design changes, even the system and acceptance tests must be constantly updated; if not, they will begin to break, and the team will lose confidence in the system. In summary, consulting code and tests to see the design of a system demonstrates with confidence what the system actually does, not what it was intended to do and not what it might have done last month.

Many advocates of this approach are also dedicated followers of TDD. To learn more, read about the practice in Chapter 8, "Testing."

In-Code Commenting

Many agile teams are content to comment thoroughly within the code. Many teams also will follow some common standard that allows them to automatically extract and produce design documentation via a tool such as JavaDoc. The resulting document in some organizations may be used to fulfill all design documentation requirements.

It is worth noting that some Agilists (and specifically many XPers) reject code commenting as a viable form of documentation. Their justification is that the blocks of text above methods and classes must still be updated apart from the code and tests, those blocks of text too often go neglected and are not updated even during the development process, such commenting often goes ignored by the maintenance team that later takes ownership of the system, and programmers use the comments as a crutch, relying on them to express the design in a meaningful way rather than writing code that is clear enough to convey its design.

Rationale and Structure Document

Many agile teams will try to maintain a single document that provides an overview of and insight into the entire system [Martin02]. The goal of this document is to communicate the rationale and structure of the system. It may be consulted by new team members and outside programmers and architects who wish to know more about the system. It may also serve as a good reference for the team that takes over maintenance of the system. Finally, similar to the design document generated by JavaDoc, this text-based document may satisfy any design-level documentation required of the team.

Robert Martin, in his book *Agile Software Development*, recommends that the rationale and structure document be a "short and salient" text. Short means one to two dozen pages. Salient means the overall rationale and the highest-level structures of the system.

AN AGILE WBS'

One huge documentation sinkhole (though it may tax the office plotter as opposed to generating the stereotypical ream of documentation) can be found in the creation and maintenance of a hierarchical project plan, or WBS. The merits of the agile LWD (list of work to be done) versus a heavyweight WBS are discussed in Chapter 12. Building and maintaining a WBS as work is completed and the project requirements and schedule shift can become a time-consuming and frustrating process. Even fashioning a one-time WBS that is not updated after the beginning of the project can entail significant effort.

Too often, one simply gets the sense that mapping an agile project into a hierarchical WBS like the one illustrated in Figure 18.2 is a lot like fitting a round peg in the proverbial square hole.

ID	Task	Days Work	Start	Finish
1	Project Alpha	54	Mon 3/3/03	Fri 6/13/03
1.1	Initiation	4	Mon 3/3/03	Thu 3/6/03
1.1.1	Introduce Team	2	Mon 3/3/03	Tue 3/3/03
1.1.2	Meet with Stakeholders	1	Wed 3/5/03	Wed 3/5/03
1.1.3	Ramp-up Period	1	Thu 3/6/03	Thu 3/6/03
1.2	Define Phase	14	Fri 3/7/03	Fri 3/21/03
1.2.1	Requirements Gathering	7	Fri 3/7/03	Fri 3/14/03
1.2.1.1	Back End Services	1	Fri 3/7/03	Fri 3/7/03
1.2.1.2	Front End	2	Mon 3/10/03	Tue 3/11/03

FIGURE 18.2   A sample WBS breakout list.

Nonetheless, a WBS sometimes is simply demanded by the business. Usually it is a required document that cannot be gotten around. Sometimes it is the only way the business will review the project duration and cost estimates. Sometimes it is management's way of assuring the team has a plan. Occasionally it is collected and never reviewed. Whatever the reason, sometimes it must be done, and the agile WBS is a strategy for using an agile team's LWD to fashion a workable and useable WBS.

Begin with a Complete List of Work

By the time it might be required to present a formal WBS, every agile team should already have an LWD. For XP teams, this will be a list of user stories. Scrum teams will have a product backlog, and teams following FDD will have a features list. Other teams will have similar lists. The LWD will look something like Figure 18.3.

ID	Feature	Estimate	Iteration	Priority
1	Create and automate development environment, including "hello world" program that can be deployed through testing environments into production	5 days	1	1
2	Create a simple work queue where multiple users can assign generic tasks to one another	5 days	1	1
3	Allow work queue users to mark tasks as completed, escalated, deferred or deleted	2 days	1	1
4	Define and create a set of specific work queue task types that users can select from when creating a task	3 days	2	2
5	Create an admin access area where task types can be managed	4 days	2	2
6	Write a log-in screen and provide secure access to the work queue	4 days	2	2
7	Provide admin access to user and role settings	2 days	3	2

FIGURE 18.3   A sample LWD.

You will need to estimate the amount of time it would take for the team to complete all the work on the LWD. What is required here is one big number, though this number will likely need to be rolled up from estimates at the feature level. You should already have a process in place to determine a number like this, but until now you may have used it only for iterations or releases. If you have no process available, consult the estimation sections in Chapter 11. Make sure not to confuse ideal time with real time, and do not forget to add an appropriate dose of risk to one number.

Sketch the Project Schedule

Now you will need to ascertain what is most important to the business: a specific release schedule, a specific completion date, or simply that all the work in the LWD gets completed. Once you know, use whiteboard or paper to sketch out a simple schedule that plots the timing of iterations and releases (or Scrums or whatever other timeboxing mechanism your project will use). Do the dates look both realistic and acceptable to the business? What about the number of programmers on the team? Is this already decided, or is it an input you can control?

Based on the simple schedule you have devised, estimate the amount of time the team will spend on each iteration and release.

Write a Simple WBS

The synthesis between structure and agile happens here.

In your favorite project scheduling application, input the iterations and releases into the task lines of a new WBS. At this time, do not include any actual features from your LWD but flesh out the WBS with other activities that you know will need to be accomplished that are not in the LWD. Your WBS should look something like the sample in Figure 18.4.

ID	Task	Days Work	Start	Finish
1	Project Alpha	54	Mon 3/3/03	Fri 6/13/03
1.1	Initiation	4	Mon 3/3/03	Thu 3/6/03
1.1.1	Introduce Team	2	Mon 3/3/03	Tue 3/3/03
1.1.2	Meet with Stakeholders	1	Wed 3/5/03	Wed 3/5/03
1.1.3	Ramp-up Period	1	Thu 3/6/03	Thu 3/6/03
1.2	Release One	15	Fri 3/7/03	Thu 3/27/03
1.2.1	Iteration 1	5	Fri 3/7/03	Thu 3/13/03
1.2.2	Iteration 2	5	Fri 3/14/03	Thu 3/20/03
1.2.3	Iteration 3	5	Fri 3/21/03	Thu 3/27/03
1.3	Release Two	15	Fri 3/28/03	Thu 4/16/03
1.3.1	Iteration 4	5	Fri 3/28/03	Thu 4/2/03
1.3.2	Iteration 5	5	Fri 4/3/03	Thu 4/9/03
1.3.3	Iteration 6	5	Fri 4/10/03	Thu 4/16/03

FIGURE 18.4   A sample agile WBS breakout list.

Review the dates in the WBS to make sure you are comfortable with them. If necessary, have them reviewed by another set of eyes.

At this point, you may be done. You have a very simple WBS that you may submit alongside the LWD. To supplement the documents, you may write up a bit of text detailing the advantages of not pre-assigning features to iterations and releases.

On several of my projects, this has done the trick. It has also worked in response to several RFPs, where we won the contract.

If Necessary, Add More Detail

If the requester asks for more detail or you know in advance that he will want more, there are two more steps you may take. However, a word of caution here. You are about to produce and provide to the customer some hard numbers about what you will have done and when. You should to the best of your ability be realistic about the numbers you provide. Double-check everything. If necessary, review the estimation process for waterfall projects discussed in Chapter 20, "Real-World Environments." No project manager wants to hand anyone the rope they could be hanged with.

First, the requester may want to know in advance what is going into each release or even each iteration. In the LWD, assign the features to releases and iterations as necessary. Check your numbers in the LWD and WBS to ensure that you have a sufficient amount of time in each release or iteration to complete the features assigned to it in the LWD.

Second, the requester may want everything spelled out within the WBS itself. If this is the case, insert the individual features under their appropriate iterations within the WBS. This should provide all the detail anyone would require.

Keep in mind that taking either of the steps in this section will make maintaining the WBS (if this is required) a bit trickier. Of course, this assumes that the project team is actually operating in an agile fashion, where features may shift between iterations, change in size, and spontaneously appear and disappear.

DOCUMENT HANDOFFS

Document handoffs are often a sign of non-agile processes. This is because one party is generating a document for use by another party, implying that instead of communicating with one another the parties are writing and reading in seclusion. Ultimately, document handoffs invoke the same sort of criticism that Agilists level against a phased development process, where deliverables are thrown over the wall from one phase to the next. Inevitably, information is lost, and some poor fool who doesn't know how to catch gets his eye poked out. It's just a bad situation.

Obviously, as long as there are documents to be handed off, there is no way to completely avoid document handoffs. There is, for example, no way to avoid employee turnover. Also, teams that are not collocated are likely to have more documentation handoffs [Ambler03]. Try encouraging face-to-face conversations, phone calls, and video conferencing to minimize the pain of document handoffs.

ADDING DOCUMENTS

Up to now, we have discussed the vetting of existing project documentation for its usefulness and potential to be streamlined. On occasion, however, an idea may percolate from within the project bowels to generate a new form of documentation.

When this occurs, beat that bad thought down. If it does not skulk away, then here are a few questions to answer before allowing a new form of documentation to be created:

- What will be in it?
- Who will use it?
- When and how often will it be used?
- Who will update it?
- When and how often will it be updated?
- Is there enough time in the schedule to handle this additional requirement?
- Is there another way to satisfy the need for this document that does not include documentation?

These questions should assist the project in devising a living document that best suits its needs and entails as little extra effort as possible. If you cannot come up with an answer for one or more of these questions, then the new documentation should not be created.

STARTING MONDAY: PERFORM A DOCUMENTATION REVIEW

If it is within your power to initiate or you can convince the powers that be to do the initiation, then consider reviewing all the live documents on your project. Obviously, the goal is to bury as many as possible without adversely affecting the operations of anyone associated with the team.

The following questions could be used to review each live document:

- Is there still a need for it? One indication that there is no longer a need for the document is if it has been produced on previous projects but no one can recall ever actually having to use it.
- Can another document satisfy or be modified to satisfy the need for this document?
- Can this document be replaced with some other process that would take less time, such as face-to-face communication or automation?
- Who updates the document, and is this the right person for the job?

If one of the above questions cannot be answered regarding a particular document, something about the process related to that document should be altered.

A month after you implement the results of the review, hold a follow-up review. Are the team and anyone else who could have been affected fairing better as a result of the lessened amount of documentation? Essentially, did you cut too much? If there is still any doubt remaining about the cuts, hold a second review in another month.

19 People

People are the heart of an agile project, and the health of any project is integrally tied to its people. If they suffer, the project suffers. If the project is affected by external forces, they suffer.

My cynical side has repeatedly prodded me to subtitle this chapter "The Softer Side of Software," but that would do a disservice to what are very important issues. Many books on the dynamics of groups and teams have been written by professionals with big titles and lots of letters after their names. This chapter is not meant to contend with any of that. Rather, it simply discusses a few topics that should be important to everyone.

MAKING CHANGE PALATABLE

Like it or not, many people and organizations do not react well to change. Even when the project is not in flux, individuals change, people get rolled on and off of projects, and tempers wear thin. People react to change (both planned and otherwise) better when they feel informed and in some level of control.

While agile planning may be based on learning to react more quickly to demand (as opposed to predicting it), agile projects can readily benefit from addressing the people issues that may arise from change before they happen instead of reacting to them afterward. Readers who have not yet read Chapter 17, "Communication and Collaboration," may want to read the section "Engendering a Communicative and Collaborative Culture."

Finally, big changes or even several little ones can lead to a spate of acts of civil disobedience on a project. This can really rankle a team lead or project manager. Agile, by its very nature, must tolerate some dissension. Bright, skilled, and self-motivated individuals sometimes have a hard time doing what they are told, especially in non-life-threatening situations. Dissension can be a sign of many things. It may just be people blowing off steam. It may also mean that morale is suffering.

THE HONOR SYSTEM

In agile development we trust people to know what their jobs are, to know how to do their jobs, and to be responsible about doing their jobs. After all, we are supposed to be skilled professionals, right? People should be trusted to follow the team processes. If individuals feel they have a say in what processes the team follows, they are more likely to follow them.

If someone is not following a team process, it is always best to first ask him why. Perhaps he has a good reason for not following the process. Granted, it may not be appropriate for him to act in a passive-aggressive manner, but the team may still have something useful to learn. If he does not have a good reason, and if he is shirking more than a couple of team processes, then the team lead and the project manager have a problem they must address.

If two or more developers are subverting the same process, it is probably best to investigate why. Again, there is not much excuse for passive-aggressive behavior, but the team may well have a process that needs to be altered. Worse, the team might have a morale issue, and this must be addressed quickly.

Some teams inevitably consider putting processes in place to keep people honest or, put another way, to monitor or control how individuals go about their jobs. Such tactics have varied results. I have been on more than one team where the team leads decided that it was valuable for programmers to include comments with every code check-in. They hoped this would help other programmers when they were hunting down defects that had been recently introduced into the code. Obviously they should have spent more time diagnosing the actual problem instead of treating symptoms, but that is not the point of this anecdote.

On the first project, the comment field on the check-in dialogue box was made mandatory. This idea was okay because it served as a reminder to programmers that they were supposed to fill in that field. Of course it was not foolproof. One could just as easily enter "asdfghjkl" as opposed to a meaningful description, but again, we are all supposed to be skilled professionals. Ultimately, the strategy was an unobtrusive reminder to programmers to follow a team practice.

On the second project, an assistant team lead coded a quick script to stroll through the check-ins on a daily basis and e-mail him a synopsis of every programmer's check-in with comments. Can you say *Big Brother*? Admittedly, morale on that team was already flying south, but his actions only helped to make it a one-way trip.

DIFFICULT CONVERSATIONS

Keeping an agile team running in tip-top shape means keeping the team members communicating and collaborating with one another. Problems and personal conflicts that will not go away need to be addressed before they poison the culture of the project team. Such potential problems and conflicts include many of the situations discussed earlier in this book and even this chapter. These include:

- The programmer no one on the team likes to pair with.
- An important stakeholder who will not follow the rules of the daily Scrum meeting.
- A tough customer newly assigned to the project team.
- Programmers who refuse to integrate their code on a regular basis.
- A seemingly unforgivable breach of the honor system.

These are real issues that can and do happen on every project team. Typically we do not have the luxury of simply replacing such individuals with their more agreeable twins. While a command-and-control response may appear on the surface to resolve many of these issues, it often only leaves deeper, unresolved issues to fester. Sometimes, the best (or only) way to address a problem or to resolve a conflict on a project team may entail a difficult but necessary conversation, a real two-way conversation where the goal is to fix an issue and not fix a person.

We should not run headlong into such conversations. Instead, consider the following suggestions (based on the recommendations in *Difficult Conversations* by Stone, Patton, Heen, and Fisher [Stone00]).

There Are Always Three Versions of What Happened

The three versions of what happened are ours, theirs, and what an impartial party would have observed. We typically already know our own. It helps to be curious about the other party's version of events. If we ask honest questions and genuinely listen to get at the other party's version, we just might learn something. Also, it is important to keep in mind that the result of someone's actions may not be the same as the intent.

While everyone loses from playing the blame game, sometimes we need to revisit in detail how things have gone wrong in order to keep them from going wrong again. In such cases, it is best to investigate how every individual contributed to the problem and what each individual could do differently next time.

Feelings May Be a Valid and Even Necessary Part of the Conversation

Typically, we try to keep feelings out of conversations related to the project, but sometimes they are the root of the problem. Even when they are not the root of the problem, strong unacknowledged feelings can interrupt and even wreck a conversation. Before entering into a difficult conversation, we should explore our own feelings, consider whether the feelings of the other party are tied up in the issue, and determine whether those feelings should be openly acknowledged as an important component of the conversation.

Self Identity Can Complicate the Conversation

The topics of difficult conversations can get tied into the self identity of either individual because the topic of that conversation could be a threat to that individual's sense of self. A programmer whose careless mistake might have caused the rollback of a production deployment might react negatively to any criticism on the matter because a careless mistake might call into question his sense of abilities and competence. Then there is the project manager who, based on his conversations with the rest of the team, needs to make clear to that same programmer that the careless mistake appears to stem from a lack of attention, which the programmer has to work on if he wants to keep his job. The project manager, who thinks of himself as an understanding person who will stick up for the members of his team, may have problems reconciling his opinion of himself while contemplating the possibility of having to deliver a veiled threat to fire someone who made an honest mistake.

Pursue a Learning Conversation

After contemplating the above points, consider following these steps when entering into a difficult conversation:

Learn the other person's story: Additionally, attempt to distinguish his intent from whatever actually transpired.

Explain your point of view: Let him know where you are coming from. Perhaps he will listen and perhaps he won't, but give him the opportunity to understand where you are coming from and don't assume he already knows.

Devise a solution together: Even if you already have a solution in mind, see how close you can get by working with the other person to come to a solution that is acceptable to both of you. It is typically better to make a concession or two if it will result in a more amicable solution.

Ultimately, a less-than-perfect solution that both parties can agree to is more likely to succeed in the long run than a solution dictated by one of the parties to the other. Often the best (and most fair) solution is one that neither party is completely happy with [Fisher91].

Finally, when addressing issues like these, do not be shy about seeking assistance. Consult the local human relations person whose job it is to help with such things. Pick up a book (for example, the previously mentioned *Difficult Conversations*). Locate some other third party who is knowledgeable and experienced in working with people—and preferably not associated with the project—who can lend his ear and experience.

MORALE

Because the success of agile teams is so closely tied to the people who constitute them, it is hard to overstate the threat a morale issue poses to a project. The good news is that agile projects are ahead of the game on morale. In 2001, a Cutter Consortium survey indicated that projects operating within an agile software development ecosystem scored over 20 percent better on morale than other projects [Highsmith02]. But this is no excuse for not being mindful of potential morale problems and addressing any problems promptly.

Detecting Morale Problems

Sometimes a morale problem is obvious, and sometimes it blindsides the team. Sometimes it affects only a portion of the team, and sometimes it grips everyone, including the project manager. However, there are a couple of ways that agile practices may help a team lead or project manager identify a morale problem in its early stages.

Feedback During Stand Up and Daily Scrum Meetings

Daily meetings are a good mechanism for warnings on this and many fronts [Lyndvall02]. Topics that become themes, get regularly introduced with an exasperated voice, and are met with rolling eyes may seem to be only footnotes at first, but they can expand into bigger problems.

Iteration Goals Routinely Not Met

If the team is intentionally implementing stretch goals (see Chapter 14, "Executing Iterative Development") and is happy with this process, then that team is in the clear. Otherwise, this is likely the symptom of some other issue that may already be or might fester into a morale problem. Iterations, after all, do not simply fail to complete themselves.

Consider the underlying cause. Is this the result of continuous overtime? Is it the result of perpetual quality issues, or is it less pernicious? Are programmers simply underestimating their tasks and does the team need to revisit this process? See Chapter 14, "Executing Iterative Development."

Address Root Causes

Plenty of events and activities can reduce morale. Some are short term and go away. Some are long term but need to be addressed from a level above the project (such as company layoffs). Then there are the morale problems that arise from within the team, may be long term, and may only get worse.

If the morale problem on the team has already devolved into open mutiny, the project manager may need to switch to a project recovery strategy (see Chapter 20, "Real-World Environments"). One technique that might work, however, is to sacrifice one of the organization's sacred cows [McConnell96]. Let people come in late or go home early, give the team its own conference room, or tear up the WBS (if there is one). Basically, do something drastic to let the team know that you are really serious about working with them to get the train back on the track.

Hopefully it has not gotten that bad. Addressing the cause of a morale problem can take less effort and sacrifice than addressing it after it has gotten out of hand. The following sections discuss a few significant and relatively easy ways to identify threats to morale and what to do about them.

Too Much Documentation

Nobody likes busywork. Excessive documentation, such as some of the scenarios that may arise from heavy process environments, can bog down a team. Defining excessive documentation may be difficult—one person's trash is another person's treasure—but the effects may be a bit simpler to identify. If the project team is not in an explicit analysis or design phase and it goes two consecutive iterations with less than half its effort directed toward programming, then it likely has an issue with excessive documentation [Lyndvall02]. See Chapter 18, "Documentation," for some ways to reduce the team's level of documentation.

Continuous Overtime

This anti-agile practice is an obvious and regular perpetrator of moralicide, yet it is probably the cause that most often goes ignored. People have lives outside of work. They have families, friends, houses to tend to, cars to get to the shop, a ballgame to see. When work intrudes into these activities, they will begin to resent it. They may be in the office more, but quality and productivity suffer. In all likelihood, so will the Yahoo!™ Games server. And so will the outcome of the project.

Perpetual Quality Issues

Perpetual quality issues within code—regardless of whether that code is written by the team or foisted upon it—can put the project in the ditch and keep it there (though many teams may sustain a surprising amount of momentum through all that dirt, brush, and trash). Quality issues result in defects and change requests that too often lead to interrupt-driven work. Either something has broken and someone is at your cube or something someone else touched is broken and you are at his cube (but he's not). Either way, lots of time, serenity, and sanity is lost when programmers need to switch frequently between productive tasks and annoying tasks.

If the problem is the quality of the team's own code, the obvious solution is to examine existing processes and improve testing practices. Typically, the answer to this solution is, "We don't have time for that." Okay. Do we have time for couldn't-care-less programming? Do we have time for programmers to start calling in sick? Do we have time for a programmer mutiny? If quality issues really are cutting into morale, these are the kind of things that will happen next.

Potentially more harmful than issues with the team's own code is when the team is having significant issues with another project's code. This can occur when the team is sharing a codebase with or dependent upon the output of another project. If that other project cannot be infected with agile practices, then try testing, as described in Chapter 8, "Testing."

Absence of a Release

Getting code into production (or at least in front of the customer) energizes an agile team. When a team that is accustomed to releasing on a regular basis hits a patch of months where it is unable to release, not because of issues related to the project but because of external issues such as a system-wide freeze or the customer being otherwise occupied, the team will likely begin to drift off course. The loss of that regular infusion of feelings of success and satisfaction, much like a runner's high, can affect motivation and even temperament.

Second, the loss of a near-term goal, unfortunately, encourages everyone on the team to not quite complete many of their tasks. Tests are not written as thoroughly, documentation updates go undone, and features go half completed. When there is no short-term goal, this and worse can happen. Then comes the subtle but increasing dread of having to go back and clean up everything. This dread will eat at morale.

This is the same dread that starts to crawl up on you in September when you remember that you haven't updated the bookkeeping since July. That's okay, you'll catch up next month. Then in November you remember again and even have time, but by then it's so much work that you cannot bring yourself to do it. You go to a friend's cottage for the weekend instead. When the thought comes back in January, you club it down mercilessly. When tax time comes you can just black March out of your social schedule.

Addressing this issue means getting back on track. Declare an amnesty period where everyone can 'fess up to and address their cut corners. Execute a spring cleaning iteration to catch up on all that two-thirds-done work. Schedule the closest thing to a release as soon as is reasonably possible.

HIRING FOR AGILE PROJECTS

If the success of agile projects is tied to the people on the project team, then the hiring process should be viewed as an opportunity to increase the ability, potential, and effectiveness of the entire team.

What should someone look for in an agile programmer, manager, analyst, or tester? Technical skill and experience might not be as important as you think [Fraunhofer02]. Skills can be learned, and experience is something that naturally comes with time. Personal character, however, is much more difficult to change. Here are some attributes to look for in a prospective member of an agile team.

Ability to Communicate and Collaborate

The ability and willingness to communicate and collaborate effectively with other members on the project team on a frequent basis should be considered an inviolate requirement for any new member of an agile team. The person does not need to be Mr. Sunshine, and he can even be a bit rough around the edges and grumpy at times (a team will grow accustomed to that), but if he is incapable of communicating and collaborating with others on a regular basis, he simply is not going to be able to contribute to the open, free flow of ideas, ask-don't-guess environment required for a healthy agile project team.

Intellectual Honesty

An individual with intellectual integrity will provide the honesty and responsible citizenship required by agile projects. This is the type of person who readily admits to making mistakes, strives to provide realistic reports and estimates, and attempts to understand the purpose of an exception instead of simply writing code to swallow it [McConnell93].

This person will say the things that we may not want (but need) to hear. He will not commit to completing a task in two days when he believes it will take a week.

Humility

People who recognize their limitations are often superior to programmers who have more raw mental power but believe they can tackle anything. Humble programmers, for example, will take the low road to designing code and will not rely solely on their own capabilities, while the fearless programmer may challenge himself to achieve a higher level of design in his solution and trust that he got it right [McConnell93]. Humble programmers are also more likely to listen to feedback and respond to user comments constructively. While the fearless programmer is out actively searching for the next challenging problem, the humble programmer will be busy:

- breaking complicated problems into simple, easy-to-attack pieces
- programming straightforward, easy-to-understand solutions
- writing more tests

Mr. Humble or Mr. Fearless—who would you rather have on your project?

Curiosity

People who ask questions and do not simply accept the answers written on the page in front of them are more likely to spot the gaps in requirements and less-than-optimal solutions. Think of a programmer who, by being curious about the new business domain of his project, learns enough in two weeks that he is able to think critically about the requirements he is given to program. Or a project manager who is not merely interested in delivering software to the customer but also understanding the reasons behind the customer's desire to move to a new system. A curious individual, by nature of his tendency to gather information and ask questions, is more likely to spot missed requirements, realize more optimal solutions, and communicate on a deeper level with the customer.

Flexibility and Desire to Learn

There is a wide variety of activities that need to be performed on the average software development project, and often there may be more roles on the project than people. Often, for example, programmers need to pinch hit as requirement analysts, and managers may need to assist with user training and acceptance testing. To be effective at developing software in a fast-paced world, project teams (especially a small one) require people who are not simply specialists in their own activities but are able and willing to learn new roles and step in and give a hand [Fraunhofer02a] [Stapleton03].

Additionally, new management methods, programming languages, and technologies are constantly flowing into and out of the world of IT, and they can change and improve the way teams work and solve everyday problems. For example, many programming challenges related to processor speed and memory just five years ago are no longer concerns today. Meanwhile, the new speed and available space on the average system has led to all manner of opportunities for the opportunistic programmer. Individuals with a predisposition to learn new things and experiment with their newly acquired knowledge are going to be the ones who make the most of these advancements.

Agile-minded organizations are often very serious about selecting new employees based on these and other agile-friendly qualities. These organizations will ensure that potential hires are interviewed by members of the team they are likely to work with. Some organizations will even go so far as to request that serious candidates for programming positions come in for half a day of pair programming with other members in the organization.

Finally, if organizations really want to hire for agile development, like it or not, they will need to be ready to pay for above average people. One repeatedly stated explanation for the success of agile projects is their tendency to use fewer but more competent people.

20   Real-World Environments

In This Chapter

- Heavy Process
- Waterfall and Other Phased Approaches
- Scaling for Big Projects
- Project Recovery
- Agile Contracts
- Fixed Cost

When an agile project crashes headlong into a real-world environment, there is no one right prescription for a solution. Agile methodologies were founded with project teams and customers who were focused above all else on building valuable software. These agile testbeds surely had environments where processes could be altered to fit new ideas and values, and they surely included programmers, managers, and customers who respected each other's abilities and were willing collaborators. One major premise of this book is the observation that not all project environments will be so conducive to an agile approach. This chapter, however, addresses some environments that can sometimes make the pioneering agile team feel that the world is dead set against them: most notably, those using a heavy process and a waterfall approach. The discussion then moves on to environments that pose both challenges and promise for agile teams. These are fixed-cost, large, and recovery projects.

HEAVY PROCESS

Heavy process environments are those in which the way of doing things (and the tools and templates used to do it) are set in stone by a company, an IT organization, or a project management office before a project team is even assembled. A team that works in such an environment often must appeal to the organization to make any changes in the way the team goes about doing things, and sometimes those appeals must be made prior to the onset of the project. Audits are performed to ensure that the project team is not varying from the plan, and too often these are checklist audits where the auditors have little interest in the effectiveness of the project team's modifications.

Too much process in software development is akin to wearing too much protective clothing when trying to do work around the house. Most handymen will wear glasses when running the table saw. The carpenter wears a mask when sanding. But no one ever dons a glove sufficient to not smash his thumb before swinging a hammer because he would be unable to hold the nail in place. Heavy process environments try to throw down covers and drop cloths to protect everything. Programmers are not given the ability to change metadata within the development databases, programmers are told that they may not do any coding before they design and document, managers are told that they must build detailed plans for a year out before the project is even funded, and no one on the project team is allowed to speak to the business; he must communicate through an information manager. Such processes are meant to keep people from breaking things, to ensure they think before they act, and to be certain that there is a plan. Too often, however, they do not address the issues they are meant to address. We smash our thumbs anyway, but this time it's because the glove gets in the way of the nail.

Heavy process environments are most often associated with such acronyms as CMM (the Capability Maturity Model), RUP (Rational Unified Process), and PMI (the Project Management Institute). None of these approaches to software development necessitates a heavy process; typically they just get interpreted that way. People learn the process and never learn the why, and it really can become absurd. At one account that I managed for more than a year, someone within the IT organization calculated how much money it would take to pilot an inconsequential change through the organization's entire development process, from the discovery period through deployment, with all the requisite trimmings. The cost: $60,000.

There is no one right set of steps to integrate agile development into a heavy process environment except to lobby for and have the majority of the process repealed. Unless a project team can make this happen, it will likely have to adopt agile development practice by practice (as discussed in Chapter 6, "Agile Practices"). Adopting several programming practices such as automated unit testing and continuous integration probably will be rather straightforward even in a heavy process environment. Lots of heavy process is also a characteristic of multi-project environments. In multi-project environments, where systems are closely integrated, agile testing practices can be more difficult to implement and maintain. Anyone working in a multi-project environment, where other project teams are actively working against related systems, will want to review the section on "Testing as the Best Defense" in Chapter 8, "Testing."

Adopting an agile management approach within a heavy process environment will likely be the hard part because processes in such environments seem to focus on what the non-programmers must do on a daily basis; analysts write requirement documents and hold meetings, and project managers keep the work schedule up to date and report progress. Tips for addressing heavy process environments permeate this book. Two chapters of particular interest may include Chapter 12, "Project Initiation," and Chapter 18, "Documentation." Other important sections include the discussion on solution sheets in Chapter 11, "Features and User Stories," and requirements tracing in Chapter 13, "Small Releases." Each chapter or section includes activities that may be used to meet the spirit of some process or documents required by heavy process environments without carrying so much of the burden. Also read the next section, "Waterfall and Other Phased Approaches," since so many heavy process environments rely on project phases.

Finally, Scott Ambler provides a fitting name for one other approach that may be used in heavy process environments: the team blocker [Ambler03a]. The individual, potentially a lion-hearted project manager, shields the rest of the team from as much of the heavy process environment as possible. Most often this becomes a job of translating everything that the team is doing from agile into the organization's heavy process. A work breakdown structure might be constantly updated (as discussed in Chapter 14, "Executing Iterative Development"). Change and deviation forms will need to be regularly completed, filed, and justified. Meetings must be attended. While the position may be no fun (and even difficult) to fill, it can provide a lot of flexibility to the project team.

WATERFALL AND OTHER PHASED APPROACHES

Waterfall, or any approach that makes only one lap around the plan-define-design-build-deploy track, is likely to encounter problems related to a lack of feedback both within cycles and over the entire project. If an organization is not very good at writing and defining requirements and a project team follows a waterfall process, the organization will not receive what it needs even if the team delivers exactly what the organization has asked for, because there would have been little means of learning that the organization was not well suited for expressing requirements until the completion of the project. Similarly—and exposing an even greater flaw in waterfall—a phased approach fails to address in any real fashion the fact that in some cases users may truly understand what they need from a system in development only after they have begun to use and understand that system. This, again, will not occur until the completion of the waterfall process.

No matter what teams do, they sometimes are forced to work within a waterfall environment. Thankfully, implementing agile development within a waterfall environment is possible. However, as with working within a heavy process environment, the exact solution will be different for every project.

Some agile methodologies may integrate rather smoothly within a waterfall environment, allowing a project team to continue working within its waterfall process while adopting an agile approach. The early phases of FDD may be extended to meet the needs of a waterfall approach. DSDM, also can be executed in a way that strongly resembles a waterfall approach (see Chapter 3, "The Agile Methodologies"). However, this approach will entail some of the drawbacks of waterfall.

Project teams following methodologies other than FDD and DSDM may be able to adjust another agile methodology or even fit a set of several agile practices and processes into a waterfall approach. Similar to working within a heavy process environment, project teams should be able to employ many programming-level practices and processes relatively easily. The real problems with using agile methods in a waterfall setting arise with the introduction of short iteration and small releases. However, there are some activities that can help almost any project team meld that iterative approach to a waterfall framework.

Shorten Auxiliary Phases and Insert Cycles

First, agile-minded projects should try to shrink any phase that does not begin with the letters b-u-i-l-d. These teams should spend as little time as is reasonable on requirement definition and design activities, sketching out only enough information to prove to project stakeholders and upper management that they have a valid understanding of and plan for the project. In some waterfall environments, teams under my management have even requested and received permission to merge the design and build phases. Similarly, our project teams have sold the use of automated unit and acceptance testing within the build phase as an alterative to a distinct test phase.

Second, project teams should try to insert cycles wherever possible. The goal is to create feedback loops within and between phases. Therefore, a team may break a yearlong waterfall schedule with one release into three or four releases, each following the completion of a short waterfall approach. Short iterations may be executed within the waterfall phases to serve as a regular feedback mechanism to measure both progress and the quality of work products. Feature-driven iterations may work best within build cycles. Meanwhile, task cycles (discussed as an agile practice in Chapter 14) may be more useful in the other phases because design decisions and the completion of entire documents, while they may be tracked as features, can run too long to be completed within one iteration.

Provide Some Upfront Detail with Estimates

Finally, when in the waterfall, agile teams may need to perform a bit of upfront estimation to break free of the plan phase safely. On agile teams, project managers and team leads are accustomed to working with the customer or alone to cleave knots of functionality into streams of stories. Experienced agile programmers, meanwhile, are accustomed to the process and perils of estimation. The key when attacking an entire project at once is to keep the process efficient.

My approach is to assemble the team in front of a whiteboard and together break the project out into a list of feature names. We identify the major elements of each feature under its name, and then I ask for broad estimates. To keep the team from getting lost in the forest of detail, we estimate in increments of three ideal days (our approximation of a single calendar week for one programmer), and we put a question mark beside the element of any feature we are not certain about. The meeting breaks up, programmers investigate the uncertain elements of each feature, and we meet a second time to refine the breakout of features and their estimates. New questions always come up, and we repeat the process of gathering information and reconvening. When we can confidently break the three ideal day barrier on a feature, we consider it adequately estimated. When we can confidently break (or at least meet) the three ideal day barrier on every feature, we consider our work complete. The project team then has a feature list from which it can provide time, effort, and cost estimates. In addition, the team also has a quality list of estimated features that it can feed into its first release planning meeting.

Many waterfall projects often follow a lukewarm process approach that is neither quite agile or heavy. On these projects, some upfront documentation may be required. In my project experience, we have often been able to produce solution sheets (discussed in Chapter 11) during this estimation period that have satisfied the documentation requirements for the project.

SCALING FOR BIG PROJECTS

Large projects can negate the effect of (and even make it impossible to implement) some agile practices, including build automation, collective ownership, the creation of an open workspace, and conscription onsite customer. This is because agile methodologies were fashioned mostly based on the work of smaller teams.

FDD seems to be the one agile methodology that was fashioned from the beginning to work with medium-size and larger teams.

One approach to consider when employing agile development is simply to not scale the project. Scaling a project always adds overhead and can cloud the visibility of immediate needs with grand ideas and big strategies. Is the whole system actually required one year from now, or might the business actually benefit more from one quarter of the functionality delivered in six months? Is the bigger team actually going to move faster? Smaller, more effective teams can perform at multiple times the productivity of a larger team [Poppendieck03]. They are easier to steer, require less formalized process to ensure communication and coordination, and lose far less productive time to resource bottlenecks and people getting in the way of one another [Lyndvall02].

Sometimes, of course, not scaling is not an option. Numerous projects have scaled agile methods with a varied amount of success. Furthermore, Scrum and DSDM both have scaling strategies built around the team of teams approach.

Two Approaches to Scaling

There is no right way to scale an agile project. One common approach is the team of teams approach. In this scenario a member of each team, typically a team lead or a programmer with some management responsibilities, functions both as a member of that team and as a member of an overall project management and coordination team. In this approach, release planning is performed by the management team, iteration planning may be performed by either the management team or the individual project teams (or some combination of both), and intra-iteration planning is typically performed solely by the individual team as it executes each iteration. The team of teams approach is illustrated in Figure 20.1. On very large projects, a customer team may be built from a similar model.

Another approach is similar to the team of teams approach but shares only one or two individuals across all the project teams, typically just a project manager, a senior programmer, or both. In this approach, there is no separate team to coordinate the activities of the teams, just shared team members who take part in the planning and execution activities of every team. I have employed this approach to manage successfully up to three teams at a time. It will certainly not scale as large as the team of teams approach, but it also reduces the amount of coordination between teams by removing the need for a standalone management team. The approach is illustrated in Figure 20.2.

Both of these approaches have common goals. One is to keep each individual development team small enough that communication and coordination with the team can be done informally, thereby keeping process costs low. Another is the attempt to establish strong communication ties between the teams so that each team

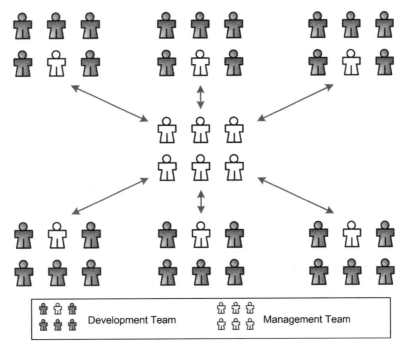

FIGURE 20.1   Scaling with a team of teams.

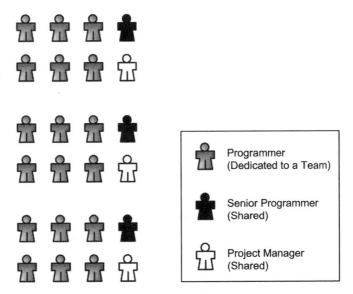

FIGURE 20.2   Scaling with a shared senior programmer and project manager.

(if not each member of each team) is aware of what the other teams are working on. Third, both support an iterative approach across the teams. Each team will not determine in a vacuum what it is working on for each iteration. Instead, each team plans in coordination with the members of other teams. Finally, the customer may still be engaged throughout the project by working with the management member of the project for planning and working with the individual teams for feature definition and development.

It is important to remember that a project may not be able to operate with multiple teams until an infrastructure has been put in place that can support such activity. This becomes even more important on projects with teams that do not work in the same geographic place. Often, a single team may need to put in place the infrastructure to manage code, tests, integration, ideas, features, and planning before additional teams can come on line. In such cases, the initial team may be made up of individuals who then disperse to the new teams, ensuring that at least a seed of knowledge is passed on to each of the new teams as the project grows.

Ten Lessons from Scaling

Recently, 35 agile practitioners gathered in Alberta, Canada, to discuss their experiences with scaling agile projects. They identified the following 10 lessons from their collective experiences [Reifer03]:

- Projects will continue to attempt to scale agile approaches regardless of what the experts say.
- More, shorter release cycles are better, even if those releases are shown only to the customer.
- Daily inter-team meetings attended by leads from each project can improve communication.
- Some upfront architecture will be required.
- A federation strategy in which many customers exist but each customer is the authority in a given area of the system can be used to scale the agile customer.
- Code interrogation and collective ownership issues may be reduced through branching, wrapping, and cloning components.
- Expectations of the overall effectiveness of agile processes need to be reduced.
- Business analysts may be employed to act for the customer as long as they do not become a blocking mechanism between the customer and the programmers.
- Teams should strive to locate and consider the lessons learned from other projects that have already experimented with scaling agile methodologies.
- A synthesis of agile and traditional approaches is appropriate.

PROJECT RECOVERY

Some teams may look to agile development as a way to salvage a distressed project. Agile projects, in fact, can perform well within a project recovery environment. Ken Schwaber, a founder of Scrum, has observed that project teams may actually have a better chance of adopting an agile methodology when they are up against a wall, because management is more willing to step in and remove roadblocks and provide other types of support [Fraunhofer02a].

Set the Project on More Solid Ground

Projects have been recovered by transitioning to an agile approach, but one must be mindful that agile practices do not represent a bag full of the same stones David used to take down Goliath. First and foremost, there may be fundamental problems that must be addressed before a team even considers applying an agile approach. For example, no amount of agile is going to help a project that is too rich in work and too poor in available time to complete it. Second, morale problems (discussed in Chapter 19, "People") may need to be addressed prior to, or at the very least apart from, adopting agile development. Third is the state of the current codebase.

Then there is the question about the state of the code and other work products produced to date. A project that is about to embark upon a recovery initiative should take the time to consider the costs associated with salvaging and retooling the work that has already been done. How significantly have the requirements changed and how much of the code was simply written against the wrong requirements? Can existing use cases and other requirements documentation be used as is or mined to create features for agile planning and management (see Chapter 11 for a discussion of how this can be done)? How much do the programmers hate the code that is in place? How many people on the team have not been there from the beginning and will have to learn the current codebase in order to get their project legs?

In short, the project team will want to have a coherent (though perhaps hastily prepared) execution strategy in place before pressing forward with a recovery program. This strategy should:

- Reduce the project's goals to something that is at worst very aggressive and not unattainable.
- Stem any fomenting people and morale issues.
- Identify the intended uses of existing documentation and code.
- Trim processes on the project to only those required to support a successful recovery.

Fold In Agile Practices

Even after fundamental issues such as these are addressed, there may be additional issues that may not be resolved by implementing one or more agile processes. Such non-fundamental problems may include resource bottlenecks, insufficient knowledge of the technology, or communication problems. Figure 20.3 recommends a process (modified from one discussed in Chapter 6) for selecting the next agile practice to adopt, taking into account the project recovery situation.

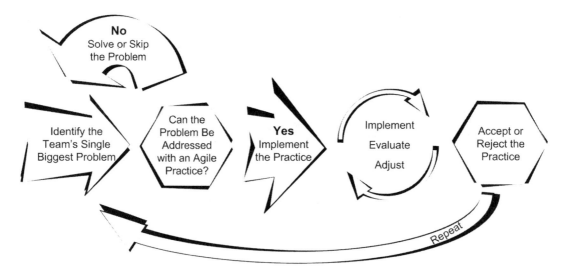

FIGURE 20.3   Implementing practices in a project recovery environment.

Agile practices and processes that the team may consider implementing first will depend upon the nature of the team's problems. Practices to consider should include build automation, testing, collective ownership, and feature teams for integration problems; stand up meetings, daily Scrums, pair programming, or onsite customer for communication issues; and user stories, small releases, and short iterations for problems having to do with getting functionality complete and out the door.

Finally, sometimes the best approach may not be to use agile to set the project right. Instead, an organization or project team may choose to use brute force, determination, and gallons of elbow grease to get the project off its fender and out of the ditch (in this case meaning to complete a shippable release). Once the project is fixed, a project team could then begin applying agile practices and processes in earnest. While not always the most appealing approach, this has worked for some projects [Schuh01a]. Like most any other recovery process, it would require a management philosophy geared toward providing the project team with whatever it needs to get the job done.

AGILE CONTRACTS

The tricky bit about agile development and contracts is that agile projects get messed up in fixed price or fixed date contracts. There are several reasons for this, including:

- A purely agile project, because it accepts and even encourages the changeability of requirements and whole features, can be extraordinarily difficult (some would argue impossible) to estimate in terms of time or cost.
- Refining system requirements to the level at which they can be accurately estimated for time and cost may take significant upfront analysis and design, which could take a sizable bite out of the benefits an agile approach would bring.
- Fixed price, date, or scope pits the customer and the vendor against one another. The customer will look to slide in as much as he can to get the most for his money, while the vendor will do as little as possible to try to make the most he can from the contract.

There is much validity to these arguments, but there are some faults of logic as well.

Optional Scope

Agilists prefer a time-and-materials contract, but to accommodate the fact that most customers do not prefer these types of contracts, they have a couple of other options.

Kent Beck has proposed the *optional scope* contract (a.k.a. negotiated scope contract or delivered-feature contract) [Beck99] [Highsmith02]. This contract provides a fixed number of developers for a fixed number of iterations or a fixed period of time. For example, the client may agree to pay a fixed amount for six programmers completing eight two-week iterations (four months total). For the customer, this arrangement makes cost predictable (it can even give a delivery date), but it does nothing to ensure the scope of the delivery.

The optional scope contract may be altered somewhat to provide the customer with a bit more leverage by allowing the customer to cancel the contract any time after the first two iterations. This, the customer may feel, might encourage the vendor to maintain a certain level of quality and performance because the continuation of the contract is completely at his—that is, the customer's—discretion.

Target Cost[1]

Another approach to agile contracts is one advocated by Lean Software Development. The target-cost contract intends to tie both the customer and the vendor to a mutual win-win (or, conversely, lose-lose) scenario. Although no contract can guarantee that one party cannot exploit an engagement to its sole benefit, the target-cost contract seeks to encourage the customer and vendor to collaborate toward meeting at or under a specific total dollar amount for the engagement.

An engagement based on a target-cost contract is begun with an agreed-to dollar figure. This figure will include the total cost to complete the functionality, including changes and corrections. Since the figure will be the target cost for both parties, and since all requirements certainly cannot be identified in advance, the customer and vendor may spend some time working toward an agreement on this number. Once the figure has been agreed upon and the project has begun, both parties are expected to work together to define, build, and deliver a sufficient amount of functionality to meet the goal of the project while meeting or staying below the target cost.

The target-cost contract is structured so that both parties benefit if the total cost of the engagement comes in under the agreed-to price. Conversely, both parties will end up paying extra if the engagement runs over the target cost. A good example of a target-cost engagement is one where the vendor is paid only the actual cost of his services until the project has been completed, at which point he receives a previously agreed-to fee. This fee is the vendor's profit. If the engagement finishes below cost, the vendor's team will have worked less time than planned, and by receiving the fixed fee, the vendor will receive a higher profit margin. Meanwhile, the customer benefits because he will have had to pay the vendor less than the planned target cost for the engagement. If the engagement finishes above the target cost, the vendor's team will have spent more time working at cost, and the vendor will receive an overall lower profit margin. In this scenario, the customer will have had to pay more overall for the engagement. To summarize, the contract for the engagement is structured so that a lower actual cost for the customer translates into a higher profit margin for the vendor. As the actual engagement cost increases, the vendor's profit margin grows smaller.

The target-cost contract can also be structured to meet a specific schedule for a customer whose concern is not overall cost but speed of delivery.

FIXED COST

Finally, fixed-cost engagements really are possible for agile projects. I managed an account with a large client successfully for almost two years where we performed agile development solely on a fixed-cost basis, with two to three project teams developing at one time and each under a separate fixed-price contract. The teams ranged in size from four to eight people, and each contract ranged in duration from four to eight months. A contract was completed only when working software was delivered, although we did receive interim payments for meeting agreed-upon milestones. The teams followed the majority of agile programming practices, executed on one-week iterations, and the customer was even allowed to introduce new functionality into an existing contract as long as the team was allowed to scope out a comparable amount of functionality. One of the projects released to production six times over an 18-month period without a single defect.

Why Do Fixed Cost?

Besides the obvious reason that they gave us no choice, there actually is a valid argument for a vendor to engage in fixed-cost work.

Customers sink untold sums of money into software projects that can make or break their futures. Vendors need to claim victory at the end of every project regardless of a project's actual outcome or see their reputations sullied. Customers want to control the hazardous materials of scope and cost by selling risk to vendors. Vendors typically avoid buying risk because of the increased likelihood of being implicated in failure.

Projects can go awry any number of ways. Risks include—but are by no means limited to—missed requirements, design flaws, and incompetent management. Projects that succumb to one or more of these risks do not merely hemorrhage cash. They slip schedules, absorb additional resources, reduce employee morale, and imperil business reputations. We can assume that all of these things eventually translate into lost income. This is why customers typically are willing to pay a premium on fixed-cost contracts. They understand that, in addition to contracting a service, they are selling off risk.

Risk is a hot potato that nobody wants to be caught holding at the end of the dance. What if the vendor put his energy toward cooling off the potato? The vendor might then be able to reduce risk much more effectively then either the customer or the competition. In this scenario, the customer will still pay the same fixed cost (risk premium included) to see the work completed, but the vendor will stand to make a tidier profit because he has actually found a way to reduce the risk of the engagement. Correctly implemented, agile programming and management practices and processes can in fact reduce risk on a project. This is because an agile approach leads to fewer defects, a system that is more responsive to change, and a focus on delivering functionality that actually has value to the customer.

To be clear, not all risks can and should be bartered. Vendors are not insurance companies and should in all cases shelter themselves from such risks as the customer's ability to manage his own resources and the outcome of the customer's other projects. Conversely, customers should not be forced to assume the risk of a vendor's own inability to perform.

Skilled Teams and Repeat Customers

Executing fixed-cost work is easiest with an established customer, in a known domain, and with a succession of contracts. An established customer relationship should enable flexibility between the customer and the vendor. Since each party has a history with the other and presumably each party has come to respect the other, there is a greater likelihood that the two will collaborate within the scope of the contract instead of seeking to exploit it. If the vendor is performing fixed-cost work within a domain that he already knows, his teams should be able to come up with relatively reliable estimates that, coupled with a risk premium, should keep him from taking a loss in any but the worst case scenario. Next, an engagement that is based on a succession of contracts can provide a level of security for the vendor. If one contract does not go well for the vendor, he has a good chance to make up his costs on the next one.

On fixed-cost engagements, the project team needs to be skilled both in the technology and in agile development. Of course, not every member of the team has to be highly skilled in both areas, but there should be a good deal of experience distributed across the entire team. Finally, once an agile vendor gets comfortable with completing fixed-cost initiatives in a known domain with a known customer and a high likelihood of repeat work, that vendor may be able to branch out to new domains and new customers.

Building a Fixed-Bid Proposal

Any vendor that chooses to engage in fixed-cost work will likely devise a method for pricing that will fit his exact needs and environments. The steps provided here are an approach that has worked for teams under my management in the past. Typically we used a small proposal team that consisted of two or three senior programmers and a manager who worked together through the processes of estimating and pricing a new project. It is highly recommended that the majority of individuals who complete the initial estimation and pricing for a contract be the same individuals who then fulfill the contract.

Step 1: Understand the Work

The team reviews whatever documentation is available, such as a Request for Proposal (RFP) or any available requirements documentation, to get the best possible understanding of the system that is being requested. If enough information can be gleaned from the documents, the team then creates a list of features for the system.

The list includes questions for each feature that the members of the team could not find answers for within the documentation.

Members of the team set up one or more meetings with domain experts, stakeholders, or users of the system. Basically, these should be people the team knows can best answer their questions, best understand the system that the customer wants built, and the customer is comfortable with the team talking to. Members of the team then meet with these individuals, both to verify the team's understanding of the system and to get answers to the questions in the draft features list.

Step 2: Estimate the Features

Once an initial list of features has been identified, the team begins to estimate each feature. The approach we used for estimating an entire set of features in this fashion is discussed earlier in this chapter, in the section "Waterfall and Other Phased Approaches." This estimated feature list becomes the initial plan for the project if and when a fixed-cost bid is accepted.

Step 3: Write Up a Solution Sheet for Each Feature

Solution sheets are introduced and discussed in Chapter 11. The team should write up a solution sheet for each feature, focusing on the major requirements of each feature, the identified risks, and things that specifically would not be done as part of the feature. These feature sheets serve two purposes. First, they ensure that the entire proposal team understands and is in agreement on each feature. Second, they form the bulk of the proposal that is delivered to the customer along with the fixed bid.

Sometimes additional information that affects the estimate of a feature is shaken out of that feature when the solution sheet is written. When this happens, the entire proposal team convenes to re-estimate the feature.

Step 4: Price the Contract

Finally, the manager needs to price the contract. For my teams, this process is based on four inputs. First is the total number of ideal days the team has estimated for the proposal. Second is the average velocity at which we believe the team will complete work during the engagement (basically, how many actual days it will take to complete an ideal day's worth of work). The third input is a coefficient for risk. This coefficient was meant to cover anything that could go wrong, such as estimates being too low, requirements having been missed in the estimation process, unexpected technical issues, the Blackout of 2003, and so on. This number was based both on the gut instinct of the team for the specific engagement and on experiences from previous contracts. Fourth is the blended day rate for a team member.

The initial price for the bid ended up being the total number of estimated ideal days, multiplied by the ratio of ideal days to actual days, multiplied by the risk coefficient. An example of this is illustrated in Figure 20.4.

Estimated ideal days to complete contract		Number of actual days required to complete an ideal day of work		Risk coefficent		Blended day rate per programmer		Estimated contract cost
58	×	1.5	×	1.3	×	$800	=	$90,480

FIGURE 20.4 Calculating an initial fixed-cost bid.

We would then validate this price by identifying the likely duration of the contract and the individuals who would most likely be assigned to it. We would then cost out a few different scenarios with individual billing rates and durations until we were comfortable with a final price. Also, if the time for a part-time manager (all that was ever needed) had not been baked into the estimates, then the bid was adjusted accordingly.

Finally, if we knew that a particular customer was going to try to negotiate us down by a significant amount (some purchasing departments at large corporations can be rather predictable), we adjusted our proposal accordingly.

21

Seeking Additional Assistance

In This Chapter

- Online Resources
- Other Books
- Courses, Certification, and Coaching
- Ask the Author

Obviously, if you are serious about going agile, you will soon need to arm yourself and your team with much more than just this book. Most agile methodologies and practices discussed in this book are followed by a short list of online and print resources. This section lists resources that relate to agile development in more general terms.

ONLINE RESOURCES

Here are a few good places to start when going online for additional assistance and resources on implementing agile development.

The Agile Alliance Web Site

Located at *www.agilealliance.com*, the Agile Alliance Web site is a good launching point to find additional resources on agile development. The site has three sections of particular interest. First, the Roadmap section provides links to other useful and informative sites on agile methodologies, practices, and tools. Second, the Articles section categorizes and provides a limited search capability of a small library of articles on all things agile. Finally, if you are interested in hooking up with an agile-oriented group in your area, try the User Groups section.

The Wiki

Also known as the Wiki Wiki Web and Ward's Wiki, the Wiki is a great resource for information related to agile development. Developed by Ward Cunningham, the Wiki is a forum where agile-minded individuals share ideas and information. The pages are added, updated, and refined by a multitude of participants, and the browser should keep in mind that the information can at times be very subjective. You can get a good introduction to the Wiki at its welcome page at *http://www.c2.com/cgi/wiki?WelcomeVisitors*.

Because of its nebulous nature, it can take a bit of time to get used to navigating the Wiki. Searches can be performed from *http://www.c2.com/cgi/wiki?FindPage.*

If you simply want to browse the Wiki beginning with agile development and see where it takes you, start with *http://www.c2.com/cgi/wiki?agileSoftwareDevelopment.*

Discussion Groups

There are dozens of discussion groups related to agile development. Most are located at Yahoo! Groups (browse to *http://groups.yahoo.com*) include Agilists of almost every persuasion and point of view. Groups tend to form around methodologies, practices, and geographical areas. Participants tend to engage in rather high-level discussions about all manner of things agile, but they are also generally happy to help newcomers with questions about both tricky agile issues and real-world problems.

OTHER BOOKS

Here is a short list of good books for further reading:

- Robert Martin's *Agile Software Development* provides a very illustrative presentation of agile at the programming level, with lots of code snippets and examples [Martin02].

- Steve McConnell's *Rapid Development* is a wonderful resource for practical, implementation-level information on many practices and processes used in agile development, even though it does not include the word agile in its title [McConnell96].
- Jim Highsmith's *Agile Software Development Ecosystems* provides a lot of detail on both the major agile methodologies and the major agile methodologists behind them, in addition to more general high-level discussion on agile development itself [Highsmith02].
- Boehm and Turner's *Balancing Agility and Discipline* discusses the agile and traditional perspectives of software development as distinct approaches that have "home grounds" where they work best. The book also discusses how the perspectives might be bridged and the approaches combined to address projects that do not lie within the home ground of either approach [Boehm04].
- Alistair Cockburn's *Agile Software Development* gives insight into much of the softer side of agile development, focusing on individuals, communication, and fitting the methodology to the team [Cockburn01a].
- Rob Thomsett's *Radical Project Management* provides a refreshing and practical interpretation of much of the heavy process found in traditional project management. It will likely be too much formalism for the truly agile minded, but it might be just the right thing for the project management professional (PMP) who needs additional assistance bridging structured management processes with the practical-minded, let's-get-it-done agile culture [Thomsett02].
- Andrew Hunt and David Thomas's *Pragmatic Programmer* takes a simple, back-to-basics, and disciplined approach to programming. It is a good reminder that programming is an expert's craft, and nearly everything in the book can be applied to agile practices [Hunt99].

COURSES, CERTIFICATION, AND COACHING

It is the belief of many Agilists that teams can train themselves in agile development, and this applies particularly to the XP, FDD, Scrum, and Crystal methodologies [Lyndvall02]. This belief is based on the wide availability of material on agile development and the tendency of agile principles to promote a communicative and collaborative environment where knowledge is easily transferred and shared. Additionally, the success of an agile project is more likely dependent on the team's experience in building systems than it is on the team's familiarity with agile.

If a project desires a more formal approach, it might send several individuals (or even the whole team) to a course on the project's intended methodology. Conferences also can be a good place to plunk into and steep in agile development. Projects may also consider bringing an expert to the team site for on-site training.

If time is of the essence, risk must be kept to a minimum, or you have more money than you know what to do with, it may be beneficial to seek the assistance of a coach. Agile coaches are not cheap, but the good ones can start from the beginning with many of the right questions, steer the project clear of known pitfalls, and serve as a mentor to each individual on the team. An agile coach can provide other benefits for the team. First, the backing of an expert can help to lend credence to decisions made by the team. Second, his outsider status may afford him the ability to address issues that are taboo for those within the organization but may need to be brought to light to remove obstacles from the project's path.

As an alternative to an external coach, the project might choose to develop a coach from within. This could be done by sending a promising individual to a rigorous training or certification program (that is, if your project's agile methodology of choice has a certification program). When the individual returns, he should be given time apart from his project-related duties to work with and mentor other members of the team.

One final note on certification as it regards to extreme programming. There has been a decision among XP gurus in general and Kent Beck in particular not to provide formal certification for XP. This should not be confused with the training courses provided by ObjectMentor or other well-known and respected XP practitioners. The decision against formal certification is based on the dubious effectiveness of a certification process, the nature of XP as a flexible and relationship-driven process as opposed to technical and procedural, and a desire to avoid the creation of an exclusive set of practitioners [Beck04]. Any group purporting to offer XP certification should be treated with a good dose of skepticism.

ASK THE AUTHOR

I would happily receive feedback and, to the extent that time allows, will field questions related to the topics discussed in this book. Feel free to e-mail me at *integrating-agile@peterschuh.com*.

Endnotes

CHAPTER 1

1. © 2001. Kent Beck, Mike Beedle, Arie van Bennekum, Alistair Cockburn, Ward Cunningham, Martin Fowler, James Grenning, Jim Highsmith, Andrew Hunt, Ron Jeffries, Jon Kern, Brian Marick, Robert C. Martin, Steve Mellor, Ken Schwaber, Jeff Sutherland, Dave Thomas. This declaration may be freely copied in any form, but only in its entirety through this notice.

CHAPTER 3

1. The source for the majority of the information in this section is *DSDM: Business Focused Development*, Second Edition and the DSDM Web site at *http://www. dsdm.org* [Stapleton03]. The nine principals of DSDM are reprinted with the permission of the DSDM Consortium. DSDM is a registered trademark of the DSDM Consortium.

2. The source for the majority of the information in this section is *Lean Software Development: An Agile Toolkit for Software Development Managers* [Poppendieck03].

CHAPTER 7

1. Portions of this section first appeared in my article "7 Simple Ways to Add a Little Agile Without Going to Extremes" in *Better Software* magazine [Schuh04].

2. Ibid.

3. The source for the majority of the information in this section is *A Practical Guide to Feature-Driven Development* [Palmer02].

CHAPTER 8

1. Portions of this section first appeared in my article "7 Simple Ways to Add a Little Agile Without Going to Extremes" in *Better Software* magazine [Schuh04].

CHAPTER 9

1. The source for much of the information in this section is my paper, "Easing Test Object Creation in XP," presented at the XP Universe conference in 2001 [Schuh01].

2. The source for much of the information in this section is my paper, "Agility and the Database," presented at the XP2002 conference [Schuh02b].

CHAPTER 12

1. The source for the information in this section is *Crystal Clear: A Human-Powered Methodology for Small Teams* [Cockburn04a].

CHAPTER 13

1. The source for the majority of the information in this section is *Extreme Programming Explained* [Beck99].

CHAPTER 14

1. Portions of this section first appeared in my article "7 Simple Ways to Add a Little Agile Without Going to Extremes" in *Better Software* magazine [Schuh04].

CHAPTER 16

1. The source for the majority of the information in this section is *A Practical Guide to Feature-Driven Development* [Palmer02].

2. The source for the information in this section is *Agile Project Management with Scrum* [Schwaber01a].

3. The source for the information in this section is *Agile Software Development* [Cockburn02].

CHAPTER 18

1. The source for much of the information in this section is my article, "A Pragmatic Work Breakdown Structure" [Schuh03].

CHAPTER 20

1. The source for the information in this section is *Lean Software Development* [Poppendieck03].

References

[Abrahamsson02] Abrahamsson et al. *Agile Software Development Methods: Review and Analysis.* Available at *http://www.inf.vtt.fi/pdf/publications/2002/P478.pdf.*

[Ambler02] Ambler, Scott and Ron Jeffries. *Agile Modeling: Effective Practices for Extreme Programming and the Unified Process.* John Wiley and Sons, 2002.

[Ambler03] Ambler, Scott. "Agile Documentation." Available at *http://www.agilemodeling.com/essays/agileDocumentation.htm.*

[Ambler03a] Ambler, Scott. "Running Interference." *Software Development.* July 2003.

[Ambler04] Ambler, Scott. Available at *http://www.agiledata.org.*

[Anderson02] Anderson, David. "The Case for Class Ownership." *The Coad Letter.* February 2002. Available at *http://bdn.borland.com/article/0,1410,31957,00.html.*

[Anderson04] Anderson, David. *Agile Management for Software Engineering.* Prentice-Hall, 2004.

[Astels03] Astels, David. *Test Driven Development: A Practical Guide.* Prentice-Hall, 2003.

[BCS04] British Computer Society. "The Challenges of Complex IT Projects." Royal Academy of Engineering, 2004.

[Beck99] Beck, Kent. *Extreme Programming Explained: Embrace Change.* Addison-Wesley, 1999.

[Beck99a] Beck, Kent and Dave Cleal. "Optional Scope Contracts." Available at *http://www.xprogramming.com/ftp/Optional+scope+contracts.pdf.*

[Beck00] Beck, Kent and Martin Fowler. *Planning Extreme Programming.* Addison-Wesley, 2000.

[Beck02] Beck, Kent. *Test Driven Development: By Example.* Addison-Wesley, 2002.

[Beck04] Beck, Kent. "Is It XP." Extreme Programming Discussion Group Post. Available at *http://groups.yahoo.com/group/extremeprogramming/message/91267.*

[Boehm04] Boehm, Barry and Richard Turner. *Balancing Agility and Discipline: A Guide for the Perplexed.* Addison-Wesley, 2004.

[Clark04] Clark, Mike. "A Dozen Ways to Get the Testing Bug in the New Year." Available at *http://today.java.net/pub/a/today/2004/01/22/DozenWays.html.*

[Coad99] Coad, Peter et al. *Java Modeling in Color with UML: Enterprise Components and Process.* Prentice Hall, 1999.

[Coad03] Coad, Peter. "What Is Test Driven Development?" *The Coad Letter,* Issue 93. 2003. Available at *http://www.coadletter.com/article/0,1410,29690,00.html.*

[Cockburn97] Cockburn, Alistair. *Surviving Object-Oriented Projects.* Addison-Wesley, 1997.

[Cockburn01] Cockburn, Alistair and Jim Highsmith. "Agile Software: The People Factor." *IEEE Computer.* November 2001.

[Cockburn01a] Cockburn, Alistair. *Agile Software Development.* Addison-Wesley, 2001.

[Cockburn02] Cockburn, Alistair. "Interview with Alistair Cockburn." Available at *http://www.cutter. com/consultants/cockburna.html*.

[Cockburn04] Cockburn, Alistair. "Crystal Main Foyer." Available at *http://alistair.cockburn.us/crystal/*.

[Cockburn04a] Cockburn, Alistair. *Crystal Clear: A Human-Powered Methodology for Small Teams, Including the Seven Properties of Effective Software Projects.* Addison-Wesley, 2004.

[Cockburn04b] Cockburn, Alistair. "The 'Cone of Silence' and Related Project Management Strategies." Available at *http://alistair.cockburn.us/crystal/articles/cos/coneofsilence.htm.* University of Michigan.

[Cohn03] Cohn, Mike. "Introducing an Agile Process to an Organization." *IEEE Computer.* 2003.

[Cohn04] Cohn, Mike. "The Scrum Development Process." Available at *http://www.mountaingoat-software.com/scrum/*.

[Cohn04a] Cohn, Mike. *User Stories Applied: For Agile Software Development.* Addison-Wesley, 2004.

[DeLuca04] DeLuca, Jeff. "Agile Software Development using Feature-Driven Development." Available at *http://www.nebulon.com/articles/fdd/*.

[Dollery01] Dollery, Bryan. "Migrating to XP." *Computer World (New Zealand).* October 2001.

[DSDM04] DSDM Consortium Web site. Available at *http://www.dsdm.org/*.

[Fisher91] Fisher, Roger et al. *Getting to Yes: Negotiating Agreement Without Giving In* (Second Edition). Penguin USA, 1991.

[Fowler99] Fowler, Martin et al. *Refactoring: Improving the Design of Existing Code.* Addison Wesley, 1999.

[Fowler01] Fowler, Martin and Matthew Foemmel. "Continuous Integration." Available at *http://martinfowler.com/articles/continuousIntegration.html*.

[Fowler03] Fowler, Martin. "The New Methodology." 2003. Available at *http://martinfowler.com/ articles/newMethodology.html*

[Fraunhofer02] "Summary of the First eWorkshop on Agile Methods." Fraunhofer Centre for Experimental Software Engineering. 2002. Available at *http://fc-md.umd.edu/projects/Agile/ Summary/SummaryPF.htm*

[Fraunhofer02a] "Summary of the Second eWorkshop on Agile Methods." Fraunhofer Centre for Experimental Software Engineering. 2002. Available at *http://fc-md.umd.edu/projects/Agile/ SecondeWorkshop/summary2ndeWorksh.htm*

[Fraunhofer02b] "Summary of the Third eWorkshop on Agile Methods." Fraunhofer Centre for Experimental Software Engineering. 2002. Available at *http://fc-md.umd.edu/projects/Agile/3rd-e Workshop/summary3rdeWorksh.htm*.

[Gamma95] Gamma, Erich et al. *Design Patterns.* Addison-Wesley, 1995.

[Glasser65] Glasser, William. *Reality Therapy: A New Approach to Psychiatry.* HarperCollins, 1965.

[Highsmith00] Highsmith, James. *Adaptive Software Development: A Collaborative Approach to Managing Complex Systems.* Dorset House Publishing, 2000.

[Highsmith00a] Highsmith, James. "Retiring Lifecycle Dinosaurs: Using Adaptive Software Development to Meet the Challenges of a High-Speed, High-Change Environment." *Software Testing and Quality Engineering.* July/August 2000.

[Highsmith02] Highsmith, James. *Agile Software Development Ecosystems.* Addison-Wesley, 2002.

[Hunt99] Hunt, Andrew and David Thomas. *The Pragmatic Programmer: From Journeyman to Master.* Addison-Wesley, 1999.

[Hunt03] Hunt, Andrew and Dave Thomas. *Pragmatic Unit Testing in Java with JUnit.* The Pragmatic Programmers, 2003.

[IEEE86] Software Engineering Standards Subcommittee of the Technical Committee on Software Engineering of the IEEE Computer Society. *IEEE Standard for Software Unit Testing.* IEEE, 1986.

[Jeffries00] Jeffries, Ron et al. *Extreme Programming Installed.* Addison-Wesley, 2000.

[Jeffries01] Jeffries, Ron. "Essential XP: Card, Conversion, and Confirmation." 2001. Available at *http://www.xprogramming.com/xpmag/expCardConversationConfirmation.htm.*

[Jeffries02] Jeffries, Ron. "Refactoring Isn't Rework." *XP Magazine.* 2002. Available at *http://www.xprogramming.com/xpmag/refactoringisntrework.htm.*

[Kearns04] Kearns, Eamon. Private interview, 2004.

[Lyndvall02] Lindvall, Mikael et al. "Empirical Findings in Agile Methods." *Extreme Programming and Agile Methods—XP/Agile Universe 2002.* Springer, 2002: pp. 197–207.

[Mackinnon01] Mackinnon, Tim et al. "Endo-Testing: Unit Testing with Mock Objects." Available at *http://www.connextra.com/aboutUs/mockobjects.pdf.*

[Manifesto01] "The Agile Manifesto." Available at *http://www.agilemanifesto.org.* 2001.

[Mar04] Mar, Kane and Ken Schwaber. "Scrum with XP." Available at *http://www.controlchaos.com/XPKane.htm.*

[Marick04] Marick, Brian. "Agile Methods and Agile Testing." Available at *http://www.testing.com/agile/agile-testing-essay.html.*

[Martin02] Martin, Robert. *Agile Software Development—Principles, Patterns, and Practices.* Prentice Hall, 2002.

[McBreen02] McBreen, Pete. "Pretending to Be Agile." Available at *http://www.informit.com/articles/article.asp?p=25913&redir=1.*

[McConnell93] McConnell, Steve. *Code Complete.* Microsoft Press, 1993.

[McConnell96] McConnell, Steve. *Rapid Development: Taming Wild Software Schedules.* Microsoft Press, 1996.

[Meyer04] Meyer, Eric. Private interview, 2004.

[Middleton03] Middleton, James. "Websites Don't Like Mondays." Available at *http://www.vnunet.com/News/1140934.*

[Oldfield03] Oldfield, Paul. "Mix and Match—Making Sense of the Best Practices Jigsaw: Attainability." 2003. Available at *http://www.aptprocess.com/whitepapers/MakingSenseOfTheBestPracticesJigsaw_Attainability.pdf*

[Palmer02] Palmer, Stephen and John Felsing. *A Practical Guide to Feature-Driven Development.* Prentice Hall, 2002.

[Palmer03] Palmer, Stephen. "Feature Driven Development and Extreme Programming." *The Coad Letter,* Issue 70. 2003. Available at *http://www.thecoadletter.com/article/0,1410,29684,00.html.*

[Poppendieck01] Poppendieck, Mary. "Lean Programming." *Software Development.* May 2001.

[Poppendieck03] Poppendieck, Mary and Tom Poppendieck. *Lean Software Development: An Agile Toolkit for Software Development Managers.* Addison-Wesley, 2003.

[Poppendieck03a] Poppendieck, Mary. "Lean Software Development." *C++ Magazine.* Fall 2003.

[Reifer03] Reifer, Donald et al. "Scaling Agile Methods—Ten Top Issues and Lessons Learned." Available at *http://can.cpsc.ucalgary.ca/ws2003/ScalingAgile%20V1_1_.pdf.*

[Rising02] Rising, Linda. "Agile Meetings." *Software Testing and Quality Engineering.* May/June 2002.

[Rueping02] Rueping, Andreas. *Agile Documentation: A Pattern Guide to Producing Lightweight Documents for Software Projects.* John Wiley and Sons, 2002.

[Schuh01] Schuh, Peter and Stephanie Punke. "Easing Test Object Creation in XP." Available at *http://www.xpuniverse.com/2001/pdfs/Testing03.pdf.*

[Schuh01a] Schuh, Peter. "Recovery, Redemption and Extreme Programming." *IEEE Software.* November/December 2001.

[Schuh02] Schuh, Peter. "Standards versus Agility: Working Toward Success in Software Testing." *Cutter IT Journal.* August 2002.

[Schuh02a] Schuh, Peter. "A Pocketful of Practices." *Cutter Information Corp, Executive Update,* 2002.

[Schuh02b] Schuh, Peter. "Agility and the Database." *XP2002 Conference Proceedings,* 2002.

[Schuh03] Schuh, Peter. "A Pragmatic Work Breakdown Structure." *Cutter Information Corp, Executive Update,* 2003.

[Schuh04] Schuh, Peter. "7 Simple Ways to Add a Little Agile Without Going to Extremes." *Better Software.* July/August 2004.

[Schwaber01] Schwaber, Ken and Mike Beedle. *Agile Software Development with Scrum.* Prentice Hall, 2001.

[Schwaber04] Schwaber, Ken. *Agile Project Management with Scrum.* Microsoft Press, 2004.

[Shalloway00] Shalloway, Alan. "Estimation as Hypothesis." Available at *http://www.netobjectives. com/ap/download/est_as_hyp.pdf.*

[ScienceDaily00] "Working Together in 'War Rooms' Doubles Teams' Productivity. University of Michigan Researchers Find." Science Daily. Available at *http://www.sciencedaily.com/ releases/2000/12/001206144705.htm.*

[Shapiro97] Shapiro, Stuart. "Splitting the Difference: The Historical Necessity of Synthesis in Software Engineering." *IEEE Annals of the History of Computing.* Vol. 19, No. 1. 1997.

[Stapleton03] Stapleton, Jennifer, editor. *DSDM: Business Focused Development,* Second Edition. Addison-Wesley, 2003.

[Stone00] Stone, Douglas et al. *Difficult Conversations: How to Discuss What Matters Most.* Penguin USA, 2000.

[Thomsett02] Thomsett, Rob. *Radical Project Management.* Prentice Hall, 2002.

[Venners03] Venners, Bill. "Collective Ownership of Code and Text: A Conversation with Ward Cunningham, Part II." 2003. Available at *http://www.artima.com/intv/ownership.html.*

[Wallace02] Wallace, Nathan et al. "Managing XP with Multiple or Remote Customers." *XP2002, Conference Proceedings.* 2002: pp. 134–137.

[Williams00] Williams, Laurie. "The Collaborative Software Process." University of Utah Department of Computer Science (Dissertation) 2000.

[Williams02] Williams, Laurie and Robert Kessler. *Pair Programming Illuminated.* Addison-Wesley, 2002.

[Wiki04] The Wiki Wiki Web. Available at *http://c2.com/cgi/wiki.*

Index

A

acceptance tests
  implementation, 115
  opportunities and obstacles, 115–116
  overview, 113
  purpose and benefits, 114–115
  requirements tracing, 173, 201–202
  total number of, 260
  user stories, 171–172
Adaptive Software Development (ASD)
  adaptive lifecycle, 35–37
  collaboration, 36–37
  learning process in, 37
  overview, 2–3, 35
  resources, 37
  speculation, 35–36
Agile Alliance Web site, 328
agile development
  adopting, 50–51, 100
  assessing project environment, 14–16
  common themes, 17–18
  described, 2
  discontinuing processes, 58, 259
  embedded XP, 47–48
  false practitioners and projects, 59–60
  gradual adoption, 51
  implementing by the book, 46–48
  iteration zero, 57–58, 137
  measuring adoption progress, 60
  mix and match implementations, 48
  modified or partial implementations, 47
  principles of, 5–6
  project characteristics, 7–8
  projects benefiting from, 13–14
  resistance to, 51–54
  right approach to, 46–48
  starting with bare minimum, 55
  support for, 13
  team readiness, 49–50
  vs. traditional approach, 43–46, 180–182
  transition to, 50–51

values, summary of, 3–4
See also environments; methodologies
"Agile Documentation" (Ambler), 288
agile practices
  acceptance tests, 113–116
  adopting before tools, 65–66
  agile data management, 143–151
  automated deployment, 74–76
  biggest bang for buck, 63
  blitz planning, 189–192, 197
  build automation, 71–74
  collective ownership, 83–87
  collocated teams, 279–282
  continuous integration, 76–80
  current worst problem, 63
  daily Scrum meetings, 24, 272–273, 276–278, 283, 306
  described, 4–5, 66–68
  design simplicity, 80–83, 172
  easiest thing first, hardest second, 64
  FDD practices, 26–28
  feature teams, 26, 85, 87–91
  implementing in recovery, 320–321
  methods for selecting next practice, 63–64
  MockObjects, 138–143
  ObjectMother, 98, 133–138
  pair programming, 20, 66, 95–99, 100, 141
  plan for implementing, 61–63
  planning game, 197, 202–207
  refactoring, 92–94, 126
  rejecting, 64–65
  stand up meetings, 272–276, 283, 306
  task cycles, 232–239
  test-driven development (TDD), 116–118
  XP practices, 20–21
Agile Project Management with Scrum (Schwaber), 278
Agile Software Development (Martin), 294
Agile Software Development with Scrum (Schwaber, Beedle), 281
Ambler, Scott, 288
analysts and agile development, 53–54, 98
Anderson, David, 87, 91